THE PREHISTORY OF
DICKSON MOUNDS:
THE DICKSON EXCAVATION

by
Alan D. Harn

ILLINOIS STATE MUSEUM
REPORTS OF INVESTIGATIONS, No. 36
Dickson Mounds Museum Anthropological Studies

Illinois State Museum
Springfield, Illinois
1980

First edition, 1971
Second Edition (revised), 1980
ISSN 0360-0270
ISBN 0-89792-085-6
Printed by Authority of the State of Illinois
(P.O. 18270—3M—6-80)

TO THE LATE DON DICKSON
A small chapter has been
added to the story of
your people.

Frontispiece: The Dicksons' Excavation.

CONTENTS

TABLES

FIGURES

PLATES
(following page 146)

Plate 1.
a. Don F. Dickson near Tent Covering Original Excavation, 1927.
b. Don F. Dickson and First Temporary Frame Building over Original Excavation,
1927.

Plate 2.
a. View of First Temporary Frame Building, 1927.
b. First Permanent Building over the Dickson Excavation, 1928-1967.

Plate 3.
a. Marion H. Dickson and Don F. Dickson in the Dickson Excavation.
b. Thomas Dickson Examining Dog Burial at University of Chicago Excavations at
Dickson Camp, 1932.

Plate 4.
a. Don F. Dickson and Probably Raymond Dickson in the Area of the Original Excavation, 1931.
b. Don F. Dickson and T. W. Routson in the Second Excavation, 1927.

Plate 5.
a. Beginning of Excavation inside Second Temporary Frame Building, 1927.
b. View of Excavation from Northwest, 1928.

Plate 6.
a. Don F. Dickson Lecturing in the Excavation, 1930.
b. View of Excavation from Southwest, 1928.

Plate 7.
a. General View of Burials, 1930.
b. The Dickson Excavation as It Appears Today.

ACKNOWLEDGMENTS

Without the assistance and encouragement of many people, this publication would never have appeared in its present form. Foremost is my deep indebtedness to the late Dr. Don F. Dickson who, until his death in 1964, provided much encouragement and the inspiration which led to the completion of the original work. The late Mrs. Irene Dickson, Ms. Louise Fike, Mrs. Fern Dickson, and the late Mr. Marion H. Dickson were of great assistance in providing much of the information on the early history of Dickson Mounds as well as offering many helpful suggestions.

Dr. Patrick J. Munson, University of Indiana, and Mr. Lawrence A. Conrad, Western Illinois University, gave helpful criticisms. Many thoughts incorporated in the original manuscript were the result of the writer's long association with Dr. Munson.

Dr. Howard D. Winters, New York University, Dr. Robert L. Hall, University of Illinois at Chicago Circle, and the late Dr. Joseph R. Caldwell, formerly of the Illinois State Museum, provided valuable suggestions and criticisms. The helpful assistance of these individuals over several years of research will not soon be forgotten.

The late Dr. Georg K. Neumann, Indiana University, contributed much to the publication through his excellent criticisms and his kind offer of the use of his notes on the skeletal population of the Dickson Mounds. He is absolved, however, from any errors in interpretation made by the writer.

Dr. Dan Morse, formerly of the Peoria Municipal Tuberculosis Sanitorium, aided the writer in locating certain pathological specimens in the Dickson excavation. Dr. A. J. Novotny, Orthopedic Surgeon, Peoria, kindly offered his assistance in identifying certain bone diseases as well as his criticism of the pathology section; and Dr. John Taraska, Methodist Medical Center of Illinois, Peoria, provided X-ray analysis of the pathological specimens with Burial 216.

Dr. Stuart Struever, Northwestern University, offered many suggestions and served as a source for reference material. His continual encouragement was much appreciated.

The assistance and cooperation given by the Staff of the Illinois State Museum is especially appreciated: Dr. Paul W. Parmalee, presently of the University of Tennessee, identified the faunal remains; Dr. Richard L. Leary identified the lithic material; Dr. Alfred C. Koelling and the late Dr. Glen S. Winterringer provided much helpful information on the plant distribution and identified many of the plant species; Ms. Orvetta Robinson spent many hours critically reading the manuscript and offered many helpful suggestions as did Dr. Bonnie Whatley Styles; Mrs. Fay Garvue, formerly of the Museum Staff, offered thoughtful suggestions and criticisms concerning my errant art technique. Mr. Dennis Guernsey was responsible for the lettering on Figures 1 to 55 and 59, and Mr. William Weedman performed a variety of tasks and offered suggestions that greatly aided in the completion of the graphics. Mr. Marlin Roos provided the photograph for Plate 7a and reproduced all photographs in Plates 1 to 7.

A special acknowledgment goes to Staff members of the Dickson Mounds Museum for their contributions during the manuscript revision. Ms. Carol Slaubaugh provided expert typing and proofreading assistance while the close scrutiny of the early photographs and Dickson notes (and decipherment of the handwriting) by Mr. Mark Blaeuer was instrumental in clearing up the confused movement of many artifacts within the excavation.

My wife, Ruth Ann Harn, undertook many of the more drudging tasks throughout the course of the original writing, enthusiastically assisting in every phase of research from fieldwork to the monotony of final proofreading. Her cheerful cooperation and understanding throughout both the original research and the current revision have been deeply appreciated.

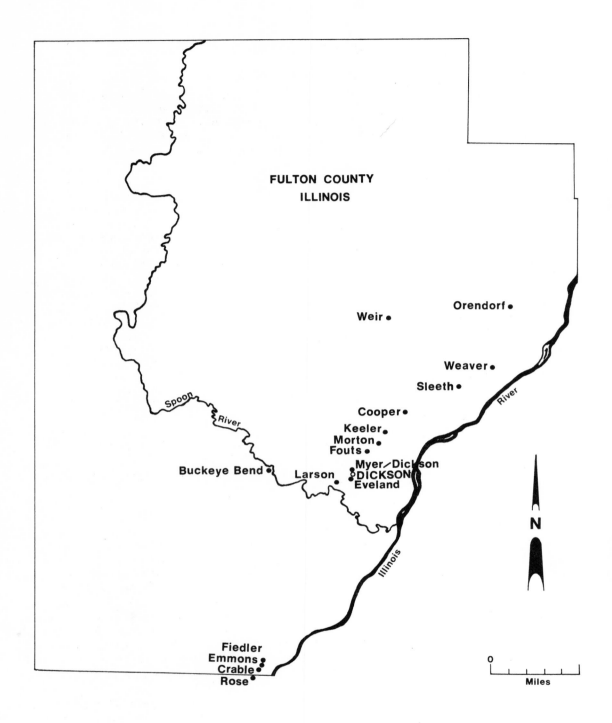

Figure 1. Map showing location of Dickson and selected Spoon River Tradition sites.

THE PREHISTORY OF DICKSON MOUNDS:
THE DICKSON EXCAVATION

INTRODUCTION

Fulton County, Illinois, has long been known as having within its boundaries the greatest concentration of prehistoric archaeological sites in the State. At the time of this writing, nearly 3,000 mound and village sites have been recorded in the county; and as public awareness of archaeology continues to grow, additional sites are being reported with regularity. An unusually well-balanced natural environment provided optimum living conditions throughout most of the period of human prehistory, inviting continuous aboriginal occupation of the area. Every phase of prehistoric cultural occupation known in central Illinois occurs in Fulton County. Although there are a number of early references to historic Indians living throughout the area, no sites of this period are presently recorded within the county. Only two historic Indian burials dug intrusively into a prehistoric mound have been excavated by the Illinois State Museum.

From the time of its earliest European settlement, Fulton County has been known to contain an abundance of prehistoric remains. Early work by professional institutions in the Illinois River Valley was very scanty (cf. Thomas 1894). Field methods oriented in part toward the acquisition of museum display objects resulted in the recovery of disconnected data and facts which tended to be isolated and somewhat nebulous. Although these cursory explorations made it apparent that a number of archaeological manifestations were evident locally, little attempt was made to group them into cultural complexes or relate them in terms of chronology.

No great interest in the archaeology of the area was taken until 1927 when Don F. Dickson, an amateur archaeologist, began the partial excavation of a Middle Mississippian burial mound on land owned by his father. This excavation soon became a focal point of attention for professional anthropologists, stimulating further research in the immediate vicinity. The first of these scientific explorations was undertaken by the University of Chicago field parties under the direction of the late Fay-Cooper Cole. Between 1930 and 1932, Dr. Cole carried out a systematic project of testing and/or analyzing a total of 48 sites of ar-

chaeological importance in Fulton County. The material findings and data were separated into artifact categories, grouped into cultural complexes, related chronologically, and published in *Rediscovering Illinois* (Cole and Deuel 1937).

The Dickson Mounds Cemetery (F⁰34) presents an unusual opportunity to study the Spoon River variant of the Mississippian Pattern in the Central Illinois Valley. Much has been written pertaining to the chronological position of the Spoon River variant people, but little has been done to relate them to other prehistoric manifestations in the Midwest. Situated as it is in the Central Illinois Valley, the Dickson Site is at the gateway to the north and west. Its cultural personality reflects the Mississippian influences from the south combined with established traditions of the indigenous Woodland people which were, in turn, subjected to regional influences from the Plains area. A comparison of Dickson Mounds with these neighboring cultural manifestations creates a basis for a better understanding of both local and regional cultural development.

The skeletal material and accompanying burial furniture in the Dickson excavation remains *in situ*. This is quite advantageous to the researcher when analyzing material, eliminating hours wasted rummaging through dusty storage rooms and file cabinets in search of misplaced bags and the seemingly insurmountable, and sometimes impossible, task of deciphering the recorder's handwriting. Material left *in situ* also provides the opportunity to recheck any questionable occurrences that inevitably appear after a specimen has been removed and to achieve a certain thoroughness that otherwise might be impossible.

The greatest value may be that it affords all persons an equal opportunity to study the remains and arrive at their own conclusions. There are certain disadvantages, however, the major problem being the limitation for overall analysis imposed by the many skeletons which are only partially uncovered due to the presence of other burials directly over them. Only slightly more than 40 percent of those in the Dickson excavation are adequately exposed to be completely usable in all phases of analysis. Also, as will be discussed later, it is perhaps inevitable that some movement of materials will transpire in an exhibit of this type.

In 1964, Don Dickson and the writer agreed to collaborate in an attempt to write the story of these prehistoric people as the Dicksons have presented it over the years and to include, in a story fashion, the more detailed analysis usually found in a site report. It was soon decided to write two separate publications: the first, a detailed report; the second, the Dicksons' story. Only the illustration of the material and the preparation of a rough outline were completed when Don Dickson passed away that same year. Dr. Dickson's many papers, notes, and maps have been of great assistance in the preparation of this paper.

The manuscript of this monograph was submitted for publication in January, 1967, and printed in 1971 as "The Prehistory of Dickson Mounds: A Preliminary Report" (*Dickson Mounds Museum Anthropological Studies*, No. 1). It generally reflected the knowledge and terminology of the time of its writing except for some minor text changes updating the Spoon River terminology made just prior to printing in 1971.

From 1966 through 1968, massive excavations into other parts of Dickson Mounds were undertaken, producing more than 800 burials and a tremendous wealth of additional data. It was regretted at the time that some of these excavation results could not be incorporated into the original manuscript along with several revisions felt to be required in light of new data (Harn 1971b:2). Fortunately, the decision was made to publish the manuscript as it was.

Final analysis of the 1966-1968 excavated materials, intensive excavations at other local Spoon River sites, and a new series of radiocarbon dates for Spoon River Mississippian manifestations presented a far less foreboding framework than was anticipated for revision of the original manuscript. As this publication will show, our basic concepts have remained unchanged although the new data have added greater analytical precision by clarifying certain aspects of cultural change and continuity at Dickson Mounds.

Some years after the passing of Irene Dickson, Dr. Dickson's widow, her sister, Ms. Louise Fike, presented to Dickson Mounds Museum a large collection of black-and-white photographs showing the original Dickson excavation in progress as well as views of the external burial area (Plates 1-7). These were apparently owned by Dr. and Mrs. Dickson. Also donated were boxes of newspaper and magazine articles, records, and memorabilia relating to Dickson Mounds, accumulated over a period of more than four decades. Among these materials were the original, handwritten, Dickson excavation field notes, supposedly stolen and destroyed some 40 years previously (Harn 1971b:11).

The receipt of the field notes and early photographic records came at a most opportune time since the current revision of the original Dickson report was nearing completion. Although these records necessitated extensive revisions of the revisions, they have cleared up a number of discrepancies which finally allows us to employ the Dickson excavation data with a high degree of confidence.

The analysis of the field notes was very exciting from one standpoint because it frequently presented a totally different view of the Dickson excavation than that to which I had become accustomed over the previous 15 years. New, strong patterns of age and/or sex versus burial furniture emerged to replace often-confused or weak patterns which had existed previously. One by one, most of the discrepancies disappeared as the notes were interpreted and the data crosstabulated. The field notes suggested the existence of additional artifacts, and several pieces were rediscovered, buried by the decades of dust and cobweb accumulation or shoved into nooks and crannies beneath burials.

The study of the field notes and the subsequent reanalysis of the data were much like excavating and reporting a vibrant new site, with the many discoveries normally spread over a period of years being compressed into less than three months' time. On the other hand, analysis of these early records continually reminded us that those previous studies of Spoon River mortuary and social organization, which employed the Dickson excavation as a data base, had been adversely affected in varying degrees. As the analysis progressed, it became evident that some 21 percent of the burial furniture had been moved from one burial to another, over 46 percent of the artifacts appeared in wrong positions with the burials, and possibly 17 artifacts and one skull had been added to burials in the excavation (apparently for use as graphic aids during lectures by the Dicksons). These artifacts, listed in the original report, are excluded from this revision: one mussel shell (D275), one arrowpoint (D37), 3 bone awls (D127, D128, D133), bone shuttle (D132), bone needle (D129), bone flaker (D126), sandstone abrader (D123), necklace of river pearls (D96), 4 *Busycon* spp. pendants (D36, D138, D236, D341), bone hairpin (D125), and two pottery jars (D97 and D94). The latter vessel was found to have been associated with a burial from the smaller of the original Dickson test areas which is later described (Plate 4b).

No one could doubt the sincerity with which the movement of artifacts was made. Most were moved vertically upward in an obvious attempt to display to the visiting public interesting or unique specimens which happened to be in unviewable locations with lower graves. In so doing, multiple specimens were sometimes divided between two or more upper burials. In a few cases, artifacts appear to have been moved closer together to demonstrate similarities, but any lateral movement was generally quite limited. Intraburial artifact movement probably took place during periodic cleaning of the exhibit. Badly damaged skulls and long bones were sometimes exchanged with less-viewable specimens nearby to enhance the appearance of the exhibit. This situation has since been partially corrected.

The Dickson notes indicate that several burials, primarily disarticulated or fragmentary fetus and infant skeletons, were either partially or totally removed during the original excavation process; and the early photographs show others which have since partially or totally disappeared, probably with repeated cleaning of the excavation. Also some fetuses were moved slightly from their original positions to facilitate cleaning or to protect them from foot traffic during lectures.

Early photographs of the excavation in progress reveal that at least two partially articulated burials were removed by the Dicksons in order to facilitate excavation of lower graves (See Burials 72, 79, and 106). Neither was mentioned in the field notes. How many other upper burials met a similar fate is unknown; but it is doubtful that the number was significant or that it included complete skeletons.

The Dickson field notes were handwritten by two different individuals — one undoubtedly Don F. Dickson, the other possibly Raymond Dickson who may have been the only other person actively involved toward the end of the excavation. The notes are not actually field notes, that is, not a daily log of activities now commonly associated with archaeological excavation; they are essentially an inventory made after the excavation was completed. Each burial and artifact was numbered, and all burials were described with regard to body position, association with other burials, and estimates of age, sex, and occasional pathological conditions. Associated artifacts and their placement were accurately described, often in some detail with precise measurements, tracings, and drawings. Various questions and brief theories were often interjected into the burial descriptions.

The artifacts were numbered in ink, and a separate "relic" notebook gave even greater detailed description of the burial furniture; however, it was not completed beyond Burial 35. Many of the original Dickson numbers are still evident on artifacts in the burial exhibit, saving considerable time in matching specimens with original owners.

Little reinterpretation of the Dickson notes was required. Only one notebook page, apparently elaborating somewhat on the artifacts with Burial 90, was found to be missing, and only two obvious mistakes were found.

Analysis of the Dickson notes allowed us to surmount all but one minor problem — that of the occurrence of mussel-shell fragments inside several pottery vessels. While altered and unaltered mussel-shell valves appear with great frequency in Mississippian burial vessels throughout the Spoon River area, the occurrence of shell fragments inside vessels is unique to the Dickson excavation. We are inclined to view this material as grave fill which was placed in convenient receptacles either during excavation or later during cleaning activities.

From the time of the original excavation until the publication of the first Dickson Mounds report in 1971, some 17 artifacts had been lost or stolen from the Dickson excavation. Included were two copper-covered wood earspools, three bead necklaces, a bead bracelet, a bone bracelet, over 100 beads from three burials, three "irregular shaped rocks," possibly two *Busycon* spp. pendants, and a chert flake and arrowpoint. In the eight years since publication, 17 more artifacts have been stolen during at least five break-ins into the excavation: 13 arrowpoints (D3, D4, D40-D45, D71-D74 and D202), one elbow pipe (D48), two knives (D148, D167), and one bead necklace (D191). A newly installed alarm system should preclude the loss of additional materials.

DESCRIPTION OF THE CENTRAL ILLINOIS VALLEY

PHYSICAL GEOGRAPHY

The Dickson Mounds Cemetery, F°34, is located about three miles southeast of Lewistown, Illinois (SE½ SW½ Sec. 1 T4N R3E, Havana Quadrangle).

Situated on the eastern edge of a region of gently rolling plains and high on a point of the Illinois River bluff over 90 feet above the valley floor, the mounds provide a beautiful view of the Illinois and Spoon river valleys to the east and south (Fig. 1).

The bluff itself is a thick deposit of yellow to yellow-brown loess that mantles the underlying tacky, glacial drift clays of the Buffalo Hart moraine. Recent testing in areas immediately north of the mound revealed that the deposit of loess is at least 30 feet deep. Like all bluffs in the immediate area, it is deeply incised by many small stream valleys and washes that cut back into the uplands. Small springs and seeps are quite common along the slopes of many of these valleys, especially at the juncture of the glacial deposits and Pennsylvania shales. Slumping, resulting from the continuous wetting of the plastic clays and shales, is also common.

The next valley west of the mound contains a large spring that apparently was used time and time again over the millennia. Archaic people who had a small camp area in this valley were probably the first to exploit this water resource. Evidence implies that the spring continued to be used by the Woodland and Mississippian groups; and it was used as recently as the 1930's by the Dickson family to water their livestock.

Situated between the upland and the Illinois River floodplain is the Havana Terrace. To the east of the mound, alluvial fans sweep outward into the low, wide valley.

The Illinois River Valley, a remnant of the old Mississippi, is about four miles wide at the Dickson Mounds area. The eastern edge of the valley is defined by 30-foot-high ridges which constitute the Havana and Manito terraces. These terraces are mostly sand dunes and flat sand country. On the west the valley is bordered by 90- to 130-foot-high bluffs which mark the edge of the flat uplands.

Down the valley nearly four miles to the southeast of Dickson Mounds, the Spoon River merges with the Illinois. For some time after the turn of the century, much of this area was still a maze of large lakes and meandering channels. The largest of these, Thompson Lake, was drained in 1923 by Joy Morton, the "Salt King." However, many sloughs and low pondlike areas still remain. Manmade levees presently surround this part of the valley and crisscross through it along property lines, permitting much of this lowland to be cultivated. However, certain parts of this area are still so low that, in the event of a wet spring, crops may not be realized from them.

Some of the local geological conditions were particularly beneficial to these prehistoric peoples. Sandstones, useful as smoothing and abrading stones, outcrop along many stream valleys. Hard stones such as granite, diorite and basalt, which were used in the manufacture of tools and for other domestic purposes, are also available in many of the creekbeds. Products of the glacial drift, the hard stones are often accompanied by low-grade chert pebbles that could have been utilized in the manufacture of some of the smaller tools although little of this low-grade material appears to have been used. No outcroppings of fine-grained chert are exposed anywhere in the immediate area, and only three outcroppings of low-grade, friable siliceous material could be located in the area. However, this material was seldom used. About 92 percent of all chert used by the Dickson Mounds people came from the Avon quarries located 30 miles northwest. An abundance of fairly high grade chert is available at this quarry which appears to have been worked extensively.

Many sources of clays containing enough montmorillonite, illite, and kaolinite to be useful in potterymaking are available throughout the area. Of the Pleistocene-age clays, the glacial drift, loess, and recent alluvial deposits, all having high montmorillonite content, are the most suitable sources for the manufacture of pottery.

The clays most often used by the Mississippian people seem to have been the alluvial and glacial drift clays. The latter is easily recognized, when fired under oxidizing conditions, by its high iron content which becomes nearly brick red in coloring. Weathered shale and underclays were seldom used by late prehistoric potters.

HARN: PREHISTORY OF DICKSON MOUNDS

Outcroppings of weathered shale are abundant locally in the Pennsylvanian deposits. Most of these underclays are primarily composed of illite, but the basal Pennsylvanian underclays, which are entirely noncalcareous, are predominantly kaolinite. Local clayworking plants and kilns have used both clay and shale sources in the manufacture of brick and tile throughout the last century (Savage 1921:57-58).

Great quantities of bituminous coal outcrop along nearly every major stream and river in the area, but there is no evidence that it was used for fuel by the Dickson Mounds Indians. The Dicksons found two large discs of smoothed and polished cannel coal associated with burials in the now-destroyed upper layers of the mounds. Both discs were found in pottery vessels and may have been used as smoothing tools. It is also supposed that coal could have been used as a source of pigment for making black paint.

Today, the climate of this area is temperate with an average growing season of 177 days (Wanless 1957:15). The annual average temperature is 51 + degrees. The mean monthly temperature at Havana ranges from 26.6 F. in January to 77.5 F. in July. Annual precipitation averages 34 inches, and the unmelted snowfall averages 20.9 inches. As the runoff is about one-fourth the total rainfall, disastrous flooding of the major rivers sometimes follows periods of concentrated rainfall. Today, this is partially controlled by levees.

BIOGEOGRAPHY

The natural habitat is an important consideration in the cultural position of Dickson Mounds and its related sites in the Spoon River area. Complex floristic communities afforded ideal environments for many economically important forms of wildlife. White-tailed deer (*Odocoileus virginianus*), raccoon (*Procyon lotor*), opossum (*Didelphis marsupialis*), woodchuck (*Marmota monax*), porcupine (*Erethizon dorsatum*), squirrel (*Sciurus* spp.), gopher (*Geomys* spp.), rabbit (*Sylvilagus* spp.), various small rodents and some elk (*Cervus canadensis*) appear to have been common in the uplands and forested areas. Turkey (*Meleagris gallopava*), passenger pigeon (*Ectopistes migratorius*), prairie chicken (*Tympanuchus* spp.), bobwhite (*Colinus virginianus*) and various passeriformes were probably dominant among bird populations of these zones.

Until the time of its draining, Thompson Lake provided both commercial and sport fishing and hunting for thousands of people each year. The output of rough fish for this area reportedly totaled over one million pounds annually. Undoubtedly this area also provided an abundance of game during prehistoric times. Remains of several kinds of waterfowl and riverine birds and animals were found in association with the Dickson Mounds occupants. These included species of ducks, geese, and swan (?), muskrat (*Ondatra zabethica*), beaver (*Castor canadensis*), various species of freshwater mollusks and fishes, turtles, and frogs.

Nuts, fruits and berries, seeds, and roots and tubers contributed substantially to food requirements and, together with many kinds of drug and fiber plants, served a variety of domestic uses by the prehistoric inhabitants.

Probably little difference in flora existed between the last prehistoric occupation and the first concentrated European settlement of this area in the Illinois valley. At least no major climatic change had occurred during this short span of time to influence a change in the floristic conditions.

The first white inhabitants to trickle into this region were trappers and hunters; and since they practiced little agriculture, they had relatively little influence on the ecological situation prior to the first quarter of the nineteenth century. Between that time and the beginning of the Civil War, however, this European invasion was greatly accelerated; and by the termination of the war, the population of the Dickson Mounds area was nearly equal to (if not larger than) that of the present day. The majority of these newcomers were farmers who tilled the clay hillsides and "stump farmed" (cut down trees and farmed between the stumps). These two practices, plus the practice of burning to reduce vegetation, have resulted in the drastic alteration of the original flora.

According to local tradition, the clay hillsides were the first to have their natural vegetational covers altered. Next were the benches or terraces adjacent to the floodplain. However, little of the prairie was farmed prior to the introduction of the steel plow. Years later, when the land reclamation projects were begun, great portions of the floodplain were opened to cultivation. The only areas in the floodplain that retain their primitiveness today are the gaps between levee districts which allow intrusive tributaries to reach the main rivers. Since these gaps are subject to frequent overflow, they are rarely farmed, thereby giving a fair picture of the prereclamation-era flora of the valley.

Two other areas or zones have escaped deforestation to a certain degree: the stream valleys, usually not cultivated but frequently grazed, and the talus slope or hillside forest. The hillside forest is quite often (by modern standards) in a nearly primitive state. Occasionally used as a source of lumber and firewood, it was frequently found to be too steep to farm; consequently, a fairly natural situation still exists in some areas.

A predominance of certain types of vegetation usually exists in each of the three major floristic zones. To simplify a discussion of this, the area will be divided into three zones: the uplands, the floodplain, and the transition zone separating these two. Further divisions of these zones are listed below.

    A. The Upland Zone
        1. The upland prairie
        2. The upland forest
    B. The Transition Zone
        1. Hillside talus-slope forest
        2. Transition forest
    C. The Floodplain Zone
        1. The floodplain prairie
        2. The floodplain forest
        3. The lakes and sloughs

The Upland Zone

Flora on the upland prairie in this area is practically nonexistent. Farming and other domestic agencies have altered it so greatly that one can only guess what the original vegetational cover may have been. Early settlers noted that much of the upland prairie was covered with tall grasses (probably species of *Andropogon*, *Spartina* and *Panicum*), limited patches of which still occur today. Weed types, too numerous to mention, border fields and gullies where cultivation is impossible. Since the majority of these had little or limited economic value to the aborigine, they will not be discussed in detail here.

While only a few permanent shrubs have penetrated this plant monopoly, they are fairly well represented in a floral analysis. Among the most common are:

    Poison ivy *(Rhus toxicodendron L.)*
    Fragrant sumac *(Rhus canadensis L.)*
    Smooth sumac *(Rhus glabra L.)*
    Elderberry *(Sambucus canadensis L.)*

    Rough-leaved dogwood *(Cornus drummondii C. A. Mey.)*
    Buckbrush *(Symphoricarpos orbiculatus Moench.)*
    Hazel *(Corylus americana Walt.)*
    Sassafras *(Sassafras albidum [Nutt.] Nees)*

The persimmon *(Diospyros virginiana L.)* and the wild crabapple *(Malus ioensis [Wood] Britton)* occur occasionally in this habitat and would provide a fairly good food source in the late fall.

Few areas of virgin forest remain undisturbed; and through clearing and cutting, many tree species are nearing extirpation in the region. Cherry and walnut have been exploited for the manufacture of furniture and cedar for use as fence posts. Other species which are commonly cut include oak, maple, and hickory.

Some large trees still remain. Increment borings made by Patrick J. Munson of several large trees in the Dickson Mounds area proved that many had surpassed the century mark in age. However, a high percentage of the trees over 100 years old have hollow centers, making it difficult to determine the exact age beyond the 90- to 100-year barrier. At least where there are many trees this size accompanied by adequate numbers of smaller trees, small-tree species and seedlings, one can feel more justified in believing that a situation such as this would be nearly representative of the primitive upland forest. The trees most commonly found are listed here according to dominance.

    White oak *(Quercus alba L.)*
    Black oak *(Quercus velutina Lam.)*
    Northern red oak *(Quercus rubra L.)*
    Shagbark hickory *(Carya ovata [Mill.] K. Koch)*
    Mockernut hickory *(Carya tomentosa [Poir.] Nutt.)*
    Sugar maple *(Acer saccharum Marsh.)*
    White ash *(Fraxinus americana L.)*
    Pignut hickory *(Carya glabra [Mill.] Sweet)*
    Black walnut *(Juglans nigra L.)*

The pawpaw *(Asimina triloba [L.] Dunal)*, wild plum *(Prunus americana Marsh.)*, and black cherry *(Prunus serotina Ehrh.)*, although not dominate, would also provide a good food source.

Since few of the smaller trees and shrubs are as beneficial to the aborigine as the above-mentioned species, only the three most common fruit-bearing types will be listed.

    Redbud *(Cercis canadensis L.)*
    Hazel nut *(Corylus spp.)*
    Smooth sumac *(Rhus glabra L.)*

Woody vines and herbaceous plants are present locally in good numbers. The more important of these will appear later.

The Transition Zone

As mentioned previously, the vegetational types of this zone are often undisturbed. This situation often offers a good opportunity to study nearly primitive forest conditions.

Usually the upper portions of the slope mirror the situation of the upland forest, with the oak-hickory forest usually extending down over the hillside. Maples (*Acer* spp.) and walnut (*Juglans* spp.) are more dominant in this zone, as are the American and red elms (*Ulmus americana* L. and *Ulmus rubra* Muhl.). The American elm, by far the more numerous of the two, has been virtually destroyed by the Dutch Elm disease that swept through the area in the late 1950's. Basswood (*Tilia americana* L.) is commonly found in this zone.

Different types of small trees and shrubs occur occasionally in this habitat, but they are usually so similar to the small trees and shrubs recorded with the upland forest that they will not be repeated.

Herbaceous plants and several varieties of vines are again present in this zone, and many of these will appear in the Summary.

Beginning at or near the foot of the talus slope and extending down the gentle slopes toward the lake and river areas is the transition forest that binds the talus slope and floodplain flora. The underlying soil is mainly rich hillside wash with some alluvium soil and clay deposits noticeable closer to the floodplain.

This zone commonly combines some of the floristic elements of both adjacent forest zones. The bottomland types most commonly represented are the American elm (*Ulmus americana* L.), bur oak (*Quercus macrocarpa* Michx.), honey locust (*Gleditsia triacanthos* L.), silver (soft) maple (*Acer saccharinum* L.), pecan (*Carya illinoensis* [Wang.] K. Koch), and sycamore (*Platanus occidentalis* L.). Walnut (*Juglans nigra* L.), redbud (*Cercis canadensis* L.), and an occasional butternut (*Juglans cinerea* L.) are the most common hillside trees, that would be a food source for human inhabitants, to be found in the transition zone. The American elm, sycamore, bur oak, and pecan attain their maximum concentrations here and dominate much of this zone. Pecan groves at one time covered large areas of the west bank of Thompson Lake in the vicinity and were so fruit-ful that, as late as the early 1920's, each local family would gather "several large, horse-drawn wagonloads of nuts each fall" (Don F. Dickson, personal communication).

As is true of the transition of trees, the transition of hillside to floodplain herbaceous plants also occurs in this zone. Two of these types found in this area are especially worthy of mention as a food source. Lamb's quarter (*Chenopodium* spp.) is especially noticeable along with a sprinkling of pigweed (*Amaranthus* spp.). Both are well represented.

This abundance of natural food was undoubtedly relied upon heavily, even by the later plant-raising people. The availability of *Chenopodium* and *Amaranthus*, their rapid maturity, the number of seeds per plant, and the relative ease with which the seeds could be gathered would, in some instances, make their harvest even more desirable than that from the more laborious processes of corn-planting. In fact, Sauer (1950) presents rather convincing evidence concerning the productivity of the grain amaranths and contends that the yield of grain amaranths per unit of land may be greater than that of corn.

The Floodplain Zone

The floodplain prairie is almost completely cultivated at present. The original Federal land surveys suggest that large expanses of the floodplain were covered with grasses and herbaceous plants, but few of these conditions remain. Possibly, the original conditions were dominated by slough grass (*Spartina pectinata* Link.) and sumpweed (*Iva ciliata* Willd.) in the riverward part of this zone, becoming associated with bluestems as the bluffs were neared.

The floodplain forest is usually confined to a belt bordering the river channels and their entering tributaries, lakes and sloughs. Three previously mentioned trees — the American elm, soft maple, and pecan — are again dominant in this habitat; and another, the pin oak (*Quercus palustris* Muench.), is also well represented. The cottonwood (*Populus deltoides* Marsh.), hackberry (*Celtis occidentalis* L.), and, occasionally, a big shellbark hickory (*Carya laciniosa* [Michx.] Loud.) will also be noted, but they are usually in a minority.

An additional food source, the persimmon (*Diospyros virginiana* L.), is occasionally present in this habitat. Many species of woody vines are normally present in this forest area.

The banks of the lakes and sloughs are worthy of some discussion. These areas supported quantities of vegetation (many species favored as food by migratory birds) that made the waters attractive spots for wildfowl. Reed grass *(Phragmites australis* [cav.] Steudel*)* and cattail *(Typha latifolia* L.*)* were also present and probably served a variety of domestic uses of the prehistoric inhabitants in the valley. On the banks of nearly all bodies of water in the lowland and even wet areas of the uplands, the willow *(Salix* spp.*)* is by far the most dominant species of tree.

SUMMARY

One will readily note that in this study of the local flora, only the most dominant species are mentioned. Other floristic types, although sometimes not appearing in great numbers, were of equal importance to prehistoric people as food sources.

Grass and Weed Seeds
   Ragweed *(Ambrosia* spp.*)*
   Reed canary-grass *(Phalaris arundinacea* L.*)*
   Sunflower *(Helianthus* spp.*)*

Fruit and Berry Plants
   Mayapple *(Podophyllum peltatum)*
   Strawberry *(Fragaria americana* and F. *illinoensis)*
   Black raspberry *(Rubus occidentalis* L.*)*
   Grape *(Vitis* spp.*)*
   Gooseberry *(Ribes* spp.*)*
   Blackberry *(Rubus pennsylvanicus* Poir.*)*

Trees
   Black haw *(Virburnum prunifolium* L.*)*
   Kentucky coffee tree *(Gymnocladus dioicus* [L.] Koch*)*
   Mulberry *(Morus rubra* L.*)*

Roots and Tubers
   Hog-peanut *(Amphicarpa comosa* [L.] G. Don*)*
   Wild onion *(Allium tricoccum)*
   Arrowhead *(Sagittaria latifolia* Willd.*)*
   Bulrush *(Scirpus validus* Vahl.*)*
   Jerusalem artichoke *(Helianthus tuberosus* L.*)*
   Wild potato-vine *(Ipomoea pandurata* Meyer.*)*
   Wild ginger *(Asarum reflexum* Bickn.*)*

Vines
   Bittersweet *(Celastrus scandens* L.*)* innerbark used
Herbs
   Spikenard *(Aralia racemosa* L.*)* fresh shoots used
   Pokeweed *(Phytolacca americana* L.*)* leaves and stalks used
   Common milkweed *(Asclepias syriaca* L.*)* buds used
   Butterfly-weed *(Asclepias tuberosa* L.*)* buds used

Several species of trees, shrubs and plants could produce vegetal fibers to be used in the manufacture of fabrics. The milkweed *(Asclepias* spp.*)*, Indian hemp *(Apocynum cannabinum)*, red cedar *(Juniperus virginiana* L.*)*, nettle *(Urtica dioica* L.*)*, and red elm *(Ulmus rubra* Muhl.*)* would produce usable fibers. Probably the best sources of fibrous material would be the inner bark of the pawpaw *(Asimina triloba* [L.] Dunal*)*, dogbane *(Apocynum androsaemifolium* L.*)* and the inner bark of the basswood *(Tilia americana* L.*)*.

Although horticulture was probably relied on more heavily during the Mississippian period in the Dickson Mounds area, it was undoubtedly supplemented through the warmer months by the wealth of natural resources. Since the ripening period of some berries begins as early as June and other fruits, berries, roots, seeds, and nuts continue to mature into late fall, an exploitation of the floristic environment could have provided an important nutritional additive for the diet of these people.

Through centuries of continued practice, an ever-increasing familiarity with the habitats which would produce certain edible plants and animals at definite times throughout the year undoubtedly came about and, with this establishment of "Primary Forest Efficiency" (Caldwell 1958) available to complement their plant-raising, a greater residential stability could be easily maintained. The writer believes that even with locally dense prehistoric occupations, an intelligent utilization of the floristic environment could have nearly displaced any need of corn-raising. In fact, any early intense plant utilization may have given way to selective breeding which, in turn, may have paved the way for the acceptance of corn when it was finally introduced into the Illinois valley.

MOUNDS DESCRIPTION

Curved around the brow on a point along the Illinois River bluff, the Dickson Mounds reportedly resembled a single, large, thickened crescent with blunt points. However, recent excavations suggest a slightly different shape (Fig. 2).

Because of the amount of disturbance of the burial area, the original shape has been somewhat altered and nearly leveled in some areas. In addition to some destruction in 1900 and the ravages of previous excavators, many areas were leveled to erect outbuildings. These combined factors were found to be instrumental in the disturbance of at least 43 burials in the Dicksons' controlled excavation. In fact, out of the total 60-foot length of the vertical profile on the east side of the excavation, all but a few feet had been previously disturbed by uncontrolled digging.

Many broken and displaced bones can be attributed directly to tree roots and the pressure of the overlying soil. The overburden has also been instrumental in the crushing of most of the skulls of the children under twelve years of age. Many adult skulls and some of the pottery vessels found in the lower levels of the mound were affected by this factor. Rodent burrows were also a major problem. Known locally as "groundhog clay," this soft, easily dug loess is ideal for rodent burrowing. Groundhogs have honeycombed the hill with dens and tunnels and the mounds were no exception. Several burials have been disturbed as a result of this activity.

Mounds of this type are ideal for archaeological exploration. The loess soil has a high calcium oxide content and contains almost none of the acids which break down the general structure of the bone. Thus the skeletal remains are in a nearly perfect state of preservation. Loess is further advantageous to the archaeologist because it is soft, easily troweled, and unusually stable. A vertical profile of this soil will stand for decades without slumping.

Portions of at least two burial mounds were exposed by the Dickson excavation, as well as a few burials which may have been included in the pre-mound cemetery. Most of the skeletons are dorsally extended although many bundle burials and some prone and semiflexed burials also are present. Quantities of grave offerings accompany the dead.

The majority of the first burials were apparently placed in graves dug into the hill surface. Burial mounds were added later in the burial sequence. The hill surface may have been scraped clean or otherwise prepared prior to burial since there is a near absence of humus lines in the existing profiles. However, any existing humus line may have been destroyed by intensive grave digging on the part of the Indian. Humus lines were evident elsewhere in the burial area during the 1966-1968 excavations.

More than ninety burials, all of which are below the level of the original hill surface, are exposed in the excavation. Only six burial pits or graves could be isolated for these individuals. However, this is partly due to the fact that the floor of the Dickson excavation is level, for the most part, and does not necessarily follow the original hill contour; therefore, most of the pits were completely removed. The bottom of the excavation is many feet below the base of the mound in some areas along its eastern perimeter. Because of the absence of good profiles and the removal of all earth down to the level of a given burial, it is difficult to determine the relationship of some burials to the original hill surface.

Many graves were dug intrusively into the mound as it was built up, but most of these pits can not now be detected because of the leaching of the loess soil. Intrusive burials are easily detected only where they intrude earlier interments, which occurs at least 18 times. Little reverence was paid the burials encountered; while some disturbed bones were gathered and replaced in a stack nearby, many were thrown aside, and other bones and bone fragments were included in the fill over the newly placed bodies.

The locations of the first burials placed on the hill may never be known. The hilltop was not built up in even layers, and there was a certain amount of horizontal expansion as well. The 1966-1968 excavations disclosed that the burial area was actually comprised of several small pre-mound cemeteries, at least 10 separate burial mounds, and a small truncated pyramidal mound which was later enlarged and used for burial purposes (Harn n.d.). These mounds and the earlier areas of pit burial were concentrated into a cemetery along the crest and bluff point which partially encircled a large aboriginal borrow pit. These factors underlie the term *Dickson Mounds Cemetery*.

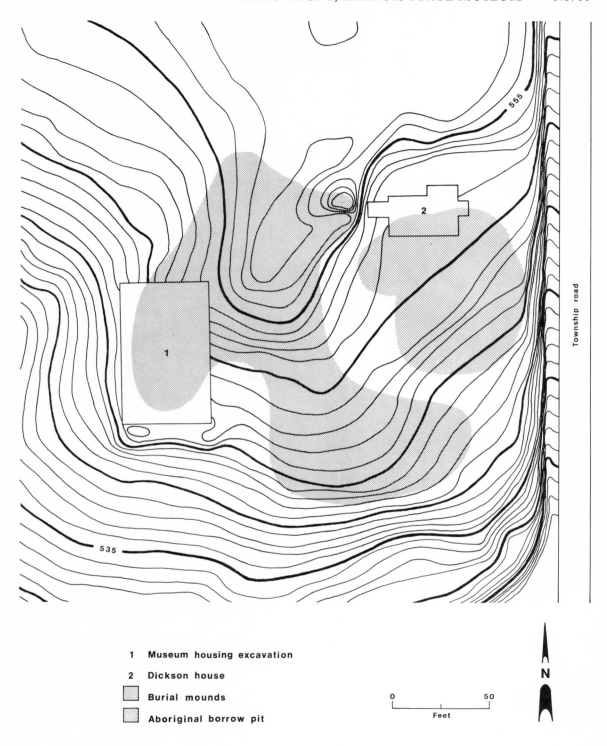

Figure 2. Contour map of the Dickson Mounds Cemetery and accompanying aboriginal borrow pit (now filled). Contour interval, one foot. (Adapted from Anderson and Associates 1966.)

The borrow pit is adjacent to the eastern edge of the mound (Fig. 2). According to the first white occupants of the site, the pit was approximately 80 by 90 feet in diameter and 27 feet deep. A comparison of the soil in the hole with that covering the burials revealed that both were silty loess, suggesting that this pit resulted from the continued use of this spot as a source of earth to cover the dead. If the pit were roughly hemi-spheroidally shaped, it would have contained over 75,000 cubic feet of fill. If it were more straight-sided, the amount could have been in excess of 100,000 cubic feet. These figures are substantially more than the estimated 65,000 cubic feet of earth required to create the mounds. Recent testing suggests that the borrow pit was slightly smaller and less deep than the original estimate.

HISTORY AND EARLY EXCAVATIONS

The Dickson Mounds Cemetery was originally included in a designated tract of land in Illinois known as the "Military Tract." This area was laid out following the War of 1812 to be given as payment to the soldiers of that conflict. Its broad expanse lies between the Mississippi and Illinois rivers and extends north to the north line of Bureau and Henry counties — one of the most fertile areas in the Midwest.

The entire area, abundant with natural resources, was particularly attractive to early man. No river or major stream in the Tract is without sites of archaeological importance. In Fulton County, bordered by the Illinois River on the east and bisected by the Spoon River, a number of rich Indian sites were noted by early settlers. Among these was the Dickson Mounds site. The early historians' factual accounts and descriptions of the Fulton County area often contain valuable information, listing exact locations of archaeological features, such as rows of house depressions in village sites or original heights and pyramidal contours of temple mounds (History of Fulton County, Illinois, 1879). Today these once well-defined locations often appear only as indiscernible low areas in a field or obscure rises and humps, altered by cultivation until all distinguishing features are obliterated. Far from being mere references, these early accounts are often amazingly keen observations even though they were written nearly a century ago.

Reference to the Dickson Mounds was made years previous to the finding of burials there. Occupying a conspicuous position curving around the brow on the point of the bluff, this large structure caused much speculation by local residents. It was a generally accepted fact that the mounds probably contained burials, a supposition made because cultivation of similar structures in the area produced human bones; how-ever, the mounds remained untouched until soon after the termination of the Civil War. William Dickson migrated from Kentucky in the late 1830's and settled the land that encompassed Dickson Mounds. In the late 1860's he cleared the burial area of brush and trees in preparation for the planting of an orchard. Human bones encountered when digging holes to set out the young trees were taken to another area and reburied. This practice was continued for several years and only occasionally was an artifact saved.

No great interest was taken in the burial area by collectors until late in the 1800's. W. S. Strode, a local doctor and naturalist, reportedly dug in the mounds on numerous occasions but no record was made of any of his findings. The mounds became a popular source for collectors; and their uncontrolled digging, coupled with unchecked soil erosion, gradually reduced the skeletal population and number of artifacts for nearly four decades.

One enterprising collector, Dr. Perine (a veterinarian from Chandlerville, Illinois), had a somewhat unique method of transporting his excavated pottery. Saving only the unbroken pieces, "he would place these side by side, separated by a little straw in an old high-sided farm wagon, the bottom of which was also covered with straw. When a layer was completed, it was covered in a like manner. This was repeated until the wagon was full" (Don F. Dickson, personal communication). This man reportedly "salvaged" three wagonloads of pottery. Most or all of this pottery has since been sold or scattered. In addition to this quantity of material, Thomas Dickson originally had an extra bedroom "about half filled with bowls" also from the mounds. These were sold and some were given away; the majority were purchased around 1920 by Mr. Harris, a buyer for the Payne Collection. However, no records were made of this material. Don Dickson, son of Thomas Dickson, mentioned that the pottery types were mostly plain ware (sometimes black-polished), beakers, and effigies and that hooded water bottles were more frequently found than they were in his later excavations. Antler or bone(?) rings were commonly noted as were strings of marine-shell beads. Copper-covered wood ornaments (discs with center holes) were found in a few graves as were four or five long brown-flint knives (Ramey knives of Mill Creek chert?) and several stone pipes. These items will be discussed later in the text.

In 1932, collector Edward W. Payne passed away, and the next year Don Dickson agreed to appraise and direct the sale of the Payne Collection. A few of these items were recognized as originally coming from the Dickson Mounds. Governor Horner provided funds in order that they could be purchased and returned to Dickson Mounds where they are currently on display.

According to oral tradition, considerable destruction to the burial area was effected in 1900 by Thomas Dickson during preconstruction activities associated with the erection of a house adjacent to the mounds. It was estimated that several feet of earth containing some 800 burials were removed from the crest and eastern portion of the mound by horses and a slip scraper and used to fill the adjacent aboriginal borrow pit (Harn 1971b:10-11). The house reportedly was then built in the filled pit, using the mounds as a partial shield from winter winds. Unfortunately, the oldest informant of these activities would have been only five years of age in 1900, and there remains no creditable first-person account.

Subsequent excavations of the burial mounds, borrow pit, and adjacent areas suggest a chain of events quite contrary to the above (Harn n.d.). None of the mounds near the borrow pit appeared to have been altered by grading. Mound L, a truncated pyramidal structure situated adjacent to the borrow pit on the west, retains its ramp-sided, flat-topped contour to the present day. Except for extensive pitting by relic collectors, contours of other mounds in the area of the reported destruction appear little changed. Equally as contrary to oral tradition was the situation in the borrow pit where only fragments of human bone were discovered. The pit was found to be filled, not by skeletons and mound fill, but by a more sterile clay-loess mixture obtained by scraping a notch into the hillside adjacent to the borrow pit on the north. The depth of

the scraping removed possibly ten horizontal feet of the shallow, northern edge of the borrow pit. The Dickson house was then built primarily on the stable loess subsoil in the artificial notch instead of in the newly filled borrow pit as reported, a procedure that certainly would have been more architecturally sound. However, the south side of the house was built on pit fill, but it was situated over a compacted area filled by silting prior to 1900. The extreme northern limit of the borrow pit shown in Figure 2 represents its approximate configuration prior to alteration in 1900, the edge line being partially extrapolated from vertical profiles recorded by excavations in 1968.

In the late 1920's Don Dickson decided to excavate more of the cemetery, a decision made not for the purpose of obtaining relics but because of his interest in pathology. Dr. Dickson's primary concern centered on the presence of the many individuals who had died and were buried together. He hoped to find some correlation between mass graves and bone pathology. It long has been held that his first excavation was begun in February, 1927. As is discussed below, this date may or may not have marked the beginning of the actual Dickson excavation, but one fact is abundantly clear: A new attitude prevailed at the cemetery; for instead of exhuming skeletons bone by bone, the shovel was abandoned for a hand trowel, small brushes, and similarly sized equipment in order that the burials could be carefully excavated. It was this simple decision to preserve that provided the stimulus for advanced archaeological research in Illinois, if indeed not throughout the eastern United States, directly affecting the lives of many of us who were to follow.

In retrospect, it now appears doubtful that the full-scale excavation was actually started in February. Two points would argue for this position: (1) Unless the winter was unusually mild, excavation would have been nearly impossible, or at best very difficult, because of the normally frozen ground; and (2) there is no record of newspaper coverage of the excavation which precedes early April of that year. Once excavation was begun in earnest, massive attention was focused on the site by the media, and hundreds of associated newspaper articles are preserved in the Dickson scrapbooks.

Two areas were originally opened on the mound. The larger of these, midway down the west slope of the burial area, was located in what is now the northeast corner of the burial exhibit

(Plate 4a). A smaller excavation was positioned on the east slope some 50 feet away (Plate 4b).

Three semiflexed burials found in the smaller test area were exhibited to the public during 1927 and 1928. They were protected by a small A-frame hog shed until the hole was finally backfilled in the fall of 1928. Artifacts from this group were removed, with the pottery vessel eventually ending up near Burial 67 in the Dickson excavation (See D94 Harn 1971b: Fig. 22). Its associated shell spoon has not been found.

It is possible that the reported February testing of the mound developed into the smaller excavation that was covered by the A-frame shed as local tradition dictates. But newspaper accounts suggest that this excavation was actually undertaken sometime after the larger excavation was opened. Its presence is not indicated prior to mid-April.

Work in the larger excavation was begun about April 1, 1927, according to various newspaper reports. At that time Dr. Dickson was assisted by unidentified relatives, probably his father and father's brothers. Also involved was the late T. W. Routson, a fellow chiropractor about Dr. Dickson's age (Plate 4b). By April 8, more than 20 burials had been exposed by these gentlemen; but by mid-April, Dr. Routson had been "obliged to resume his practice," according to the April 14, 1927, *Peoria Star*. It is doubtful that he assisted on a regular basis after that time.

At first this excavation area was covered only by a small canvas tent which sheltered the area and workers during the excavation (Plate 1a). By May 1, the Dicksons had erected a more substantial woodframe structure measuring some 20 by 20 feet, its sides covered with glass cloth to enhance interior lighting (Plate 1b). This move toward permanence was greatly influenced by the interest of Dr. Strode and the continued encouragement of Dr. Warren King Moorehead. In a paper presented in 1929 at the Twenty-Second Annual Meeting of the Illinois State Academy of Science, Dr. Moorehead (1930:27) referred to the Dicksons' work as being "the most important exhibit *in situ* in this country."

It is at this point that the process of excavation and the individuals involved become less clear. We do know that Dr. Dickson's father, Thomas (Plate 3b), and his father's younger brother, Marion (Plate 3a), continued working with him in the excavation and that a cousin, Raymond Dickson (Plate 4a), eventually joined these three. However, the extent of their individual contributions is unknown except in the case of Marion Dickson. Marion soon left Dickson Mounds (after aiding in the excavation of Burials 73 and 74) to direct excavations at the Middle Woodland Ogden Mound in the valley below.

With the discovery of each new item at Dickson, interest in the excavation intensified, and a second frame building measuring 20 by 28 feet was soon built in the area which is now the southwestern corner of the excavation (Plate 2a). These were replaced in January, 1928, by a 46- by 76-foot tile block building that housed the excavation until recently (Plate 2b). Excavation progressed until the summer of 1929 when the last of the 234 burials were exposed. Four years later, on May 1, 1933, a tornado partially destroyed the tile block structure. Some archaeological material in display cases was lost along with some artifacts from the excavation, but overall destruction of skeletal material was minimal.

Periodically throughout the decade following 1927, small tests were made in other parts of the burial mounds in an effort to determine its dimensions and the density of burials. All burials encountered were carefully exposed and occasionally photographed; but they were left *in situ* and reburied. Artifacts found with these burials were undoubtedly removed if the A-frame excavation is an indication of normal procedure.

Many of the most prominent figures in archaelogy of that era, such as Warren King Moorehead, Henry Clyde Shetrone, and Fay-Cooper Cole, were frequent visitors to Dickson Mounds. Since this was the first place where prehistoric materials were left *in situ* for public viewing, much publicity was given this formerly secluded spot in Fulton County. Tourist traffic soon became a major problem, and the flow of visitors was so great that most of the Dicksons' workday was spent in explaining their work to these people. Later in 1927, a fee was attached to viewing the remains to help defray the expenses of the new building and other planned public facilities. This charge was not relinquished until the mounds and their confines were sold to the State of Illinois in 1945 and placed under the Department of Conservation, Division of Parks and Memorials. The Park was transferred from the Department of Conservation to the Illinois State Museum in 1965. A new museum of anthropology was opened at Dickson Mounds in 1972.

One of the major problems has been the preservation of the exposed skeletal remains. Varnishes and shellacs were first tested on bones which had eroded out of the mound. These coatings discolored the bone, leaving an unnatural sheen, and further testing of these solutions was curtailed. Other solutions, such as hot paraffin, were tested without success. The paraffin was applied only to the most porous bones (vertebrae and joint areas), but it became cloudy and was easily discolored by dirt. Occasionally it penetrated the cracked bone and split it further. Diluted ambroid was used for a period of time but it also was unsatisfactory. A mixture of Alvar 7-70 and chemically pure acetone proved more successful. The Alvar mixture was more easily applied, had good penetrating qualities, and sealed out the air without producing an unnatural appearance. It is hoped that repeated applications of this solution will effectively reduce any corrosion of the bone surface, protecting the skeletal material indefinitely.

INVENTORY OF ARTIFACTS

All artifactual material from the Dickson excavation is associated with mortuary activity. In this respect, these items are "ceremonial" in that they reflect certain attitudes regarding death. Because of their implied use or function, most also reflect the technology and to a lesser degree the subsistence activities of this period. Many burial items probably represent special efforts which influenced the quality and stylistic design. While some of these items were probably not indicative of everyday utilitarian equipment and others may have been contributed gifts not actually owned in life by the deceased, none are regarded as being specialized funerary equipment manufactured expressly for inclusion with the dead.

Traditionally, artifacts have been grouped and described according to the various kinds of raw materials from which they were made. The recent trend has been toward classification in terms of functional categories (cf. Winters 1969:30-87). This analytical trend is followed regarding the Dickson Mounds material.

This functional division of artifacts is arbitrary and further studies may justify including some of these items with different groupings; this may be especially pertinent regarding the "ceremonial" division.

Below is a list of the artifacts, followed by a functional classification and discussion of each artifact type.

GENERAL UTILITY TOOLS
  Unaltered flakes
  Scrapers
    side
    end
    thumbnail

Knives
  large blades
  simple flakes

WEAPONS
  Projectile points

FABRICATING AND PROCESSING TOOLS
  Needles (?)
  Bone Awls
  Weaving tools
  Drills
  Grooved sandstone abraders
  Flaking tools

DIGGING OR AGRICULTURAL TOOLS
  "Hoes," shell
  Hoes, stone

ORNAMENTS
  Shell bead bracelets
  Shell bead necklaces
  Beads, marine-shell
    disc-shaped
    hemispherical
    spheroidal
    truncated-cone
    whole *Olivella jaspidea*
  Beads, fluorite
  Pendants, mussel-shell
  Pendants, *Busycon* spp.
  Arm rattles or clackers, mussel-shell
  Ankle rattles, mussel-shell
  Bracelets, bone
  Hairpins, bone
  Antler rings (hair ornaments?)
  Copper-covered wood earspools or plugs

DOMESTIC
  Spoons, shell
  Trowel, pottery
  Spatula, pottery
  Pottery jars
      Cahokia Cordmarked
      Dickson Plain
      Dickson Trailed
      Powell Plain
      globular
      lobed
      miniature
      incised
      plain and black- or brown-polished
  Water bottles
      short-necked
      hooded effigy
      plain
  Beakers or bean pots
      Spoon River
      Tippits
      plain and black- or brown-polished
  Shallow bowls
      plain and red-slipped
  Deep bowls
      plain
  Effigy bowls
      mammal
      bird
      plain and black-polished

FISHING
  Fishhooks, bone
  Fishhook blanks, bone

WOODWORKING TOOLS
  Celt
  Chisel, beaver incisor

CEREMONIAL ITEMS
  Stone pipe

MISCELLANEOUS
  Tool kits
  Snails
  Mussel shells, unaltered
  Deer phalanges, unaltered
  Bird bone, unaltered
  Broken rock
  Chert flakes
  Potsherds
  Scarification(?) kit

GENERAL UTILITY TOOLS (Figs. 3-6)

By far the most common artifact types in the excavation are general utility tools. Lithic materials of this category comprise five distinct artifact types: unaltered flakes, flake side scrapers, scrapers (side, end, and thumbnail), flake blades (lamellar and simple), and knives (large double-pointed blades). Nearly all of these artifacts are made from Avon chert.

Unaltered flakes occur most commonly, followed by small simple scrapers with one or two worked edges. End scrapers and thumbnail scrapers are present in limited numbers, as are blades made from simple flakes. One lamellar blade was found. Flake blades are usually present in three forms: large heavy flakes with rough to fine alternate flaking along one or more edges, thin elongated flakes with fine and even alternate flaking occurring along one or more edges, and unaltered flakes which exhibit battering along at least one edge. Some unretouched chert flakes and chunks presently listed as waste material could have been employed in a variety of domestic uses without further modification. Both categories of knives and scrapers are ordinarily manufactured from simple, uniface flakes or spalls.

Positioning of the general utility tools seems to have been somewhat correlated with sex. With male burials, unaltered single chert flakes rarely (never?) occur as separate offerings, with all flake groups included as parts of larger tool kits. These groups are placed at the head (3 instances), right hand (2 instances), and left hip and feet (1 instance each). Only one of the three females with unaltered flakes has an accompanying tool (a flake knife), with flakes positioned at either hand and the head. Unaltered flakes occur singly with sub-adults at the head and in one tool kit at the right hip-hand.

Except for one example at the right elbow, chert scrapers occur also as parts of larger tool kits with male burials, occurring at the hand (3 instances — 1 left, 2 right), head (4 instances) and left hip and feet (1 instance each). With females, scrapers occur as separate grave offerings and appear only at the right hand (3 instances), with one scraper included in a female bundle burial and the position of another scraper unrecorded. Scrapers were included only with one subadult.

Flake knives were also restricted to larger groups of artifacts with males, occurring at the head (1 instance) and the right hand (2 instances). With females, flake knives occurred only at the left hand (2 instances), once accompanied by a chert flake. Subadults had single instances of flake knives at the right hand, head, and left side, with one subadult having four knives included in a tool kit at the right hip-hand.

Six bifacially flaked knives are found with burials (Fig. 6). The four smaller knives are included in groups of other lithic artifacts while the two larger blades occur as separate offerings. Both occur in the area of the hands. Two knives are more or less double-pointed and broad, the larger of these having one of its edges less curved than the other. One other knife is more narrow and has a convex base. All three are thin and well made. Two knives are rather crude. Both are bulky and roughly chipped, and one (D167) has slight shoulders. They are included in a tool kit with Burial 90.

The original shape of the sixth knife probably resembled the broad-bladed "Cahokia" or Ramey knife (Fig. 6, D209). The flake scars on about one-fourth of the length of the piece are worn almost smooth from prolonged hafting(?) (it could also have been a polished ceremonial knife which had been reworked) and the resharpening of the cutting edges has altered the blade into a narrow lanceolate form. This knife was manufactured from Mill Creek chert.

WEAPONS (Fig. 7)

A total of 28 arrowpoints is recorded with 10 burials, and all are typically Mississippian. Two of these (with No. 179) have been missing for many years and are not included in the following tabulations. Seventeen are simple triangles with straight to slightly convex sides and nine are notched. The bases of seventeen are straight, five are slightly concave, and four are slightly convex. One (D145, Burial 90) could be a drill since it is quite narrow and has an expanding base resulting in sharply pointed tangs on each side. Seven points have multiple notches. These are essentially simple side-notched triangular points with an extra set of shallow notches cut between the basin notch and the base. Five arrowpoints have basal notches. Two single side-notched points, one with elongated indentations instead of true notches, are also present. Fine flaking on

both faces is usually characteristic of all of these points, but occasionally one face has a smooth fracture surface which is rarely worked at all. The arrowpoints do not have a great range in size, all measuring between 1.2 cm. and 3.2 cm. long with points about 2.5 cm. being most common.

The positioning of these arrowpoints varies somewhat. Arrowpoints are found over the shoulder (3 instances), between the knees (2 instances), at the head, the side, and on the chest of a fetus (1 instance each), and in tool kits (2 instances). Only the orientations of arrowpoints between the knees of burials were recorded by the Dicksons. With the exception of those specimens included in tool kits, probably completed arrows were interred with the dead.

FABRICATING AND PROCESSING TOOLS (Figs. 8 and 9)

Fabricating and processing tools include needles, awls or punches, weaving tools, drills, grooved sandstone abraders, and chert-flaking tools. These tools are associated with four burials in the excavation (Nos. 45, 90, 170, and 179), and they are included as parts of larger tool kits which also contain utility tools as well as a variety of other equipment.

Seventeen bone "needles" were found in a cluster accompanied by a fine-grained sandstone abrader inside two mussel-shell valves behind the head of Burial 90 (Fig. 32, D135-D137). The needles are all of similar size and shape, 5 cm. in length, and range from flattened to square in cross section. One appears to be round. Although they may have been employed in sewing, it is just as conceivable that their intended use was for scarification. Thus they also are discussed under the heading **Miscellaneous**.

One bone awl fashioned from the tarsometatarsus of a turkey (*Meleagris gallapavo*) was associated with a sandstone abrader behind the head of No. 90. It is moderately polished.

An apparent bone shuttle was included in a tool kit at the head of No. 45. It is a flattened piece of bird bone, probably cut from the humerus of a large goose or swan. The sides and end are worn smooth by use, while the tip (although now partly broken) is highly polished.

Seven drill bits occur with four burials. Six are crude bits on heavy flakes while one is more well made. In cross section, these tools have roughly rounded bits and flattened expanded bases. All are part of larger tool kits.

Two burials, Nos. 45 and 90, have five sandstone slot abraders in association. Two abraders with No. 45 were included in a tool kit near the head. One of the three with No. 90 occurred in association with a sewing or scarification kit; another was associated with a bone awl, and the other occurred singly. All were positioned near the head.

Two smooth pieces of sandstone in a tool kit with No. 179 could also have been employed as whetstones in grinding or shaping (Fig. 31, D316, D400). Both show indication of wear.

Nine deer antler tips are found with three burials. All were probably taken from white-tail deer *(Odocoileus virginianus)*. These tips were usually broken off and used without further modification, but in two instances tips were cut or grooved and broken. One (D315) has a curious V-shaped cut across the bottom of its base. Since the tips of these tines generally show scratches and other signs of wear, it is probable that they were used as flaking tools. All antler tips were included in tool kits in association with chert flakes, chert cores, and completed chert artifacts. Positioning of these artifacts was restricted to the right hand-waist area (1 instance), left side (1 instance), and to the feet (1 instance). Five flakers were included with No. 90, three with No. 179, and one with No. 170. Only a portion of the tool kit with No. 170 has been uncovered, however, and other unexposed artifacts probably remain.

Digging Or Agricultural Tools (Fig. 10)

While their occurrence is usually restricted to village sites, six remnants of digging tools are found in the excavation. Three of these are manufactured from shell and three from chert. The three shell "hoes," (along with several unaltered valves of common mussel shell and a shell spoon) were associated with Burial 72. All are probably made from Washboards *(Megalonaias gigantea)*. One small and apparently unpolished chert hoe is included in a tool kit at the feet of No. 170. A moderately polished hoe fragment, modified into a scraper, is associated with No. 46, and a small, lightly polished hoe fragment is with No. 152.

Ornaments (Figs. 11-15)

Olivella jaspidea shell beads occur with two infants. A single *Olivella* bead is on the chest of No. 139, while at least 103 *Olivella* beads were piled on the chest of No. 161. In this case, it is probable that the beads were strung but were not placed around the neck. All *Olivella jaspidea* beads are unaltered except for the apex which is broken or ground away to produce a continuous hole the length of the shell. One disc bead of mussel shell was found on the chest of one infant.

Busycon spp. was the most common marine shell employed in bead manufacture; over 680 marine-shell beads are found with 21 burials. While disc beads are the most common type, a variety of other shapes is represented including thickened discs, spheroidal and nearly round beads, globular beads with flattened sides, and one truncated cone.

Bead bracelets occur on the right wrist of No. 2 and on the left wrist of No. 219. The right wrist of No. 219 has not been exposed, nor has the upper body or lower legs — areas frequently involved in the display of bead ensembles.

Bead necklaces actually being worn occur with six children and infants and two adults. Beads per necklace range from a low of five beads with a fetus to 111 and 207 beads with the adults. The previously mentioned group of 103 *Olivella* beads probably represents a necklace, although it was not actually being worn.

Single disc beads of marine shell (2 instances), mussel-shell disc beads (1 instance) and a single *Olivella jaspidea* bead possibly accompanied by two disc beads appear on the chest of four infants and may have represented necklaces. This may also be true of a single rectangular-block bead of fluorspar on the chest of infant No. 73.

Two groups of disc beads were described as being either "scattered over this skeleton" (No. 141) or as "lying on the chest" (No. 164). Both may have been either scattered necklace remnants or sewn on clothing. Two infants (Nos. 50 and 211) have 10 and 2 beads placed near the head. While these may represent unworn necklaces, they could have been worn in the hair.

Single large flattened hemispherical and globular beads of marine shell are found on the chests of two females, both beads accompanied by *Busycon* spp. pendants.

A single thickened disc bead of marine shell with No. 35 may have been a forelock bead since it was found "about 1 inch above the skull."

A large truncated conoidal bead of marine shell was included in a tool kit at the head of No. 45.

Mussel-shell pendants appear on the chests of two infants (Nos. 127 and 151). The former pendant is little more than a chip of shell, drilled for attachment. It accompanied a necklace of small marine-shell beads. The other pendant is a small right valve of mussel shell drilled at the anterior end for suspension. All margins and the hinge have been altered by smoothing.

Ten marine-shell pendants (*Busycon* spp.) are found with nine burials (Fig. 13). Seven of these appear on the chest, two occur near the head of one infant, and one was placed in a pottery jar near the head of another infant. All *Busycon* pendants have been altered in some manner. The surfaces of some are simply smoothed or ground while others have portions of the whorl removed. The axis and spire were removed from one shell, leaving only the hollow outer whorl. Five have been grooved for attachment, one has been drilled, and three show no evidence of either. One (D354) was initially grooved and subsequently was drilled when the pendant broke through the groove.

Sets of mussel-shell arm rattles or clackers were associated with three burials (Fig. 12). They were found "beneath neck" at the right shoulder and included in a tool kit at the feet of a burial. Similar specimens recovered during recent excavations at Dickson Mounds were positioned at the left elbows of burials, suggesting that these specimens in the Dickson excavation may not have been in their normal area of display. Each set was made from two unaltered valves of the same shell by drilling single holes (7-9 mm. in diameter) inward near the umbones and probably loosely tying the valves together. Shell species represented include the Pimple-Back (*Quadrula pustulosa*), Purple Warty-Back (*Cyclonaias tuberculata*), and Pig-Toe (*Fusconaia flava*).

Three sets of shell ankle rattles and a single shell ankle rattle were found with three females and an infant (Fig. 12). Each set was located in the ankle region; the single rattle was found in an unspecified location with the infant. The sets with Nos. 27 and 155 contained 14 and at least 12 rattles respectively. Both ankles were adorned. The set with No. 126 contained 12 rattles which appear to be placed only around the left ankle. No coverings or interior (usually quartz) pebbles

were apparently found with either Nos. 27 or 155 and no pebbles appear with the set on No. 126. However, unless a double strand of rattles was worn, it is suspected that these 12 shells may represent both the rattles and their covers.

Bone bracelets were found with one child and three infants (Fig. 14). Two may have been found on the left wrists, but the positions of others were not recorded. Three are fragmentary, portions of at least two of these probably being overlooked and destroyed during the initial excavation. All bracelets were cut from animal bone, probably from ribs of bison. All appear to have been rectangularly shaped, the length being three to four times the width. Each was ground thin on the under side, as evidenced by striations, but the outer surface is smoothed and highly polished. One hole was apparently drilled in each of the four corners, from the polished outer surface inward. Two of the bracelets are plain, one is probably decorated with engraved, nested, zigzag lines, and one has an intricate, engraved pattern not easily described (D401). This latter specimen may or may not be the one found with Burial 12.

Bone hairpins were found with two burials, Nos. 45 and 90 (Fig. 15; D58, D131). It is probable that both pins were worn in the hair, although the Dickson notes are not entirely clear in this regard. Both pins are round in cross section and have been cut from animal bone, probably deer. The pin with No. 90 is polished but undecorated while that with No. 45 is polished and has rough striations engraved around its base.

Two wide rings of deer antler were found with No. 99 (Fig. 15, D187-D188). Short sections (17-19 mm) were cut from the main antler beam and hollowed to produce rings with wall thicknesses of approximately 3 to 5 mm. Both rings are slightly concave-sided and exterior surfaces appear to have been polished. Both were found on the left shoulder of a female and were probably worn in the hair. According to the Dicksons, other bone (probably antler) rings were found "near the heads" of several burials prior to 1900 suggesting their occurrence is probably common.

Copper ornaments have often been found in the Dickson Mounds, most of which have been copper-covered wood earspools and, occasionally, beads. One unusual copper artifact, a "rod" approximately three feet long, one-fourth inch in diameter, and possibly pointed at one or both ends, was "pulled out of the ground" in the early

1900s. None of this early material is available for examination since it was sold by Thomas Dickson prior to 1910.

Two apparent remnants of copper-covered wood earspools were reportedly found somewhere near the head of No. 195 in the Dickson excavation. Their definite association is unverified, however, since no mention of them is made in Don Dickson's original records. Only the large disc end faced with foil copper was preserved, or at least recovered, with the covering carefully crimped over the edges of the piece. Both pieces were placed on display in an exhibit case in the museum building but were lost in the aftermath of the tornado of 1933. The drawing of these specimens was based on verbal descriptions supplied by the Dicksons (Fig. 15, D404-D405).

One other burial, No. 162, has a heavy copper discoloration on the left mastoid process and mandible. No associated copper object is mentioned in the Dickson field notes, but it is possible that any specimens were removed at the time its head was damaged by previous excavators. One deer antler tip (D314) with No. 179 is thoroughly stained with copper, but no associated object of copper was found.

DOMESTIC (Fig. 16 for shell spoons and Figs. 17-29 for pottery)

Shell Utensils

Common mussel shells were of definite economic importance to the people at Dickson. In addition to their use as tempering for pottery and for "hoes," they were equally important in their use as domestic utensils. Mississippian people of the Spoon River area commonly altered these shells both to add to their general serviceability and for decoration. However, the unaltered valves associated with Nos. 54 and 152 are probably spoons since they were included in vessels.

Manufacturing techniques are usually simple. The periostracum of the shell is normally removed and the sides and margins are ground, resulting in the thin spoons with polished, round-edged surfaces. Further alteration is usually limited to cutting a simple handle on the anterior margin. Handle shapes are varied, but most common is the stubby spur type. Handles are infrequently curved or elongated by cutting a deeper notch across the width of the valve. In three cases, handles are decorated with notches.

One of these (Fig. 16, D63) also has a small hole drilled in its cup near the lower ventral margin. All shell spoons with handles are made from left valves. Handles positioned on the anterior margins of left valves would most conveniently be used by right-handed people.

The alteration of many shells is so heavy that determination of the species is difficult at best, but the deep-cupped Pocketbook (Lampsilis ventricosa) is heavily favored in spoon manufacture. Of these 30 shell spoons, 28 are probably made from this species. One (D272 with No. 166) is made from a Pink Heel-Splitter (Proptera alata) and one from a Fragile Paper-Shell (Leptodea fragilis).

Of the 30 spoons definitely associated with burials, 22 are found in pottery vessels (including one spoon lying over a miniature jar), three appear in reasonably close proximity to the head and could have been included in perishable containers, and three occur at the left hand of one burial. The position of two spoons could not be determined. Spoons are most commonly contained within jars (17 instances) and bowls (4 instances), with one questionable occurrence of a spoon within a beaker. These spoons are frequently too large to have been used as dippers to extract food from the accompanying vessel.

Potter's Tools

The potter's trowel located near the right hand of No. 82 is the only tool of its kind in the excavation. It is made of clay with a paste similar to that of St. Clair Plain. A ceramic disc, which may have been a spatula or an undrilled spindle whorl, was associated with it (Fig. 30, D111-D112).

Pottery

For the most part the ceramic complex at Dickson Mounds appears to be similar to that of the Mississippian traditions of the Cahokia and Spoon River areas. No large storage jars were recovered nor were any Wells Incised plates found, but these vessels were probably regarded as culinary and may not have been buried with the dead. Both types are commonly found in association with other Spoon River ceramics in excavations of villages, however.

The most common pottery type in the Dickson excavation is a shell-tempered plain ware similar to St. Clair Plain: Approximately 72 percent of the vessels have been assigned to this category.

Vessel forms included in this category are effigy bowls, water bottles, lobed jars, deep bowls, shallow bowls, globular and angular-shouldered jars, and beakers.

While the use of alluvial(?) clays seems to predominate in pottery manufacturing, about one-third (primarily globular jars) are made of clays from the glacial drift. A separate category is not assigned for black- or brown-polished ware. Nearly every pottery type contains plain ware plus vessels which are identical to these in paste and technique of manufacture — except that they have been black- or brown-polished.

The remainder of the ceramic assemblage is comprised of shell-tempered, cordmarked globular jars with everted rims. Certain variations among these vessels are evident and will be discussed below.

Beakers

Of the ten beakers, three are typical Spoon River types (constricted sides producing expanding mouth and base) and seven are typical of the Cahokia type, Tippits Bean Pot. Four (three Spoon River and one Tippits) are black- or brown-polished, and the six remaining Tippits type are plain and slightly polished. The former beakers have slipped and polished inner and outer surfaces; all have lips and lugs for pouring on the rim opposite the handle, and three have an extra lip on the rim opposite the pouring lip. All beakers except D366 have handles. Handle shapes are straight to upcurving spike except for one which resembles a crude fist or paw (D345).

No evidence of painting, incising, or engraving has been noticed on any of the vessels of this category, although such techniques were evident elsewhere in the Dickson cemetery and appear at most other Mississippian burial sites in the area (cf. Cole and Deuel 1937).

Shallow Bowls

Three plain vessels comprise this category. One (D189) has indented pouring channels on opposite sides of the rim.

Deep Bowls

One vessel with the scars of two lips or lugs on opposite rims has been either red-filmed or its original black-polished surfaces have been almost completely destroyed by intense firing. Only small flakes of the completely oxidized slip remain intact.

Water Bottles

Two plain vessels comprise this category. One is a large wide-mouthed variety, the other a miniature, hooded, stylized, owl-effigy type with a bail handle.

Effigy Bowls

Six effigy bowls are present. Three may have been black-polished and three are plain. The effigy heads of only three remain, one each of duck, foxlike animal, and crow(?). The typical hooded-duck type usually associated with Mississippian is not common in the Dickson Mounds area. One vessel (D107, a duck effigy) may be representative of the type Mound Place Incised. It has three unfinished, incised bands that were probably intended to encircle the vessel below the rim and dip to form a "U" under the head and tail — a decorative style often seen with local duck effigy bowls. The association of this vessel with a definite burial has not been established, however.

Miniature Vessels

Six miniature, shell-tempered plain vessels were recovered. One has loop handles and slight shoulders. Four are simple globular jars, and one is the previously mentioned hooded water bottle. One (D115) appears to have been polished black.

Plain Jars

A wide variety of vessel and rim forms is represented by shell-tempered plain jars. The plain globular shape predominates, although about 24 percent of the assemblage has slight shoulders which, although somewhat angular, do not begin to approach Powell Plain in terms of sharpness. Three lobed jars are present. Two of these are highly polished, have handles and slightly constricting, vertical rims. The other handleless specimen is plain and has a slightly expanding vertical rim.

Sharply everted rims, similar to those seen on cordmarked jars, are more noticeable with the globular forms. Slightly expanding rims are more common on the sharper-shouldered vessels. The jars with sharply everted rims are often black-polished, without handles, and their paste is made up predominantly of glacial drift clay with a high iron content. Both strap and loop handles are associated with all forms.

Trailing and incising is evident on three jars. This occurs in the form of broad-trailed meander, line-filled triangle, and incised crosshatch. Decoration is restricted to the area between the shoulder and neck of jars with slight shoulders and everted rims. Loop and strap tridactyl handles are present on two of these vessels.

Local variations of Mississippian decorative techniques are evident on certain vessels. One of the most common is the bifurcated or binoded handle which is often suggestive of erect ears or frog eyes. Single nodes on handles are also common; and bifurcated and noded decorations appear on both strap and loop handles. Also common is the addition of tridactyl appendages attached at the bottom of the handle which grip the sides of some vessels. When these handles are topped with paired nodes, a strong stylization of a frog is presented (Fig. 25, D181). Frogs are one of the most important of the local Mississippian effigies, usually appearing in the form of stone block pipes.

Powell Plain

Two variants of Powell Plain jars are represented. Both have typical rolled rims, sharp angular shoulders, and black-polished exterior surfaces. Both vessels have deep conical bases; one has strap handles, the other loop handles.

Cahokia Cordmarked

Nine cordmarked jars comprise this category. The term "Cahokia Cordmarked" (Griffin 1949:55-56) is here used to describe all cordmarked vessels in the Dickson excavation. However, it should be noted that, in addition to the expected geographical differences in clays used for pastes between the American Bottom (Cahokia) and the Illinois Valley, the cordmarking of Spoon River ceramics is more commonly smoothed or roughly brushed over than Cahokia cordmarking. Like Cahokia Cordmarked, cord impressions on Spoon River ceramics are usually vertical and cover the exterior of the vessel from the neck to the base. However, local cordmarking is occasionally confined to the area from the shoulder to the base (Dickson Cordmarked) or is sometimes diagonally applied. Some vessels have their exteriors haphazardly roughened with a cord-wrapped paddle.

Colors range from the usual oxidized, glacial drift, red clays through gray-brown. (The larger cordmarked storage jars found in associated villages are predominately oxidized red to light orange-brown.) In form, the bulk of the Dickson vessels is comprised of small, globular jars — all with medium to wide everted rims. They are comparatively soft in texture and the shell-tempering is often leached. With the exception of two vessels, D22 and D243 which have Z-twisted cords, the strands of the cord impressions on all vessels are S-twisted. The interior of one jar is painted red (D243), but no decoration other than cordmarking appears on any of the remaining eight vessels. Jar D362, which has moderate angular shoulders, is the only cordmarked vessel which deviates greatly from the globular shape. It has deep, narrow, smoothed-over cord impressions between the shoulder and the base. Another jar (D207) is cordmarked vertically to the shoulder area and diagonally to the base.

Four equally spaced pouring or decorative(?) lips are present on the rims of two vessels, and one jar has bifurcated loop handles. One jar (D346) has a small rounded opening intentionally left in its side; another (D207) has a mended area near its shoulder and a hole near its base which was repaired by inserting a pottery plug or rivet. Six cordmarked jars have no handles, one has rounded strap handles, and two have loop handles.

The paste of these cordmarked jars deserves a more detailed analysis and a closer scrutiny than is possible to observe megascopically. While all cordmarked ceramics appear to be only shell-tempered, one jar apparently has small lumps of clay or grog(?) mixed in with the clay; another has small quantities of grit. Porter (1964:12-14) noticed similar clay "pellets" in Cahokia Cordmarked pottery from the Mitchell Site in Madison County, Illinois.

Dickson Ceramic Series

DICKSON TRAILED

Two trailed vessels in the Dickson excavation comprise an as yet undefined pottery type.
Illustrations: Fig. 24, D208; Fig. 25, D181.
Type Material: This type is set up after the comparison of approximately 50 rims from the Dickson Mounds (F° 34), the Dickson Camp (F^{V}35), the Myer Site (F^{V}33), the Eveland Site (F^{V}900), Morton Mound (F°14), and the Larson Site (F^{V}1109).
Paste: Dickson Trailed is tempered with crushed shell. Texture is medium to fine in small vessels varying to coarse in larger ones. Color ranges from the predominant oxidized red to occasional gray-brown. A dark core is usually present with the gray-brown vessels.

Surface Finish: Vessel exteriors are usually smooth and may exhibit a light polish; a very small percentage of these may have black-polished slips. Cordmarking is present on many vessels, from the shoulder to the base; and one Dickson Trailed jar from the Larson Site has incising applied over cordmarking in a manner similar to Fisher pottery.

Decoration: The decorations are restricted to the shoulder area of jars. There seem to be two main types of decoration: *trailing* with comparatively wide lines, made with a blunt instrument; and *incising* with narrow lines, executed by a sharp instrument. Both types of decoration were applied when the clay was still plastic. A few engraved designs have been noticed. The decorative form commonly consists of a band of connected line-filled triangular forms (similar and often identical to designs of Wells Incised Plates) that run horizontally between the neck and the shoulder of the vessel. Chevrons and nested arc motifs are occasionally noticed.

Form: The most usual form associated with this decoration is the more weak-shouldered jar. The area between the shoulder and the neck is usually somewhat flattened to slightly convex, but the shoulder angle is never as sharp as that of Ramey Incised vessels. Everted rims are most common but some extruded rims have been noted. These may appear early in the series. Strap handles are sometimes present. Occasionally bifurcated, tridactyl and loop handles are seen. This type of decoration is occasionally found in association with beakers and rarely with wide-mouthed water bottles.

Cultural Associations: In the central Illinois River Valley, this decorative type is found in association with Middle Mississippian materials of the general Spoon River variant series and may be more prevalent in sites situated in the northern half of the Central Illinois Valley. This pottery type may have developed out of Ramey Incised.

Chronological Position: This type is commonly associated with Cahokia Cordmarked, Wells Incised, and St. Clair Plain-like materials. Consequently, its greatest use was probably between A.D. 1225 and 1325. Decorations of this type are interestingly similar to decorations of vessels from the Over Focus, Big and Little Sioux phases of the Middle Missouri tradition, Orr Focus, and Silvernale Focus sites of the Northeastern Plains and may have developed through interaction between the two areas.

DICKSON CORDMARKED

Dickson Cordmarked has characteristics identical with those of Dickson Trailed but lacks trailed, incised, or engraved decorations. The cordmarking on Dickson Cordmarked vessels is usually restricted to the area between the shoulder and the base. The area between the shoulder and lip is plain.

DICKSON PLAIN

Dickson Plain shares all characteristics of both Dickson Trailed and Dickson Cordmarked except that the surfaces of Dickson Plain vessels are never decorated or cordmarked.

Illustrations: Fig. 28, D358.

SPOON RIVER BEAKER

Three vessels in the Dickson excavation are representative of a pottery type presently undefined.

Illustrations: Fig. 19, D79; Fig. 23, D121; Fig. 24, D210.

Type Material: This type is set up after comparison of approximately 25 partial and whole vessels from the Dickson Mounds (F°34), the Myer Site (F^{V}33), The Dickson Camp (F^{V}35), The Morton Site (F°14), the Larson Site (F^{V}1109), the Crable Site (F^{V}891), and the Fiedler Site (F^{V}973).

Paste: Spoon River Beakers are tempered with crushed shell. Texture is usually fine with color ranging from the predominant gray-brown to an occasional oxidized red. A dark core is often present with the gray-brown vessels.

Surface Finish: Vessel surfaces are usually smooth and slipped. Many are black- or brown-polished, but no red-filming has been noticed.

Decoration: Decorations occur infrequently. These appear to be limited mainly to crude engraving (limited incising) applied haphazardly over much of the exterior surface or to the upper half of the vessel. No particular decorative motif is common. Single and/or multiple horizontal, straight, or wavy lines bordering bands containing combinations of chevrons, Wells-like triangular forms, zigzag lines, vertical lines, and cross hatching are sometimes seen. But all of these design elements can occur singly without bordering lines and be randomly applied almost anywhere on the vessel surface.

Form: The Spoon River Beaker appears mainly in the rather elongated (height-width ratio about 1.10:1) spool-shaped or concave-sided form. The base is usually slightly larger than the mouth.

Handles are nearly always present but are frequently placed nearer to the center on the back of the vessel than are handles of the local straight-sided and barrel-shaped beakers (Tippits Bean Pot and others) which usually occur nearer the rim. Handle shapes of Spoon River Beakers also deviate from the Tippits Bean Pot types in that they occur in a wide range of shapes and sizes, from mere nubs to long, sharply upcurving spikes. Although some handles project straight outward, most angle upward at 15 to 30 degrees. A single lip or lug pouring spout is usually present on the rim opposite the handle, with an additional lip sometimes placed on the rim directly above the handle.

Cultural Associations: This proposed pottery type is found in association with Middle Mississippian materials of the general Spoon River variant series in the Central Illinois River Valley. The Spoon River Beaker probably represents a localized variation of the Tippits Bean Pot.

Chronological Position: This type apparently postdates the Early Mississippian-Late Woodland Period and seems to make its appearance well after the arrival of barrel-shaped beakers and the Tippits Bean Pot. It is commonly associated with materials of the Dickson Ceramic Series, Cahokia Cordmarked, St. Clair Plain, Wells Incised, wide-mouthed water bottles and lobed jars. Spoon River Beakers would probably date from sometime before A.D. 1200 to possibly the beginning of the 15th century.

It was tempting, when classifying pottery for this section, to segregate the vessels with polished black and brown slips into a separate classification. To become familiar with the appearances of black- and brown-polished surfaces, the author made test firings similar to Bergmann's (Porter 1964:21), followed by swabbings of grease and submersion into other organic substances such as mud, dead leaves, grass, etc., on several newly manufactured test tiles in an attempt to produce black and brown slips. The quality of the slip and the simplicity with which it could be applied was most surprising. Support was also given to Bergmann's findings in connection with the reheating of the tiles. It was found that, with many repeated firings, the black and brown slips often burned or flaked away or turned a red-orange color but that the slips could be easily restored by simply reheating the tile and submerging it into almost any organic substance. Considering these results, a reevaluation of all plain vessels in the excavation was undertaken.

Four vessels originally listed as being unslipped showed signs of having been previously black-polished. The remnants of black-polishing on one of the vessels (D393) appeared as a faint black band, 5 mm. wide, on the inside of the rim, an area where an excess of grease(?) may have been smeared. In that position, the slip was not subjected to direct flames while in use and was still intact.

With the wide range of colors and the great variation of surface conditions evident from our observations of the polished and refired test tiles, the writer believes segregation of the polished ware in this report would be tenuous. The variation between the finest brown- and black-polished ware and the more drab slipped and sometimes plain-appearing pottery may represent only the range of differences that would be caused by normal household use and by different histories of firing. To quote Porter (1964:21):

There is no reason, as far as we can see, for making so many distinctions in these pottery types since there is no evidence to suggest a great change in techniques. The knowledge that one can obtain a perfectly black bowl by simply forming a reducing atmosphere while the vessel cools only suggests that its increase in use with time reflects the increase in demand by users. Thus the potterymaking centers, just as present business practices are guided, would continue to make a number of surface finishes depending on demand and availability of material.

As evidenced when comparing other pottery styles, the ceramics of the Spoon River variant people are rather mediocre technologically. The usual plain and drab ware, the relatively simple pattern forms, the simple all-over slip decoration, and the choice of symmetry are unappealing. While a few vessel forms are fairly skillfully constructed, the potter did not pursue the decorative possibilities to a great degree. The vestigial incising present on some vessels probably represents a degenerate Ramey technique which, itself, may have been only a simple attempt to copy the more elaborate elements from the south. While Cahokia ceramics are certainly not elaborate (when comparing them to southern styles), nonetheless, they are thinner walled, and generally better constructed, more symmetrical, and exhibit a wider variety of vessel forms, surface finishes, and artistic styles than do the ceramic expressions of the Mississippian manifestations of the Spoon River area.

Clay Sources and Comments

Local clay sources are plentiful. Loess was

available in large quantities but was apparently never used. Glacial drift clays cover the bluff areas and the Havana Terrace on which all three associated village sites (Eveland, Dickson Camp, and Myer) are located, and the reliance on this clay by Mississippian potters was fairly heavy. Many outcrops of weathered shale and "fireclays" are present in the Pennsylvanian geological formations of the Spoon River Valley. In fact, the numerous outcroppings of the refractory shales in this area establish the Spoon River Valley as one of the largest outcrop areas for low duty (refractoriness rating — Cone 15-29 min.) refractory clays in Illinois (White 1962:2 and following map). In theory, this shale would have been one of the best sources of raw materials for use in the manufacture of pottery. The gypsum on its weathered surfaces can easily be mixed throughout the paste simply by the addition of water which, in turn, reduces the refractoriness of the clay and makes the paste more plastic. However, in experimenting with weathered shale in the manufacture of test tiles, it was found that more water was required to produce satisfactory plasticity than with any other type of clay tested. This addition of extra water produced greater shrinkage of the final product — but the shrinkage could possibly have been controlled with more experimentation.

Another good clay source in the Dickson Mounds area is the flat floodplain of the Illinois River. Here, during times of high water and floods, clay and silt-sized particles carried by the water are deposited in depressions and swales, forming tacky dark gray to black "gumbo" deposits. These sources were frequently used by Mississippian potters. The pottery produced by the use of these alluvial clays is ordinarily gray to gray-brown, and since the clays are also highly organic, a dark gray to black core is normally present. The "nicer" pieces, plates, effigy bowls, water bottles, and beakers, are usually made of alluvial clays while most of the common jars, bowls, and water jugs are made of lower grade glacial drift clays.

During the summer of 1964, the writer carried out a series of experiments concerning the firing of test tiles manufactured from local clays. These tests were made primarily to confirm our own belief that the Dickson Mounds people were: (1) using local clay sources for ceramic manufacture; and (2) selecting specific clays because of availability, workability and ease of manufacture, strength and durability, and aesthetic reasons (in that order of importance). All research was geared mainly toward familiarizing ourselves with local clays (and subsequently with the paste, tempering, and surface finishes of local prehistoric pottery) and obtaining comparative data to complement similar studies recently done in the Cahokia area by James W. Porter.

Tiles used in these experiments were baked in open fires of different combinations of dried maple, oak, hickory, and elm woods. (It was found that the variety of wood made no appreciable difference in the final product; only the size of the logs seemed to be an important factor). If thrown directly into the hot coals in a fresh and somewhat wet state, the tiles often cracked; but if warmed next to the fire before baking, the tiles usually fired perfectly. All tiles were placed into the fire, covered with live coals, and baked until the fire subsided and cooled. Unfortunately, with no high temperature thermometer available, we were not able to record the temperatures at which the tiles were being fired; but using similar methods of firing, Porter (1964:5) found his open wood fires reached temperatures of 840 °C with no draft and up to 950 °C with a slight breeze. A range of 600 ° to 700 °C was found to be common around the immediate surfaces of the vessels he was making. Several different combinations of clays, grits, and shells were used in this study and some interesting results were obtained. A difficulty in obtaining satisfactory vitrification of the test tiles (at least as good as that of Late Woodland potters) was experienced when using weathered shale, and this situation was not improved when the 40 percent grit- or grog-temper was substituted for shell at various percentages ranging from 5 to 90 percent. The finished product improved only after similar weathered shale, 40 percent grit-tempered tiles were fired in a hotter open fire with coal as fuel, suggesting our open wood fire did not produce adequately high temperatures.

More success was obtained with the glacial drift clays from the Eveland Site, approximately 200 yards south of the Dickson Mounds. The finished tiles were nearly a brick red in color and were fairly durable. However, a combination of 40 percent shell-tempering and glacial drift clay appeared to be no stronger nor more durable than similar tiles of the same clay with grit as a tempering material. The higher temperatures produced by a coal fire did not improve the final status of either the shell- or the grit-tempered products.

The greatest success was obtained with test tiles of alluvial clays. The clays chosen for this part of the study were dark gray and tacky gumbos from the floodplain approximately 500 yards southeast of the Dickson Mounds. The high organic content of the clay apparently combined well with shell-tempering to produce very durable tiles. Even in instances where the usual two- to six-inch diameter wood "logs" used as fuel were replaced by smaller sticks to produce less heat, the finished tiles were still well fired. The calcium oxide in the shell acting as a flux was probably instrumental in lowering the fusion point sufficiently to gain complete vitrification at low temperatures. When the highly organic, fine-grained alluvial clays were combined with crushed shell (flaky particles which resemble the structure of the clay minerals), some very thin and durable tiles were produced. Paddling to help align the shell parallel to the tile wall may also have been beneficial in creating a finer, more durable ware. The finished product was weakened considerably when much shell-tempering was present (75 percent). Best results were obtained when the quantity of shell was held to 50 percent or under. Between 20 and 30 percent shell-tempering produced fairly good results, but the quality of the fired tile was poor when it was under 20 percent.

While the thin-walled, shell-tempered tiles of alluvial and glacial drift clays outwardly appeared superior in quality to the grit-tempered tiles of glacial drift clay and weathered shale, they had a tendency to disintegrate after many intense firings. The grit-tempered tiles held up much better.

FISHING (Fig. 30)

Although early excavations by Thomas Dickson uncovered a "quart size" pottery bowl containing "several dozen" barbless bone fishhooks, only three were recovered in the Dicksons' later controlled excavation. Two were found near the right shoulder of Burial 165. Both hooks are about the same length, 2.5 cm., and both have been grooved for attachment. One specimen is thicker and more squared while the other is more slender and round. A bone fishhook was also apparently included in a tool kit with No. 45, but it is no longer present.

Two bone "tubes" or fishhook blanks appear in a tool kit with No. 45 (Fig. 30, D60-D61).

Both were probably cut from a tibia-tarsus of a large bird, possibly a goose or swan. They are still in their initial stages of manufacture. The ends of the smaller tube show only evidence of transversal cutting while the larger tube has both transversal cutting on the ends and longitudinal grooves along either side and nearly through the walls.

Four fishhooks are normally made from each bone tube of this type. Although large bird bones are commonly used, deer bone was also popular. The method of fishhook manufacture most often seen in the Dickson Mounds area is detailed in Fig. 41, a-d.

WOODWORKING TOOLS
(Fig. 30, D147, D239)

Stone celts are common finds in village excavations, but they are rarely interred with the dead. The only celt found in the Dickson excavation lies on the right hip beside the hand of Burial 90. Made from a dark gray granitic rock, it has a slightly flared bit and roughly squared base; and well over half of its length is covered with rough to smoothed-over pecking. It is smoothed and polished at the bit.

An incisor of a beaver (Castor canadensis) is centered on the forehead of No. 150 (Fig. 30, D239). Although this specimen may have been a chisel, its association with the burial is not definite.

CEREMONIAL ITEMS (Fig. 30, D48)

One equal-arm elbow pipe was found near the head of Burial 35. It appeared to have been made from an inferior grade of dark brown catlinite, but exact determination of the material is not now possible because of the theft of the specimen. The openings for the stem and bowl are both conically bored, with the stem opening slightly larger than that of the bowl. The piece is highly polished and is undecorated except for a small engraved line on the right side of the bowl running horizontally across it about 9 mm. down from the top. Whether or not this is an unfinished band intended to encircle the bowl is conjectural.

Several stone pipes and two unfinished, sandstone pipes were found in the early, unrecorded excavations at Dickson (Don F. Dickson, personal communication). The stone pipes were sold about 1920, but the latter ones are now in the Dickson Mounds Museum collections. One is a small rectangular block with a concave front face and conical openings in the back and top. The other is a large, undrilled, equal-arm elbow type.

MISCELLANEOUS (Figs. 31-33)

Groups of tools and related items occur with 10 burials and may be indicative of tool kits. Three varieties of kits seem to be represented: tool groups containing from two to seven chert items whose functions are limited to cutting and scraping (6 instances); groups containing a large number and wide variety of artifacts (4 instances); and a group containing a variety of artifacts probably relating to a single purpose (1 instance).

Included in the smaller kits are general utility tools — chert objects such as scrapers, flakes, flake knives, and a bifacially flaked blade. This composition seems to suggest a more mundane class of equipment probably universally employed by a large segment of the population. These kits occur most frequently at the hands (4 instances) but also appear at the head (2 instances).

Articles most commonly included in the larger kits are antler tip flakers, knives, scrapers, chert flakes, arrowpoints, drills, and some ornaments. The types and variety of tools represented indicate that the larger tool kits may have been used by specialized craftsmen. Other items of perishable material may also have been present. The placement of these groups varies. They are found at the head, feet, pelvic region and left side. The third class of tool kit contained somewhat mutually dependent tools (needles and sharpener) encased in mussel shells. A functionally specific activity such as sewing or scarification is suggested. Placement of the kit was at the head.

At least 13 valves of common mussel shells are recorded with burials, not including those specimens previously identified as spoons. These shells do not necessarily represent grave offerings since they are unaltered and frequently fragmentary. Because their positions were not always recorded at the time of excavation, exact provenience is frequently lacking. Today these fragmentary shells often appear in a pottery vessel accompanying the burial, probably having been placed there to prevent their loss. Five species of shells are represented: Pocketbooks (*Lampsilis ventricosa*), Fragile Paper Shells (*Leptodea fragilis*), Three-Horned Warty-Backs (*Obliquaria reflexa*), Pink Heel-Splitters (*Proptera alata*), and Muckets (*Actinonaias carinata*).

The study of broken rock and clinker associated with burials proved uneventful. All lithic material, other than chert, is either of local origin or can be attributed to local glacial deposits. Five distinct categories of rock are present: sandstones and conglomeratic sand, mudstones, granitic rock, diorite, and hematite (represented by one unworked piece). One small (and probably modern) clinker or cinder was included in the fill around Burial 161. Probably much of the scattered debris, the broken rock, pottery sherds, and chert flakes, were unintentionally included in earth fill obtained from the village area.

Since it is especially common to find one species of terrestrial snail (*Anguispira alternata*) scattered throughout loess soil (and loess mounds), it is not surprising that several of these snails are present in the Dicksons' excavation. They are definitely associated with a burial in one instance. A bowl near the head of No. 21 contains 123 shells of this species (Fig. 32, D406). None have been altered, but it is possible that they represent raw materials intended for ornament manufacture — although they could be indicative of food offering. Neither use by Mississippian people has been previously documented for common snails in the Dickson Mounds area, however.

Five unaltered deer phalanges (*Odocoileus virginanus*) were found in a tool kit at the head of No. 45 (Fig. 32, D64-D68). Their use is unknown although they may represent raw materials for use in the manufacture of gaming pieces.

One possible scarification kit was found at the head of No. 90 (Fig. 32, D135-D137). Sixteen split bone "needles" and a fine-grained sandstone abrader were contained inside two valves of common mussel shell. The needles range from flattened to square in cross section and are all about 5 cm. in length. One does appear to be round. Since it is conceivable that this kit may have been used in sewing instead, it is also discussed under the heading FABRICATING AND PROCESSING.

SUMMARY OF ARTIFACT ASSOCIATIONS

Grave goods and items which can be considered "necessary equipment" are associated with 102 burials (Table 1). These items frequently include a wide range of artifacts which relate to the normal day-to-day activities of the individual, contributed goods, "gifts" not actually owned by the dead person, pieces appropriate to the person's normal task performance, and items that are intimately associated with the deceased, i.e., personalities in the sense of Binford's (1962) usage of the term. The latter category includes a variety of the more nontransferable items of personal adornment. Competitively contributed goods, grave offerings far in excess of the quantities that would normally be considered necessary or adequate for the person's life in the afterworld, seem to be absent. The lack of excessive mortuary offerings suggests that little or no importance of validating the status of the deceased or perpetuating the status positions of the remaining members of his family was attached to any of the burials.

Several items may be contributed gifts or items probably not actually owned in life by the deceased. Recognizable recipients of this category are infants and children who are buried with adult or "adult-sized" items. Children with probable contributed gifts are: No. 50 and possibly No. 12 with adult-sized bone bracelets; No. 55 with a large water bottle; possibly No. 123 with a large jar and ceremonial(?) knife; No. 179 with a large tool kit; and possibly No. 211 with two marine-shell pendants placed behind the head. Likewise, some newborns and infants are buried with simple possessions, such as chert flakes and flake knives, which they obviously could not have used and were probably not associated with prior to burial. These classes of artifacts contrast with various items of personal adornment and eating equipment found with fetuses which, although probably never used in a majority of the cases, may have been prepared in anticipation of the birth of the particular individual with whom they are buried.

Assemblages of contributed goods and necessary equipment associated with the dead cover a wide range of artifacts and occur in the form of finished and raw materials, tool kits, facilities, and possibly food.

Ownership of general utility tools and their positioning with the body is at least partially dependent upon sex. Unaltered chert flakes occur only with males as parts of larger groups of artifacts (i.e., tool kits) but can occur singly with subadults and females. Positioning with the body seems to be restricted to the area of the head and the hands.

Scrapers also appear to be restricted to inclusion in tool kits with males but do occur as separate grave offerings at the right hands of females.

Flake knives were also restricted to tool kits with males but occurred singly at the left hands of females. These implements appeared singly with subadults at the right hand, head, and left side.

Large chert blades seem to be exclusively male possessions. Three convex-based blades are associated with No. 90 and double-pointed blades appear with Nos. 115 and 138. One subadult, No. 123, also has a double-pointed blade in association. The single blades are found at the hands while those with No. 90 were included in a tool kit.

Hunting tools or weapons are associated with 10 burials, primarily with older males. One child had a tool kit containing two crude arrowpoints and one infant had an arrowpoint and pile of beads on its chest. One older female (No. 41) supposedly had arrowpoints in association. Placement of these artifacts varies, occurring on or over the shoulder, between the knees, in tool kits, and at the head, chest, and side.

Fabricating and processing tools are associated with four burials, three older males and a child of three years. Artifacts of this category are included only in tool kits with other types of equipment.

One chert hoe is included in a tool kit at the feet of No. 170, a male, and three shell hoes were found at some undesignated position with No. 72, a female.

Marine-shell beads and *Olivella jaspidea* beads, bead bracelets, and bead necklaces occur with 23 burials. One bead of mussel shell and one of fluorspar were also found. Certain age and sex correlations are apparent.

Disc bead bracelets of marine shell are found on the wrists of two adult males.

Disc bead necklaces actually being worn occur with six infants and children and two adult females. Groups of beads not actually being worn (includes bead piles, beads scattered over the burial, etc.) and single or small numbers of beads on the chest are seen primarily with children and one female. Large nondisc beads accompanied by *Busycon* spp. pendants also appear with two females.

Males with beads include No. 45, which has a truncated cone bead of marine shell included in a tool kit, and No. 35 which may have a forelock bead.

Mussel-shell pendants are associated with two infants.

Marine-shell pendants *(Busycon* spp.*)* are included with nine burials, usually being worn on the chest. Although most commonly seen with infants and children, these pendants were also reported as being worn by both adult males and females. If the Dickson records are accurate, this may be very significant, for no individual in our sample of over 800 burials in the Dickson cemetery wore a *Busycon* pendant beyond the age of puberty (Harn n.d.).

Clackers or arm rattles of mussel shell are associated with three mature males. None of the three sets was apparently being worn at burial.

Sets of ankle rattles of mussel shell were worn by three mature and elderly females. A single rattle was found at an unspecified location with an infant.

Bone bracelets occur with three infants and one child. Two of these specimens may have been on the left wrists, but the positions of the others were not recorded.

Bone hairpins were found with two adult males. Although their positions were not pinpointed by the Dickson notes, both occurred at the head and probably were worn in the hair.

Antler rings were found with one female. Both were possibly being worn in hair laid over the left shoulder.

Copper-covered wood earspools may have been found with one burial (No. 195). However, there is some discrepancy about this association and position of the artifacts with the body.

Domestic equipment such as pottery vessels and mussel-shell spoons are widely distributed among both sexes and throughout the various age groups. There seems to be no particular correlation of style or type with either age or sex.

Potterymaking equipment appears at the right hand of one female. Such equipment is probably exclusively female, since only female burials have been associated with potter's tools in the area (Harn n.d.).

Bone fishhooks were found at the right shoulder of one male and in a tool kit at the head of another. The latter tool kit also contained bone fishhook blanks.

One stone celt was present. It is located near the right hand of No. 90, a mature male.

One beaver incisor, possibly used as a chisel, was found on the forehead of a burial. It may have been included with the grave fill.

One equal-arm elbow pipe is located near the head of No. 35, a male of 50 years.

Eleven tool kits appear with 10 individuals. The six smaller kits, containing only general utility tools, appear primarily at the hands with secondary emphasis on the area of the head. A quasi-tool kit, comprised of only a flake knife and chert flake, is with a female; the remainder are with mature males.

The four larger tool kits, containing a wide variety of artifacts, are with males and one child. They appear in the pelvic region and at the head, feet, and side.

One possible scarification kit or "sewing" kit, containing bone needles and a sharpening stone enclosed in a mussel-shell container, was found at the head of No. 90, a mature male.

Most of the other items included in the **Miscellaneous** category represent disturbed materials and grave fill or are not of sufficient quantity to assess their importance in understanding artifact-burial relationships.

It is noteworthy that most of the items assigned to the assemblages of contributed goods and necessary equipment (discounting pottery vessels and shell spoons — which are more equitably distributed among ages and sexes) have definite age/sex correlations. The division is decidedly adult male-oriented, however, the only exceptions being lone scrapers found with several females, flake knives found with both sexes and all ages, and probably potterymaking equipment with females (although only one example is present). Two child burials (Nos. 123 and 179) also conflict with this pattern, having a large blade and a tool kit in association. However, the tool kit association may or may not be valid since the child was buried on top of an adult male with the kit placed on the body of the child. With these exceptions, necessary equipment was placed with males of not less than 20 years nor older than about 50 years. This may well represent the period of greatest male productivity and/or social influence.

Personalities are not so restricted. Each sex and age group claims definite identifying forms of sociotechnic items. Mussel-shell clackers, bone hairpins, shell-bead bracelets, and probably pipes and forelock beads are items which may be exclusively male in character. Because of the small sample size, mussel-shell ankle rattles are the only sociotechnic items clearly associated with females; but bead necklaces occur only with females (along with a large number of infants and children) as do antler rings. Bone bracelets occur only with children; but while they are found primarily with children elsewhere in the cemetery (Conrad 1972; Harn n.d.), at least one was found on the arm of a female. The two mussel-shell pendants also occur with infants.

The only sociotechnic item shared by both sexes in the Dickson excavation is the *Busycon* spp. pendant. These adornos were apparently worn by both adult males and females as well as infants and children. This is a decided contrast with the situation elsewhere within the Dickson Mounds Cemetery where no individual wore a *Busycon* spp. pendant past the age of puberty (Conrad 1972; Harn n.d.). *Busycon* spp. shells (some of which were modified into pendants) were found with adults during the recent excavations at Dickson Mounds, but these artifacts were not being worn. Some of these were included in tool kits and larger groups of artifacts, but many had been disturbed by grave-digging activities and were reinterred with the new grave fill. Perhaps it was in this latter context that *Busycon* spp. pendants originally occurred with adults in the Dickson excavation and were later interpreted as belonging to those individuals.

Advanced age does not seem to have been important in assuring great esteem. The oldest female (No. 27, 70 years) does have associated shell ankle rattles, but the oldest male (No. 48, 75 years) has nothing. Of the nine burials (3 males, 6 females) in the sixty-plus age category, only two females have accompanying burial furniture.

However, discounting domestic equipment, which seems to be universally buried with the dead, and items most commonly associated with infants and children (single beads, shell-bead necklaces, bone bracelets), burial furnishings are only infrequently placed with infants and younger children and rarely occur with older children and adolescents. In fact, the average age of both male and female recipients is quite high (42 and 31 years respectively) with only two males under the age of thirty years having such

grave offerings. Although still quite evident, this age pattern is not as rigid with offerings falling under the category of GENERAL UTILITY TOOLS, where some young adult (18-25 years) females and one young adult male are represented.

In this light, it is possible that increased age (maturity) was one requisite for gaining some measure of social esteem but that it was probably coincidental with gradually accumulating wealth or increased individual productivity — both of which also may have been interrelated with increased sociopolitical participation. It is probably significant that the average age range represented by a majority of the artifact associations coincides with the probable period of greatest individual productivity and social involvement.

A general view of the mortuary practices in the Dickson excavation provides several limited insights into social organization. Most obvious are the facts that not everyone was accorded the same mortuary treatment but that there was an apparent order to the division of certain types of artifacts by age and sex. There seem to be no important or sacred areas of burial within the Dickson excavation, nor do there seem to be persons of unusual importance represented. At least no exotic ceremonial regalia or quantities of artifacts are represented which suggest superordinate social positions.

In fact, there is little indication of social stratification evident beyond the presence of certain items, probably of relatively minor ritualistic nature, which may have functioned as symbols to distinguish individuals ranking as heads of office or holding other subordinate positions within the local group. Among these paraphernalia might be included the pipe, possible scarifier, and ankle rattles, for which there are widespread ethnohistoric documentations of their association with status positions. Similar associations may be indicated by the earspools, bead bracelets, and forelock bead, and possibly the arm rattles or clackers and bone hairpins. Adults with bead necklaces also may have been distinguished individuals. It is probable that the other classes of "ornaments" placed with the dead were not included solely for the purposes of individual beautification. However, the small comparative sample of all categories of artifacts presently precludes any attempt at understanding the social dimensions of inheritance or acquisition and internal ranking within the groups represented by the Dickson excavation.

Burial No.	Age	Sex	Orientation	Extended	Semiflexed	Bundle or secondary burial	Indeterminate	Chert flake	Knife	Scraper	Arrowpoint	Sewing(?) kit	Bone awl	Weaving tool	Drill	Slot abrader	Smooth sandstone	Antler flaker	Shell hoe	Chert hoe	Shell bead bracelet	Shell bead necklace	Single bead
								General Utility			Weapons	Fabricating and Processing							Digging				
1	24	M?	WNW-ESE	X																			
2	45	M	E-W	X						1	2										1		
3	46	M	E-W	X				1		6													
4	Fetus		E-W	X																			
7	47	M	NNE-SSW	X					1	1	1												
8	2		NNE-SSW	X																		1	
9	11	F	NNE-SSW		X																		
12	6						X																
14	5	F	NNW-SSE	X																			
15	32	F	E-W	X																			
17	2 +		N-S	X																			
19	22	F	N-S	X																			
21	44	M	N-S	X																			
27	70	F	NNE-SSW	X																			
28	28	M	NNE-SSW	X						1													
29	59	M	NNE-SSW	X																			
31	28	F	N-S	X																			
35	50	M	NNE-SSW	X						2	6												1
39	24	M	NNE-SSW	X																			
41	47	F	NNE-SSW	X							5												
42	2		NNE-SSW	X					1														
45	32	M	NNE-SSW	X				2		3					1	1	2						1
46	20	F	WNW-ESE	X						1													
47	40	F	WNW-ESE	X																			1
50	Infant		WNW-ESE	X				1															
51	Infant		WNW-ESE	X																		1	
54	38	F	NNE-SSW	X																			
55	Infant		NNE-SSW				X																
63	45	F	WNW-ESE	X																			
67	10		E-W	X																			
72	46	F	ENE-WSW	X																3	1		
73	2		N-S				X																1
74	2 +		N-S				X																1
79	35	M	NNE-SSW	X						1													
81	28	F	NNE-SSW	X																			
82	48	F	WNW-ESE	X																			
85	41	M	N-S	X																			
86	24	F	NNE-SSW	X																			
87	Fetus		NNE-SSW				X																
88	60	F	N-S	X																			
89	21	F	N-S	X																			
90	49	M	N-S	X				5	3	10	4	1	1		4	3		5					
93	2		NNE-SSW				X		1														
94	42	M	N-S	X																			
96	6		N-S	X																		1	
98	Fetus		WNW-ESE				X																
99	41	F	NNW-SSE	X																			
100	20	F	E-W	X				1															
101	41	F	N-S	X																		1	
103	2		N-S	X																		1	

*Grave fill or disturbed item.
(continued)

ASSOCIATED ARTIFACTS

Ornaments									Domestic							Fishing		Wood-working		Cere-monial		Miscellaneous							
Bead group	Mussel-shell pendant	Marine-shell pendant	Mussel-shell ankle rattle	Mussel-shell clacker	Bone bracelet	Bone hairpin	Antler ring	Copper-covered earspool	Mussel-shell spoon	Potter's tool	Jar	Bottle	Beaker	Bowl	Effigy bowl	Bone fishhook	Bone fishhook blank	Celt	Chisel, beaver incisor	Stone pipe	Tool kit	Snails	Mussel shell, unaltered	Deer phalanges, unaltered	Bird bone, unaltered	Broken rock and clinker	Chert flake (random)	Potsherd	Scarification(?) kit
1			3						1		1/1/1										1/1	1				*/*			
	1			1					1/*		1/1/*												*						
		14							1		1/1				1							123				*			
									1		1				1					1	1		*			*			
1	1			1		1			2				1/1			1	2				1		*	5					
	1								1			1	1		1							1							
	1	2							2/1	1/1			1									5	*						
									*/1/1/1	2/1/1/1/1				1															
	1	1				1			1/1		1/1/1		1					1			2		*						1
							2		1/1		1/1/1			1												*		1/*	

(continued)

Burial No.	Age	Sex	Orientation	Extended	Semiflexed	Bundle or secondary burial	Indeterminate	Chert flake	Knife	Scraper	Arrowpoint	Sewing(?) kit	Bone awl	Weaving tool	Drill	Slot abrader	Smooth sandstone	Antler flaker	Shell hoe	Chert hoe	Shell bead bracelet	Shell bead necklace	Single bead
								General Utility			Weapons	Fabricating and Processing							Digging				
104	3						X																
105	Fetus						X	1															
115	34	M	WNW-ESE	X				2	1	2	1												
118	Infant		WNW-ESE	X																			
119	37	M	N-S	X																			
120	65	F	NNW-SSE	X																			
122	52?	M	NNW-SSE	X							5												
123	9		WNW-ESE	X					1														
126	35	F	WNW-ESE	X																			
127	0		ENE-WSW	X				1		1												1	
128	37	M	WNW-ESE	X				1	2	2													
133	25	F					X	2															
134	2		WNW-ESE	X																			1
138	20	M	E-W	X					1														
139	Fetus		WNW-ESE	X																			
140	Infant		E-W	X																			
141	7	F	E-W	X																		1	
142	Infant		E-W	X																			1
147	7		E-W	X																			
148	51	F	E-W	X						1													
149	27	F	E-W		X					1													
150	20	F	NNW-SSE			X																	
151	2		E-W	X																			
152	18	F	E-W	X				1	1														1
154	46	F	N-S		X																		
155	55	F	E-W	X						1													
161	Infant		E-W	X							1												1	
164	20	F	WNW-ESE	X																			
165	42	M	WNW-ESE	X																			
166	36	F	NNE-SSW	X					1														
167	50	M	E-W	X				1															
168	49	M	NNE-SSW		X																		
170	46	M	ENE-WSW	X				20		10	1				1		2	1	1				
179	3		E-W	X				18	5	1	2				1		2	3					
182	2		WNW-ESE	X																			
185	49	F	N-S	X																			
190	13	M	NNE-SSW	X																			
191	Infant		E-W	X																			
192	Infant		WNW-ESE	X																			
193	12	F	WNW-ESE		X					1													
195	46	F	WNW-ESE				X																
197	19	F	NNE-SSW				X																
206	40	F				X																	
211	2		NNE-SSW				X	1															
214	8	F	N-S	X																			
215	Fetus		N-S	X																		1	
219	28	M	WNW-ESE	X																	1		
221	17	M	N-S	X																			
223	3		N-S				X																
227	30	M	WNW-ESE				X																
230	6		WNW-ESE	X																			
232	Infant		E-W	X																			

*Grave fill or disturbed item.

ASSOCIATED ARTIFACTS *(concluded)*

Ornaments									Domestic							Fishing		Wood-working		Ceremonial		Miscellaneous							
Bead group	Mussel-shell pendant	Marine-shell pendant	Mussel-shell ankle rattle	Mussel-shell clacker	Bone bracelet	Bone hairpin	Antler ring	Copper-covered earspool	Mussel-shell spoon	Potter's tool	Jar	Bottle	Beaker	Bowl	Effigy bowl	Bone fishhook	Bone fishhook blank	Celt	Chisel, beaver incisor	Stone pipe	Tool kit	Snails	Mussel shell, unaltered	Deer phalanges, unaltered	Bird bone, unaltered	Broken rock and clinker	Chert flake (random)	Potsherd	Scarification(?) kit
											1																		
											1																		
			1								1										1								
													1																
											1																		
			12								1																		
1											1																		
											1										1								
1																													
											1	1																	
									1		1																		
									1		1																		
	1																		1							*			
		1							1		1										?								
											1																		
			12								1															*		*	
1											1																		
																2													
									3						1														
		2							1					1							1								
									*												1								
							1				1																		
	*								1		1	1														*			
									1		1															*		*	
									*			1																	
								?	1		1	1														*			
												1																	
1		2									1																		
														1															
																										*		*	
									1		1													*				*	
									1		1				1														
											1																		
		1							1		1												*				*		

INVENTORY OF BURIALS

In the following pages, a brief description and discussion of each burial will be given, and for brevity each individual burial will then serve as a unit within the site. These units will, when necessary, be internally associated with burial practices such as internal relationship to other burials and the inclusion of grave goods and externally associated with other phenomena outside the excavation (e.g., artifact similarities to other sites). A detailed consideration of some of the more important aspects brought to light by the coming discussion will be included in the "Summary of Burials."

While 248 complete and fragmentary individual burials have been exposed, there are only 234 burial numbers. Occasionally, one number is assigned to a group of bones (such as a bundle burial) in which parts of more than a single person are represented (e.g., Burial 105 actually contains the bones of four fetuses). If all fragments scattered in the fill around the main burials were assigned a separate burial number, the total would probably double. It seems more appropriate to number only the complete or intentional burials and to discuss the fragments for what they usually are: evidences of later intrusive graves. The scattered remains have been recorded and are discussed in the text, and an attempt has been made to relate them either internally to nearby burials or externally to burials that are now destroyed. By determining what factors combined to reduce them to their present fragmentary and disarticulated state, we were able to ascertain the original positions of several disturbed burials. In doing this, much information was salvaged concerning many earlier burials which had been almost completely disturbed by intrusive graves. Many laborious hours of comparing and matching "loose" fragments accompanying intrusive burials with the disturbed burials in the vicinity were necessary to gain what seemed to be only a few positive evidences to offset the many which were not. This information, which could not have been gained had we disregarded the obvious presence of these sometimes minute bone fragments, filled in many missing gaps and provided a better understanding of the situation.

In the following pages, the reader will often confront references to graves and see these features outlined in the accompanying drawings.

Due to the excavation technique employed by the Dickson family, these features are rarely evident in their entirety — or as they now appear in the drawings. The outlined area usually represents only the *approximate* area originally occupied by the grave. The placement of the outlined areas was largely determined by: (1) the presence of definite graves excavated as such by the Dicksons (3 examples) and by the Illinois State Museum (1 example); (2) the existence of partial grave outlines or definite color changes, usually in profile (3 examples); (3) the fact that intrusive grave pits had cut through earlier burials (18 examples); and (4) the presence of certain burials lying in undisturbed clay or loess well below the level of the original hill surface (32 examples).

Since the publication of the original Dickson report in 1971, efforts to define the mound base by facing some of the dried profiles have met with some success. It now appears that an additional 60 burials are below the level of the original hill surface and were probably in graves. All of these have been mapped enclosed in grave outlines. Future study will probably document additional examples. The grave outlines, as they appear in the illustrations, are useful only for identification of individuals in intrusive pits and to determine superimpositon. *They should not be used* for purposes of comparison concerning grave shape or dimension. For the most part, these graves could not be traced through the mound fill and into the loess or hardpan subsoil because of the removal of superimposed earthen profiles. A majority of the graves were identified because of their relative vertical positions in relation to the original hill surface level evident in nearby profiles. The shallow depths below the original hill surface attained by most of the graves suggest that they were cut through the mound and into the natural hill; but only occasionally can such verification be positively made.

At the time of the initial publication in 1971, the original positions of most of the skulls could not be determined for a variety of reasons. Some of the crania had been moved in excavating, in cleaning, and in taking skull measurements. Consequently, a large number of skulls were in a nearly perfect "face up" position. The recent recovery of the Dickson field notes and of many early photographs taken nearly perpendicularly from a catwalk once suspended over the excavation not only show clearly original head positions for a majority of the burials but also indicate that in many instances damaged or missing skeletal parts have been replaced with appropriate substitutes. Original positions of some limbs also have since been changed, probably as a result of movement during periodic cleaning. The burial illustrations in this publication primarily are based on this early photographic record, with positions of burial furnishings based both on these early photographs and on the Dickson field notes.

The positions of many of the artifacts have likewise changed for the same reasons and several specimens have been stolen. Fortunately, a number of the more significant artifacts remain *in situ*, and most others have had their positions adequately pinpointed in Dr. Dickson's original field notes, allowing greater interpretive confidence than was suggested by our original study (Harn 1971b:32).

The various parts of the skeleton considered in sexing were the skull and teeth, pelvis, sternum, long bones, vertebral column, scapula (when available), and clavicle.

Estimation of the individual's age was based on tooth eruption, bone size (of fetuses and some infants), epiphyseal union, pubic symphysis, the skull and its suture closure, and dental attrition.

Burial 1 The first burial found in the Dickson Mounds Cemetery is an extended, supine adult (male?) — 24 years of age. The long axis of the body is generally west-northwest to east-southeast with the head to the west. To the left of the head is a (previously) polished black, strap-handled Powell Plain-like jar that contains a fragmentary mussel shell (probably *Lampsilis ventricosa*) (Figs. 17, D2; 31, D1). The shell was probably included in the fill over the burial, but it has since been placed in the jar to prevent its loss.

Because of the lack of space for burial and artifact numbers on Fig. 36, Burial 1 is shown only on Fig. 34. However, it lies one foot below and parallel to the right side of No. 2.

Burials 2, 3, 4 and 30. Lying above and parallel to No. 1 and partially covering the legs of Nos. 28 and 29 is a mass burial of two adults and two infants (Fig. 36). The two adults overlie one infant, No. 30, with the other infant resting between them. The long axis of each burial is east to west with head to the east. The arms are to the

sides and the legs of the adults are missing — possibly having been disturbed by previous excavation.

Number 2, a male of 45 years, has three associated chert artifacts. Over the left shoulder are two projectile points (Fig. 7, D3-D4): one, a simple triangle; the other, five-notched. A thin scraper or knife on the pelvic area may have been thrown in with the mound fill (Fig. 3, D8). A smoothed-over cordmarked jar containing a mussel-shell spoon (probably *Lampsilis ventricosa*) is situated just above the left pelvis (Fig. 17, D5 and Fig. 16, D6), while a bracelet of 51 disc beads of marine shell appears on the right wrist (Fig. 11, D7).

Number 3, a male of 46 years, has a set of two mussel-shell clackers or arm rattles and one fragmentary clacker which were found "beneath neck" (Fig. 12, D9-D11). The species of the two clackers (which are mated valves of the same shell) is Pimple-Back *(Quadrula pustulosa)*. A possible tool kit containing six scrapers, one chert flake, and one unaltered piece of diorite rock was found around the head (Fig. 3, D12, D14-D17; Fig. 31, D18-D19). The chert flake and the rock were not mentioned in the Dickson field notes.

Number 4, an 8½-month fetus, has a small *Busycon* spp. shell pendant on its chest (Fig. 13, D20).

Number 30, a newborn infant, has only the back of its skull exposed. There are no associated artifacts.

The two adults (Nos. 2 and 3) are interesting in that their physical characteristics are nearly identical. This is especially noticeable in the striking similarity of the facial structure of the bones. Both are affected with arthritis and, interestingly enough, both have about the same degree of involvement on the same joints. These similarities, along with the closeness of their ages, suggest that they may have been closely related in life — possibly brothers.

Burials 5 and 26. Number 5, a 20-year-old male, covers No. 26, a 45-year-old female in a grave cutting through the mound and into the original hill surface (Fig. 35). The long axis of each body is west-northwest to east-southeast. The head of No. 5 is to the east, the head of No. 26 to the west. Since these individuals are below the legs of Nos. 28-29 and the bodies of Nos. 2, 3, 4 and 30, only the head and feet of No. 26 and the upper body of No. 5 are exposed. Because of the lack of space for burial and artifact numbers on Fig. 36, they appear only on Fig. 35. These burials lie along the same axis and are centered nearly two feet below Nos. 2, 4 and 30 and extend out behind the heads of the adults in that group. Only the back of the skull of No. 26 is shown on Fig. 36. No artifacts are exposed.

Burials 6, 7, 8 and 9. Numbers 6 to 9 are associated in a mass group apparently placed in a shallow grave dug through the mound and into the original hill surface (Fig. 35). The grave disturbed the left side and skull of No. 10, an earlier flexed burial. Number 7 is covered by Nos. 8 and 9 while No. 6 was placed slightly above and left of No. 7. The left side of No. 6 is greatly slumped because of disintegration of the other three. Each burial is oriented north-northeast to south-southwest with the head to the south.

Number 6, a 12-year-old female, has no associated artifacts.

Number 7, a 47-year-old male, has a flake knife and a scraper at the side of the head which may represent a small tool kit (Figs. 3 and 5, D25-D26). A triangular arrowpoint is on top of the shoulder (Fig. 7, D130), and a large, strap-handled, cordmarked jar is to the left of the head (Fig. 17, D22). A water-worn pebble may have been included in the grave fill or may have been a recent intrusion (Fig. 31, D27). The second right rib has a healed fracture.

Number 8, a child of 26 months, has a small necklace of 10 marine-shell beads on its chest (Fig. 11, D28).

Number 9, a child (female?) 11 years of age, is the only member of the group that is not in an extended supine position. It is resting on its right side with the knees and left arm flexed right. A loop-handled, shell-tempered plain jar is to the right of the head (Fig. 19, D23). A mussel-shell spoon (D24), only partially excavated, is in this vessel.

Burial 10. The flexed burial of a male, 32 years old, rests close to or below the original hill surface (Fig. 35). This skeleton is flexed on its back with the legs to the right and arms folded to the chest. The body axis is generally north-northwest to south-southeast with the head to the south. It was disturbed by the intrusive mass grave of Nos. 6 to 9; the entire upper left side is disarranged, and the humerus, clavicle and many ribs are missing. The skull, now repaired, was found in scattered fragments near the feet of No. 7.

Burials 11, 14-23, and 175. At least 12 skeletons, representing possibly 8 separate interments, are situated in the northeastern corner of the excavation (Fig. 34). Burial 23 may have preceded all other interments. This burial and No. 175 were disturbed by the placement of Nos. 19-21, and No. 18 may have been disturbed by the grave of No. 16. Burials 11 and 22, placed in a common grave, are slightly east of the main group and may have been contemporaneous with nearby Burial 175. The grave containing Nos. 19-21 was superimposed by Nos. 16, 17, 14, and 15 in that order. Only No. 15 is oriented east to west with the head to the east. The long axis of all other bodies is generally north to south or north-northwest to south-southeast with the head to the south. The seven upper burials were apparently placed within a short time span as most exhibit various degrees of posthumous shifting caused by the deterioration of the lower bodies. All were placed in graves, the majority of these cutting through the mound and into the original hill surface.

Number 11, a male of 46 years, is one of the lower members of this group. It has a newborn infant (No. 22) placed on its right pelvic area and a bundle burial (No. 18, a male of 52 years) — which is covered by two small children (Nos. 16 and 17, age 9 months and 26 months) — placed on its upper left side. A small shell-tempered plain jar with rough loop handles was found just above the forehead of No. 17 (Fig. 18, D31). The bundle burial (No. 18) is listed as representing only a single adult; however, closer inspection revealed that it also contains the remains of at least one child of about 10 years. This bundle is not compact but is scattered over a larger area than is normally occupied by a secondary burial; possibly it is the remnants of two or more burials disturbed by the interment of intrusive graves and replaced with the fill.

Number 14, is a child (female?) of about 5 years. It is oriented north-northwest to south-southeast and the head is to the southeast. Only the head and the lower two-thirds of the legs are exposed. The lower body and the right side of the upper body are greatly slumped to the right and the head is tilted upright. To the right of the head is a miniature shell-tempered plain lobed jar (Fig. 18, D21).

Number 15, an extended female of 32 years, is situated at a right angle to the lower burials. The long axis of the body is east to west with the head to the east. The arms are to the sides with the left hand over the pelvic area, and the head rests approximately 2 feet over No. 16 and 17. The body covers parts of Nos. 14, 19, 20, 21, and 175. Scattered in with the bones of this burial is a right humerus of a child (10 years?), a left humerus of a smaller child and other bone fragments. Probably these are remains of burials disturbed by the grave. The older child's humerus may actually belong to the child mentioned in No. 18, as both seem to be from children of similar age and both had been apparently disturbed. The right valve of the Mucket (*Actinonaias carinata*) is in the fill below and to the left of the feet. A shell-tempered plain jar was found in the fill beneath the left shoulder of this burial (Fig. 19, D30). It is not known if this specimen was associated with No. 14 or was disturbed by the grave of No. 15 and included in the fill. A mussel-shell spoon originally included in this jar is missing. Although this woman is a later interment, the level of her body is below the level of the head of No. 14, implying this was an intrusive grave.

Number 19, a female of 22 years, was probably wrapped; the arms are tight to the sides and the shoulders are pulled in toward the face. A small, black-polished, Powell Plain-like jar was found to the right of and slightly above the head (Fig. 18, D32). A mussel shell or spoon originally in this vessel is missing.

Number 20, a male of 53 years, also has the shoulders pulled in toward the face giving a suggestion of wrapping. There is no accompanying burial furniture.

Number 21, a male of 44 years, is somewhat distorted by wrapping. The shoulders are pulled in to the face with the right arm over the pelvis, the left bent over the chest; the knees are together with the legs crossed at the ankles (left over right). The head is turned to the left. A shell-tempered plain effigy bowl containing 123 shells of common terrestrial snails (*Anguispira alternata*) rests to the left of the head (Figs. 18, D34; 32, D406). Both the effigy head and tail are broken off at the rim of the bowl. This burial also has a healed fracture of the right tibia.

Number 23, a 24-year-old female, is a partially disturbed burial which preceded the mass grave. Resting below the original hill surface, oriented north-northwest to south-southeast with the head to the southeast, it is flexed on its side with the limbs and the head facing to the right. There are no associated artifacts.

Number 175 is a small female, 50 years of age.

Her legs are partially covered by Nos. 19 and 20, and her body is disturbed from the pelvis upward by their grave. No grave offerings are exposed.

Burials 12 and 13. On the same level and left of the head of No. 15, two children (6 years and 26 months of age) are in a common grave (Fig. 34). The smaller child is above with its head resting at chest level on No. 12. Each has the head to the west. Both appear to have been disturbed by either rodents or previous excavation. A shell pendant (*Busycon* spp.) is on the chest of the larger child (Fig. 13, D29). Both burials protrude from the east profile wall and are only partially excavated.

Although no bone bracelet is present with No. 12, the Dickson notes contain the comment "(Include desc. of bone bracelet.)." Perhaps the missing specimen is the engraved bracelet fragment which has been for years displayed with infant No. 51. A recently obtained early photograph of the bracelet shows that a sizable portion of the specimen was once present, but only the largest of eleven fragments remains today. The caption on the photograph ("5b Bone bracelet found with child burial Sepo, Illinois. Dickson col.") contributes little toward its identification since no specific burial is indicated. But the term "child burial" implies that it was not a random find; however, it may not necessarily have been from the controlled Dickson excavation. The lack of a burial or artifact number may make any association tenuous because another photograph of the same series (photo 11b) shows a well-documented Dickson excavation artifact (D119 with No. 81) and is captioned "Lobed pot (#1, grave 3) Sepo, Ill. Dickson col." This designation seems to indicate a specific specimen in an existing field inventory (probably corresponding to the first vessel found in their third excavation area). However, the large number of pottery vessels may have necessitated a numbering system which was not needed or used for less populous classes of artifacts. Unfortunately, no other documented artifacts are pictured in the remnants of that particular photographic series. Only unidentified potsherds are shown in photograph 4b, which, under the heading "Potsherds, showing handles," is captioned similarly to the photograph of the bracelet.

Burials 24 and 25. Two males (65 and 67 years) were interred in a grave into the original hill surface (Fig. 36). Number 24 covers No. 25 and has its head on the chest of the lower. The long axis of each burial is west-northwest to east-southeast with the head to the east. Parts of the right side of No. 25 have been damaged and the feet are missing while the left foot and left humerus of No. 24 have been removed and the head damaged. There are no associated artifacts. The right humerus of No. 25 has a healed fracture.

Burial 27. The oldest female in the excavation (70 years) is buried in a grave penetrating the original hill surface a few inches behind the head of No. 26 (Fig. 36). She is in an extended supine position although the bones of most of the body and legs have been destroyed by previous excavation. The feet are crossed, left over right. The long axis of the burial is north-northeast to south-southwest with the head to the south. Scattered around the ankles and feet are 14 small mussel-shell rattles (Fig. 12, D35).

Burials 28, 29, and 176. The grave dug for No. 29 disturbed the entire right side of No. 28 and probably all of No. 176, a fetus (Fig. 36). Few of the bones of the six-month fetus remain. These burials were superimposed over Nos. 34 and 231 and were superimposed by Nos. 2, 3, 4, and 30.

Number 28 is a supine male of 28 years whose body is oriented north-northeast to south-southwest with the head to the south. The arms are to the sides with the hands on the pelvis. The partially damaged skull, pictured in a number of early photographs, was removed by the Dicksons sometime after the original excavation. Its current disposition is unknown. A chert scraper was found to the right of the skull (Fig. 3, D13).

Number 29 (male 59 years) has all of its upper portion disturbed by previous excavation. It had the same orientation as No. 28 and the angle of the femurs suggests that the legs were crossed. "Three small irregular shaped rocks" were originally noted with this burial but are not now present.

Burial 31. A 28-year-old female rests several inches above No. 32 on her left and one and one-half feet above the mass grave of Nos. 6 to 9 to her right (Fig. 35). Her grave penetrated the mound fill and several inches of the original hill surface. Orientation is north to south with the head to the south. Near the left shoulder is a shell-tempered plain, effigy bowl (missing the effigy

head) containing a mussel-shell spoon — probably *Lampsilis ventricosa* (Figs. 18, D38; 16, D39).

Burial 32. This female (35 years of age) apparently shared the same body orientation as No. 31, but her remains, from the knees up, have been destroyed by previous excavation (Fig. 35). The base of her grave is well below the original hill surface.

Burial 33. Protruding from the profile to the left of and above the feet of No. 1 are the feet of a female(?) estimated at 25 years of age. The burial orientation is east to west with the head to the east (Fig. 34). The upper portion appears to have been completely destroyed by previous excavators. No artifacts are in association.

Burials 34 and 231. A seven-month fetus and a one-month-old infant were located in a probable grave invading the original hill surface some 14 inches above and to the right of No. 27 (Fig. 36). The Dickson notes indicate that these burials were removed because of the frailty of the bones.

Burial 35. An extended male of 50 years lies in a grave dug into the original hill surface at a right angle to the left side of No. 24 (Fig. 36). Its orientation is north-northeast to south-southwest with the head to the south. This burial is twisted to the right with the shoulders pulled in (probably as a result of wrapping) and the arms are under the hips with the hands protruding below the pelvis. Eleven artifacts were associated with this burial. Included are six side-notched triangular arrowpoints: two are single and double side-notched while the remaining four are five-notched (Fig. 7, D40-D45). These specimens were clustered between the knees with the tips pointing toward the feet. A large side scraper and an end scraper, possibly indicative of a tool kit, were found near the left hand (Figs. 3, D46; 4, D282) and an equal-arm pipe of low-grade catlinite(?) was found over the left shoulder (Fig. 30, D48). A single bead of marine shell was found "about 1 inch above the skull" (Fig. 11, D47). A broken mussel shell found "near the left side of the left femur" is no longer present.

Burial 36. Situated in a grave intruding the original hill surface to the north of No. 177 is a fifteen-year-old female (Fig. 38). The long axis of this supine individual is north-northwest to south-southeast with the head to the southeast. Its grave was filled with a light-colored loess, and a definite color contrast exists between this fill and the surrounding undisturbed clay-loess. A profile of earth across the grave was left unexcavated by the Dicksons to more clearly show this. No grave offerings are exposed.

Burials 37-43 and 45. These burials are associated in a mass group of eight individuals situated in the northwest corner of the excavation (Fig. 37). The lower members (Nos. 40, 43, and 45) are below the original hill surface and are covered by Nos. 37, 38, 39, 41, and 42. With the exception of No. 45, which has its head to the north, the long axis of each skeleton is north-northeast to south-southwest with the head to the south. Number 37, a female of 46 years, was probably wrapped and buried in a prone position with her legs flexed under. Some parts of this individual were disarticulated at the time of interment: the mandible is out of position and is to the right of the head; the upper arms are articulated but the forearms are separated at the elbow joint; the right forearm with the hand attached is placed on the top of the burial and the left forearm and hand are not readily visible. It is assumed that they were placed under the body. Both legs are flexed underneath with the left leg disarticulated at the knee joint. No grave goods accompany this person.

Number 38, a child (female?) of three years, is slightly above and adjacent to No. 37. Many of its bones are slightly out of position due to the slump caused by the deterioration of Nos. 39 and 45.

Number 39, a male of 24 years, is the central figure of the group. Having been wrapped, the shoulders are pulled in toward the face, the arms to the sides with the right arm under the pelvis, and the legs crossed at the ankles (left over right). A loop(?)-handled, smoothed-over cordmarked jar (Fig. 18, D62) was found "with this burial." Although no location is pinpointed, it is probable that it was somewhere to the right of the burial.

Number 40 is a male, 41 years of age. No artifacts are associated.

Number 41, a female of 47 years, is twisted to the right due to the slump caused by the decomposure of Nos. 39 and 40. A group of five arrowpoints (four triangular and one double side-notched) was found in back of the skull (Fig. 7,

D71-D75). Only four arrowpoints are mentioned in the Dickson notes, however. This burial may have been wrapped, but exact determination is difficult because of the slump.

Number 42, 26 months of age, has some disturbance to its right side due to the slump caused by the decomposition of No. 41. At the left side is a large chert knife (Fig. 5, D76).

Number 43, a secondary burial of a 38-year-old male, is only partially excavated. It has no associated artifacts.

Number 45 (male, 32 years), covered by Nos. 37 and 38, has only part of its upper section and the legs exposed. To the left of the head is a handled beaker in which now appears a fragmentary mussel-shell spoon (probably *Lampsilis ventricosa*) (Figs. 21, D77; 16, D78). A tool kit of 19 artifacts lies to the right of the head. Included are two sandstone abraders (Fig. 9, D49-D50), one drill (Fig. 8, D51), two chert flakes (Fig. 31, D53-D54), three scrapers (Fig. 3, D52 and D55-D56), one fragmentary bone hairpin (Fig. 15, D58), one bone weaving tool (Fig. 8, D59), five unaltered deer phalanges (Fig. 32, D64-D68), two fishhook blanks of bird bone (Fig. 30, D60-D61), a notched-handled, mussel-shell spoon (*Lampsilis ventricosa*) (Fig. 16, D63), and a bone fishhook which is no longer present. A truncated conoidal bead of marine shell was found on the chest (Fig. 11, D57). Depending upon the interpretation of the Dickson notes, it is possible that the hairpin, weaving tool, and two sandstone abraders were not in the tool kit to the "right of the head" but were found somewhere nearby "at the side of the skull."

Burial 44. On a slightly lower level (probably in a grave) and about one foot to the west of this group is the burial of another 26-month-old infant (Fig. 37). It has the same orientation as that of the mass burials, and its head is to the south. While the head is turned left, there is an opposite twist to the body. This individual is in a supine position with the arms to the sides, but many of the bones are disintegrated or missing. There is no accompanying burial furniture.

Burial 46. A 20-year-old female lies at a right angle to and about one and one-half feet behind the head end of the previously mentioned mass grave (Fig. 37). Her grave appears to be well below the level of the original hill surface. The long axis of this supine burial is west-northwest to east-southeast with the head to the southeast. A scraper made from a polished hoe(?) fragment was found with this burial but its position was not recorded (Fig. 3, D397).

Burial 47. In a grave cutting into the natural hill surface two feet to the left of No. 46 is the extended burial of a 40-year-old female (Fig. 38). Exhibiting evidences of wrapping, the arms are to the sides with the hands under the pelvis and the shoulders pulled in toward the face. The burial is oriented west-northwest to east-southeast with the head to the east. Two ornaments, a shell pendant *(Busycon* spp.*)*, and a large and globular marine-shell bead (flattened on one side and the ends), appear on the chest (Figs. 13, D81; 11, D82). A brown-polished, handled, Spoon River Beaker with double lip was associated with this burial, but its exact location is unknown (Fig. 19, D79). It supposedly contained "half of a freshwater shell . . . spoon," but only a fragment remains (Fig. 31, D80).

Burials 48 and 49. A male of 75 years and an 8-month fetus are together in a grave that penetrates the original hill surface two feet south of No. 47 (Fig. 38). The long axis of each individual is west-northwest to east-southeast with the head to the east. The fetus apparently had been placed on the left arm of the adult, its head resting on the shoulder, but its bones are somewhat disarticulated due to slumping. The large male (at 5 ft. 9 in. he is the tallest man in the excavation) has his arms tight to the sides and the hands under the pelvis, suggesting wrapping. This male was afflicted with a Stage IV arthritic involvement and a possible fracture of the foot; his knees are bent and the tarsal bones of the left foot exhibit complete ankylosis. Neither burial has associated artifacts.

Burial 50. Directly to the south of Nos. 48 and 49 is the grave of an infant, 6 months of age (Fig. 38). The long axis of this supine burial is west-northwest to east-southeast with the head to the northwest. It is approximately one foot above the level of Nos. 48, 49, and 51. Lying "around the forearm bones" of this infant is an undecorated bone bracelet (Fig. 14, D89), and at the right hand is a flake knife (Fig. 5, D90). Also scattered about the right side of the skull were 10 large marine-shell disc beads which may have been worn in the hair. Only six of these remain (Fig. 11, D83-D88).

Burial 51. Lying in a grave into the original hill surface and parallel to No. 50 is a supine infant, 10 months of age (Fig. 38). The long axis of the burial is the same as that of No. 50, as is the locus of the head. A string of 59 disc beads around the neck is no longer present.

Burial 52. Four feet to the southeast of Nos. 48 and 49 is a disturbed burial, apparently that of a female approximately 47 years old. The long axis of the burial is generally east to west with the head to the east. Only the legs and pelvis remain, as the upper half of the burial was destroyed by previous excavation (Fig. 38). The grave apparently cut through the mound and into the hill surface. No associated artifacts were noted.

Burials 53 and 54. Placed in a grave into the hill and originally partially covered by No. 55 is a 38-year-old female with a neonate infant resting on her pelvic area (Figs. 39). The long axis of each is north-northeast to south-southwest with the head to the south. The head of the adult is turned to the left. Both(?) are in an extended supine position with the arms to the sides. The shoulders of the female are pulled in toward the face with the left hand over the pelvic area: the legs are crossed at the ankles (left over right), apparently the symptoms of wrapping. From the location and age of the infant, it is possible that this is a burial of a female with an unborn child in a breech position. An acute osteomyelitic involvement is evident in the female's left hand, and the extreme lightness of most available long bones suggests severe osteoporosis. Since 38 years seems to be quite late in the child-bearing period for Mississippian people, even the normal birth of a child might have been difficult without the complicating factors of infection and disease. A shell-tempered plain, shallow bowl is resting on the right shoulder of the adult (Fig. 20, D91). It contains an unaltered mussel shell *(Lampsilis ventricosa)* (Fig. 31, D264).

Burial 55. This 6-month-old infant originally rested slightly over and nearly one foot above the head of No. 54 (Fig. 39). Its grave appears to be below the level of the original hill surface. The long axis of the burial is north-northeast to south-southwest with the head to the south and the arms to the sides. The lower torso area is disturbed and the leg bones displaced to the left. A wide-mouthed, shell-tempered plain water bottle is to the left of the head (Fig. 21, D92).

Burials 56 to 66 and 178. Ten burials in a mass grave and two partially disarticulated skeletons are positioned to the west of No. 55 (Fig. 39). The long axis of each is east-southeast to west-northwest with heads to the southeast. The fill of this intrusive grave contains many loose bones and bone fragments. It is not clear whether secondary burials Nos. 56 and 178 were disturbed by this mass burial and replaced to the right of the group or if they were actually included as an integral part of it.

Numbers 56 and 178 are secondary burials of a 49-year-old female and a 55-year-old male. Most bones of No. 56 are present while only the long bones and part of the torso of No. 178 remain. Many bones of No. 178 are still articulated, suggesting that deterioration was incomplete at the time of burial. Neither has associated burial furniture.

Number 57 is an extended supine male of 39 years. As it is partially covered by No. 58, the left side is not exposed, but the right arm is folded with the hand under the chin. The head is apparently slumped and turned to the right. There are no associated artifacts.

Number 58 is an extended adult female of 34 years. Having been very tightly wrapped, the shoulders are pulled in with the arms pulled together across the front. The legs are crossed at the knees, left over right. The head is slumped and turned to the left. A healed fracture of the right ulna of this female is accompanied by an osteomyelitic involvement, and there is severe osteoarthritic involvement of the lumbar region and sacroiliac joint. No grave goods are in association.

Number 59 is an extended 38-year-old male which, covered by No. 60, has only the head and part of the legs exposed. Its head is turned right, and it has no artifacts in association.

Number 60 is a female of 17 years which is partially covered by Nos. 58, 63, and 64. The skeleton is extended with the head turned slightly right. No artifacts are exposed.

Number 61 is a 6-year-old child (female?) that is only partially excavated. It is sandwiched between Nos. 57 and 58 with its legs slightly flexed over Nos. 59 and 60. Since only the posterior surfaces of the legs and pelvis are showing, this child may have been buried in a prone position. It has no associated grave offerings.

Number 62 is another female, age 15, partially covered by No. 63. This individual is in an extended position and the head is turned to the left.

An "extra" femur of a child about 5 years of age is in the fill between the legs. There is no accompanying burial furniture.

Number 63 is a small, extended female, 45 years old. Having been wrapped, the shoulders are pulled in with the lower arms and hands under the pelvis, and the head is turned to the right. A *Busycon* shell pendant was found on the chest, but it is not the one pictured in the earliest photographs of the burial area. It is suspected that the original was stolen.

Number 64 is a female(?) estimated at 55 years, covered by No. 62 and No. 63. Only the top of the skull and the feet are exposed, but the burial is apparently in an extended position. There are no exposed grave goods.

Numbers 65 and 66 are the somewhat disarticulated remains of two small children, 5 and 2½ years (calculated according to stature). Partially covered by the smaller child, No. 65 is not completely exposed. Only the mandible, a few ribs and some of the larger bones of No. 66 remain, and the skull of No. 65 is very fragmentary. The upper left side of both burials seems to have been disturbed. Possibly Nos. 179 and 180 were intrusive and disarranged the bones of these infants. Neither child has burial furniture.

Burials 67 and 68. A child of 10 years (calculated from leg length) and an infant of about 2½ years lie above and behind the previously mentioned mass group (Fig. 39). Both are near the existing mound surface and appear to have been somewhat disturbed by farming. The long axis of each of these supine burials is east to west with the head to the east. The head and upper body of No. 67 were apparently disturbed by the intrusive grave of Nos. 208 and 209. To the right of the head area and slightly above was a fragmentary, black-slipped effigy bowl (Fig. 26, D367). This specimen and an unaltered valve of a Mucket (*Actinonaias carinata*) (Fig. 31, D368) also were probably disturbed by the later grave.

Burials 69-71. Partially covered by Nos. 72, 73, 74, and 77, three males (ages calculated at 39, 44, and 57 years) are associated in a mass grave (Fig. 41). The long axis of each burial is north-northeast to south-southwest with the head to the south. Number 71 is centered over Nos. 69 and 70. Although only the lower portions are exposed, their compactness suggests that all three burials were wrapped. Two, Nos. 69 and 70, have the legs crossed left over right while No. 71 has the legs crossed right over left. Scattered bits of bone were found throughout the fill of this grave, suggesting that it had disturbed another burial(s). No artifacts are exposed.

Burials 72 and 233. A 26-year-old female (No. 72) and the disturbed remains of a second adult (No. 233) rest in an intrusive grave above the previously mentioned burials (Fig. 41). No. 26 is oriented east-northeast to west-southwest with the head to the northeast. The arms are to the sides with the right hand on the pelvis. The feet are missing, but this may have been posthumous. This female is the latest of all burials in the area, covering parts of Nos. 69, 70, 71, and 75, cutting Nos. 73 and 74, and probably disturbing the upper body of No. 233. The left humerus of No. 233 was included with the fill over this female along with the left femur of No. 74. The remaining disturbed bones of Nos. 73 and 74 were piled on the pelvic area of No. 74.

An early photograph of the excavation in progress reveals the distal ends of the femurs, lower legs, and feet of a burial whose upper body was perfectly positioned to have been cut by the grave for No. 72 (Plate 5a, right center). We can only assume that the humerus of No. 233 belonged with this burial since the legs and feet were removed by the Dicksons sometime during the spring or early summer of 1927. The grave containing the legs and feet was intrusive, disturbing the face and upper body of No. 83.

A necklace of 207 "mussel shell" beads was found around the neck and over the rib bones of No. 72. The bead description of "¼ in. in diameter . . . ¼ in. in thickness" implies typical marine-shell beads as opposed to beads of mussel shell, however. This necklace is no longer present but does appear in a number of early photographs of the excavation (Plate 7a). Three shell hoes and five unaltered mussel shells occur with this burial, but their positions were not recorded. The five unaltered valves are Pocketbooks (*Lampsilis ventricosa*), and two are halves of the same shell (Fig. 31, D172-D176). The shell hoes are probably made from the Washboard *Megalonaias gigantea*) (Fig. 10, D168-D170).

Burials 73 and 74. Two infants, 2 years and 26 months, are buried one on top of the other (Fig. 41). The long axis of each supine burial is north to south with the head to the south. Their legs,

disturbed by No. 72, were thrown back over the pelvic area of No. 74, and the "squeezed in" appearance of the shoulders and arms suggests that they were wrapped together before interment. Number 74 covers all but the right side and skull of No. 73. Each child has a single bead on its chest: one, a large, marine-shell disc type; the other, a rectangular block bead of fluorspar (Fig. 11, D98 and D101). A plain everted-rim jar and shallow bowl were found behind the heads, the jar inverted in the bowl (Fig. 19, D99 and D102).

Burial 75. The burial of a 2-month-old infant lies in an intrusive grave on the same level and shares a common burial axis as Nos. 69, 70, and 71 to its right (Fig. 41). All four may have been interred at about the same time. Only the skull and lower legs of this infant are exposed, most of it being covered by No. 72. It has no exposed grave goods.

Burial 76. The burial of a 26-month-old infant is partially covered by Nos. 73 and 74 (Fig. 41). Its grave originated in the mound and cut into the hill surface. Orientation is north-northeast to south-southwest with the head to the south. The lower section of this burial is not exposed, and the upper portion is disturbed — possibly due to the slump caused by the decomposure of Nos. 69 to 71 below. Its head is slightly above and touching the head of No. 77. While this infant may be a later burial than No. 77, both were placed over Nos. 69 to 71 soon after the latter's interment. No burial furniture accompanies this child.

Burial 77. A male of 38 years is also partially covered by Nos. 73 and 74 (Fig. 41). Its grave appears to have cut into the original hill surface. The long axis of this supine burial is east-northeast to west-southwest with the head to the southwest. The left side of the upper section is slightly lower, apparently due to a slump caused by disintegration of Nos. 69 and 71 below left. No grave offerings accompany this burial.

Burial 78. In a grave penetrating the original hill surface to the right of No. 77 is an infant about 10 months of age (Fig. 41). The long axis of this supine individual is north-northeast to south-southwest with the head to the southwest. The arms are apparently to the sides, but the burial is greatly slumped on the left and many bones are out of position. This may have resulted from the decomposure of an unexcavated burial(s) below. No grave offerings were found in association.

Burial 79. Several inches above and adjacent to No. 78 on the right is a male of 35 years (Fig. 41). This supine burial is oriented along the same axis as No. 78, and its head is also to the south. The arms are to the sides, but the burial was disarticulated at the knees at the time of interment. The lower legs and some attached foot bones were laid back over the femurs with the feet toward the pelvis. The detached lower right arm was laid along the left forearm, according to the Dickson notes. The presence of "extra" skull fragments and a left radius of an adult suggest either an associated burial now disturbed or that this burial (No. 79) was dug intrusively into the mound and parts of the burial(s) it disturbed were thrown back into the grave with the fill. Two shell arm rattles or clackers were found near the right shoulder (Fig. 12, D104-D105). They are mated valves of a Purple Warty-Back (*Cyclonaias tuberculata*). A large chert scraper lies near the right elbow (Fig. 3, D106). Two "mussel shells" (shell spoons(?), possibly D100 and D103) were recorded near the left shoulder and a small marine-shell pendant, grooved at the neck, was reportedly resting on the sternum. The pendant is no longer present and the spoons(?) may have been moved to nearby burials 73 and 74. A mussel-shell fragment was apparently found in the grave fill (Fig. 31, D108).

Early photographs of the Burial 79 area show two things of significance. A large, Mound Place Incised-like duck-effigy bowl is consistently pictured as being positioned in the area to the left of the upper body of No. 79 (Fig. 20, D107). Although two other burials (Nos. 77 and 78) also occupy that same area, neither was exposed at the time the duck-effigy bowl first appears in a photograph. The specimen is not mentioned in the Dickson notes, however.

Nearly touching and slightly below the level of the right shoulder of No. 79 was an articulated skull and mandible shown in the earliest a photograph. The specimen is not mentioned in 5a, right edge). It was facing the opposite direction from No. 79. This skull was soon removed by the Dicksons, probably to facilitate excavation of Nos. 199-207, 172, and 169. Its whereabouts are unknown.

Burial 80. Occupying a position between the feet of No. 72 and the head of No. 81 is an infant (2½ years) (Fig. 40). This supine burial is oriented north-northeast to south-southwest with the head to the southwest. The arms are to the sides, but the lower legs and parts of other bones are missing — possibly the result of rodent activity.

Burial 81. Behind the head of No. 80 and partly covered by No. 85 is a 28-year-old female (Fig. 42). The long axis of the burial is north-northeast to south-southwest with the head to the northeast. The body may have been wrapped since the shoulders are pulled in with the arms to the sides and the hands under the pelvis. Behind the head is a lobed, strap-handled jar (originally brown-polished) that contains a mussel-shell spoon (possibly *Lampsilis ventricosa*) (Figs. 23, D119; 16, D120).

Burials 82 and 83. Two supine females are associated in a single interment: No. 83 (13 years) covers No. 82 (48 years). The long axis of each is west-northwest to east-southeast with the head to the west (Fig. 43). As their shoulders are pulled in with the arms tight to the sides and the knees and feet squeezed together, both were probably wrapped. The skull and upper body of No. 83 were somewhat disturbed by the intrusive grave of what probably was Burial 233. The feet of No. 233 originally lay on the face and upper body of No. 83 before the removal of the burial by the Dicksons sometime in 1927 (Plate 5a, right center). A potter's trowel was found near the right hand of the older female (Fig. 30, D111-D112). A rounded sherd of gray, brushed-over, shell-tempered pottery (D112), slightly larger in diameter than the widest dimension of the trowel, was found under it. This piece has worn rounded edges and because of its association with the trowel may have been used as a tool (spatula) in pottery manufacture. It may also be an undrilled spindle whorl. A fragmentary mussel-shell spoon was apparently included in the grave fill (Fig. 16, D114).

Burials 84 and 86. Two females (22 and 24 years) lie one and one-half feet below and are partially covered by Nos. 82 and 83 (Fig. 43). Both are in a grave invading the original hill surface. The lower burial (No. 86) is extended with the long axis north-northeast to south-southwest.

The head is to the northeast. Number 84 is a secondary burial that is centered over the pelvic area and femurs of No. 86 and has a similiar orientation. Both seem to have been wrapped. An everted-rim jar with traces of black polish (Fig. 21, D110) containing a mussel-shell spoon (possibly D171, Fig. 16) was associated with this burial, probably located in the area of the head.

Burial 85. A supine male, 41 years of age, covers the legs of Nos. 81 and 88 (Fig. 42). It is oriented north to south, with the head to the south. The upper quarter of the burial is missing and there is much disturbance to the left side from previous excavation. An everted-rim, smoothed-over cordmarked jar was located somewhere with this burial (Fig. 21, D109).

Burial 87. The remains of three fetuses (all 7 fetal months) originally rested behind the head of No. 99 (Fig. 44). The long axes of these were generally north-northeast to south-southwest with the heads to the south. Originally positioned in the Dickson's walkway into the excavation, the scattered bones of this burial were taken up and rearticulated on a board near the right side of No. 88. These three burials possibly represent a multiple birth. A miniature, shell-tempered plain jar with slight traces of black-slip was found near the head (Fig. 20, D115). This was covered by a mussel-shell spoon (Fig. 16, D116). Early photographs of this burial show literally dozens of bones present. The present disposition of most of these specimens is unknown.

Burial 88. A supine female, 60 years old, rests in a grave partially covered by Nos. 81 and 85 (Fig. 42). The long axis of the burial is north to south with the head to the south. Apparently having been wrapped, the arms are tight to the sides with the right hand under and the left hand over the pelvis; the knees and the feet are together, and the head is turned down and to the right. An everted-rim plain jar containing a mussel-shell spoon was found behind and to the left of the skull (Figs. 21, D178; 16, D179). It should be noted that the measurements of this vessel do not correspond exactly to those in the Dickson notes. A second pottery vessel, a handled beaker, remains *in situ* to the left of the feet (Fig. 29, D394). The unusual positioning of this beaker may indicate that it was included in the grave fill.

Burial 89. An extended prone female (21 years), partly covered by Nos. 100 and 103, lies in a grave which penetrates the original hill surface, one foot to the east of No. 88 (Fig. 44). It is oriented north to south with the head to the north. The burial may have been made when the body was partly disintegrated as the right arm is twisted over the back and the left arm is missing (although it may be covered by the burial). The compactness of the burial suggests wrapping. Fragments of an unusual strap-handled, moderately angular-shouldered jar were found near the head (Fig. 22, D183).

Burial 90. To the north of Nos. 80 and 81 is the burial of a male, 49 years of age (Fig. 40). The long axis of this supine burial is north to south with the head to the south. Undoubtedly he was a prominent person or a skilled artisan, for some 57 artifacts were buried with him. The only celt in the excavation is located near his right hand (Fig. 30, D147), as is one chert knife blade (Fig. 6, D148). A large tool kit of artifacts is situated beside the left hip. Included are 5 antler flakers (Fig. 9, D140, D142, D312-D314), 2 rough knives (Fig. 6, D149 and D167), 4 crude drills (Fig. 8, D150-D152, D410), 10 end, side, and thumbnail scrapers (Figs. 3, D153-D156; 4, D157, D158, D160, D163, D165 and D166), and 5 chert flakes (Fig. 31, D159, D161, D162, D164, and D411). Three triangular arrowpoints appeared "along the left side of the thorax" (Fig. 7, D144-D146), and the hollow outer whorl of a *Busycon* spp. shell, grooved for attachment, is centered on the chest (Fig. 13, D93).

Unfortunately, one page of the Dickson field notes seems to be missing at this point and parts of two others are very ragged. A combination of those notes and a later description of Burial 90 (Dickson n.d.:21-23) was used in the following.

At the back of the head was an awl of turkey (*Meleagris gallopavo*) leg bone (Fig. 8, D134) resting on a sandstone abrader (probably Fig. 9, D122). A bone hairpin had apparently slumped to the level of these two implements, causing its initial misassociation and identification by the Dicksons as a needle or punch (Fig. 15, D131). Near these items was a second tool kit which may have been used for either sewing or in scarification (Fig. 32, D135-D137). The kit consists of two mussel-shell valves, a Pocketbook, (*Lampsilis ventricosa*), on the bottom covered by an altered Pink Heel-Splitter, (*Proptera alata*) and a small, finely grained sandstone abrader and a group of 17 small needles which are inside the container. A third sandstone abrader lay to the right of the head (probably Fig. 9, D124) and a black-polished, handled Spoon River Beaker was probably positioned to the left of the head (Fig. 23, D121).

There is a decided discrepancy between the number and type of artifacts detailed in the Dickson notes and the artifacts traditionally displayed with Burial 90. The notes indicate a total of 35 "relic" numbers for this burial, which includes a single number assigned to the group of 17 needles and a single number for the two mussel-shell valves. By similar count, the traditional artifact total for this burial has been 50.

Unfortunately, precise identification of the original artifacts is complicated by the absence of that portion of the Dickson notes describing six of these items (Dickson "relic" Nos. 104-108 and 110). However, some insight into the problem can be gained from Don Dickson's later description of Burial 90 (Dickson n.d.:21-23) where he identifies specific objects which account for four of the six missing "relic" descriptions. The remaining two items may not have been viewed as sufficiently important to later describe, suggesting that they were not part of a group of nine other outstanding artifacts traditionally displayed with the burial. It is suspected that these additional artifacts (primarily bone tools and a sandstone abrader) were used as lecture aids since this was one burial always discussed in some detail during daily museum tours. Because they appear in all but the earliest photographs of the burial, at least three of these artifacts (D126, D129, and possibly D132, Harn 1971b: Figs. 8 and 9) probably were added even before the excavation project was completed. Others may have accumulated later as they appear only in more recent photographs. These include artifacts D123, D125, D127, D128, D133, and D138 (Harn 1971b: Figs. 8, 9, 13, and 15). None of these nine specimens has been employed in the current analysis.

By omitting these items, the discrepancy between the Dickson notes and the present burial furniture with No. 90 is considerably lessened. Present today but not accounted for in the Dickson notes are four undetermined chert artifacts (either scrapers or flakes) in the large tool kit and one arrowpoint (D143). It is even possible that these items were uncovered by cleaning or additional excavation in later years. One bone needle presently is missing from the smaller tool kit.

Burial 91. The long bones, a few ribs and vertebrae of three adults — two males 41(?) and 46(?) years and a female 26(?) years — are present in a compact secondary burial below the original hill surface (Fig. 40). The long axis of the bundle is north-northeast to south-southwest. No artifacts are associated.

Burial 92. In a grave penetrating the original hill surface slightly above and to the left of No. 91 is an extended male burial, 51 years of age (Fig. 40). It is oriented north-northeast to south-southwest with the head to the southwest. The head is turned to the left and is slightly under and several inches lower than the right forearm of No. 90. The feet are covered by Nos. 179 and 180. No burial furniture is exposed.

Burial 93. A 27-month-old infant was placed in a grave which may have disturbed the feet of No. 102 (Fig. 43). The burial is oriented north-northeast to south-southwest with the head to the southwest. It has been greatly disturbed by either aboriginal grave-digging or by previous excavation. A small mussel-shell rattle was found somewhere with this burial (Fig. 12, D177) and a knife(?) fragment was found at the right hand (Fig. 6, D180). A mussel-shell spoon (probably *Lampsilis ventricosa*) was found at the back of the head (Fig. 16, D179).

Burials 94 and 95. A male of 42 years and a child of 11 are associated in a grave below and to the right of No. 93 (Fig. 43). The child covers the adult, and both are oriented generally north to south with the head to the north. As they are partially covered by Nos. 96, 97, 101, 102 and 100, only the head, pelvic area and femurs are exposed. The head of each is turned in, facing the other, and both were probably wrapped. Either at or on the top of the heads of both skeletons is a jar, with a broad-trailed meander design and tridactyl handles, which contains a mussel-shell spoon (probably *Lampsilis ventricosa*) (Fig. 25, D181; 16, D182).

Burials 96 and 97. A child of 6 years and a female estimated at 25 years are buried above Nos. 94, 95 and 101 (Fig. 43). The child covers the left side of the adult, and both are partly covered by Nos. 82, 83, and 98. The skull of the adult has been removed by previous excavators. The long axis of each is north to south with the head to the south, and both are slumped to the left, probably due to a shifting of earth caused by the decomposure of the lower burials. A necklace of 65 dime-size disc beads, probably of marine shell, were found around the neck of No. 96. Although they appear in all of the early photographs (Plate 7a), no trace of them remains today. A poorly made plain jar was to the right of the head (Fig. 20, D117). Two fragmentary mussel shells were included in the grave fill. One was near the right arm of No. 97 (Fig. 31, D184), but the position of the other was not recorded (Fig. 31, D118).

Burial 98. Two fetuses (7½ fetal months and calculated newborn) cover the right pelvic area of No. 97 (Fig. 43). The bodies are oriented generally west-northwest to east-southeast with the heads to the west. The bones of the larger child are in fair articulation except for the legs, which have been disturbed; the smaller upper burial seems to have been almost completely destroyed. Both are close to the original surface of the mound and may have been disturbed by farming. A chert flake, probably included with the fill, is located near their left sides, while a plain jar is near the heads (Figs. 31, D185; 23, D186). The chert flake was not recorded in the Dickson notes.

Burial 99. A female of 41 years rests near the west side of the excavation in a grave penetrating the original hill surface (Fig. 44). The long axis is north-northwest to south-southeast with the head to the northwest. Suggesting wrapping, the shoulders are squeezed in toward the face and the arms are tight along the sides with the hands under the pelvis. Two wide rings of hollowed-out and polished antler are on the left shoulder (Fig. 15, D187-D188), and a heavy and roughly made, shell-tempered plain shallow bowl with pouring spouts is situated behind the head (Fig. 23, D189). Included in this vessel is a mussel-shell spoon (probably *Lampsilis ventricosa*) (Fig. 16, D190).

Burial 100. The burial of a female, 20 years of age, covers parts of Nos. 89, 101, 102, 103, 94 and 95 (Figs. 43, 44). The long axis of this burial is east to west with the head to the west. The

shoulders pulled in and the arms to the side with the left hand on the pelvis suggest wrapping. A necklace of 115 disc beads of marine shell were found around the neck. Only 111 of these remain (Fig. 11, D191). To the right of the head is a shell-tempered plain jar with flat-topped loop handles (Fig. 19, D95) which originally contained a mussel-shell spoon decorated with six notches on the handle. The spoon is no longer present and the necklace was recently stolen. A chert flake is at the right hand (Fig. 31, D412).

Early photographs of this burial indicate a complete skeleton while those taken slightly later show the head missing. Today, the skull is present, but the mandible is gone.

Burial 101. Resting in a grave along the same axis and covering Nos. 94 and 95 (but with the head to the south) is the supine burial of a 41-year-old female (Fig. 43). It is partially covered by Nos. 96, 97, 100 and 102. The feet are crossed (left over right) and the skeleton has a general compactness that suggests wrapping. The lower half of the burial is decidedly slumped, probably due to the decomposure of Nos. 94 and 95 below. All three burials may have been interred at about the same time. The grave fill to the east of the head contained several large, shell-tempered plain sherds, an unworked piece of sandstone, and burned clay(?) fragments (Fig. 31, D395; 33, D396). The clay fragments are not pictured.

Burial 102. Covering the upper portion of No. 101 is the supine burial of an 11-year-old female (Fig. 43). It was placed in a grave oriented north-northwest to south-southeast with the head to the southeast; the head is turned slightly to the left. Due to the slump caused by the decomposure of Nos. 94, 95, and 101, the pelvic area and especially the right femur is much lower than the rest of the burial. All of these burials (and possibly No. 93) were made within a short span. The fragmentary mussel shell (*Lampsilis ventricosa*) near the feet is not mentioned in the Dickson notes and may be a recent addition.

Burial 103. A two-year-old child is situated with its legs over the feet of No. 89 and approximately two feet below the chest area of No. 100 (Fig. 44). Its grave is below the level of the original hill surface. The long axis of this supine burial is north to south with the head to the south. The arms, pelvic region, and femurs have been somewhat disturbed. Scattered on the chest were 37 disc beads (estimated diameter, ¾-inch) of marine shell which are pictured in the early photographs of the excavation. According to Dr. Dickson, these were the first of the articles stolen from the excavation — which may account for the fact that they are not mentioned in his field notes.

Burial 104. The disturbed remains of a child of 3 years rest in a grave to the left of No. 103 (Fig. 44). The whole area around Nos. 104 and 105 has been greatly disturbed and parts of both are mixed and scattered over the general area. Since the artifacts are still present, probably the disturbance resulted from rodent or aboriginal activity rather than from previous excavation. A miniature, shell-tempered plain jar is at the back of the head (Fig. 22, D194).

Burial 105. In a grave behind and to the left of No. 103 is the disturbed burial of four fetuses — 8, 7, 6½ and 6 fetal months (Fig. 44). The intermingled bones were oriented generally north-northwest to south-southeast with the head area to the south. A plain miniature jar with loop handles rests near these fetuses on the right (Fig. 22, D195). A small chert flake recorded with this burial is no longer present.

Burial 106. To the right of No. 103 is the supine burial of a 40-year-old male (Fig. 46). Its grave is below the level of the original hill surface. The long axis of the burial is east to west with the head to the west. Its lower axial portion and the legs of No. 111 were disturbed by the intrusive grave of Nos. 108 and 109 and piled between its pelvic area and the heads of No. 108 and 109. No artifacts are in association. This man has healed fractures of the right clavicle and left sixth(?) rib and an irregular hole in the left frontal bone showing questionable healing (injury?). Early photographs of this burial show a skull resting on the left side and arm which has since been removed.

Burial 107 and 184. Two disturbed burials were found to the right of and slightly below the level of Nos. 96 and 97 (Fig. 43). The Dickson notes indicate that the "bones are in a poor state of preservation and their position would suggest a small B.B. [bundle burial]. This is an unusual

condition in babe's [skeletons], but in this instance they were in a small compact bundle. There were no relics found." These burials had been removed by the time Dr. Georg K. Neumann examined the skeletal population in the early 1930s (Plate 7a, right center).

Burial 108, 109, and 150. These are associated intrusive burials that rest on or slightly below the original hill surface (Fig. 46). Number 108 covers the right side of No. 109; and No. 150, a secondary burial, covers the legs of both. The group is oriented northwest to southeast with head to the northwest. Their grave disturbed the lower axial section of No. 106 and the legs of No. 111.

Number 108 is a supine female, 17 years of age. Having been wrapped, the shoulders are pulled in with the right arm under the side and the left over the lower chest area; the legs are crossed at the ankles (left over right).

Number 109, a supine male of 35 years, may also have been wrapped. The body has a general squeezed appearance, and the shoulders are pulled in toward the head. Neither of these burials has associated grave goods.

Number 150 is a secondary burial of a female of 20 years. The burial was made when much of the body was in advanced state of disintegration. Contrary to one's first impression, the individual was not dismembered. Instead, the legs were crossed above the knees (left over right) when the body was in a prone position and the upper body folded backward until its back rested on the posterior surfaces of the legs. In assuming this position, the spinal column was twisted into a U-shape with the skull and the pelvis to the north. The remains may have been wrapped, which would help explain the unusual position of the bones. Probably included in the fill was an unaltered incisor of a beaver (*Castor canadensis*) (Fig. 30, D239) and two fragments of mudstone rock (Fig. 31, D240 and D402). One of these lithic pieces has three dished-out depressions running across its unfractured side (natural?).

Burials 110-115. To the right of Nos. 108, 109 and 150 are at least six burials (Fig. 46). Although none of these is lying along the same axis as any of the others, all are touching and were interred within a short time span. The only possible exception to this would be No. 112, the first burial to be placed in this area. It was later disturbed by No. 115, and this burial was followed by Nos. 113, 111, 108-109 and 150, 110 and 114 in that order. The lowest burials of this group appear to be on or below the original hill surface (in graves?). With the exception of No. 115, none of the burials have associated grave goods.

Number 110 is a supine male of 41 years apparently placed in a grave that disturbed No. 113. The long axis is east to west with the head to the east. The arms are to the sides with the left hand over the pelvis.

Number 111, a 19-year-old female, has her left lower arm and both legs disturbed by intrusive Nos. 108-109 and 150. The long axis of this supine burial is northeast to southwest with the head to the south. This burial is also interesting in that it has hypoplastic teeth and very pronounced cradleboard deformity (See Fig. 56, F).

Number 112 is the disturbed remains of a 24-year-old male. The original position of the body was probably west-northwest to east-southeast with the head to the west. Apparently disturbed by Nos. 113 and 115, only the skull, mandible and left scapula are still in position. Its femurs and right humerus were replaced over and to the left of its skull. The grave for this burial is below the level of the original hill surface.

Number 113 is a young female, 12 years of age. It is oriented west-northwest to east-southeast with the head to the west. As the body was wrapped, the shoulders were pulled in with the arms tight to the sides and the feet crossed (left over right).

Number 114 is a secondary burial placed on the feet of No. 110. While it is listed as containing a single adult male, 37 years of age, further cleaning produced parts of another male approximately the same age (from bone condition).

Number 115, a male of 34 years, is the lowest interment of the group. It is oriented west-northwest to east-southeast with the head to the west. The arms are to the sides with the left hand over the pelvic area, and the head is turned slightly left. A tool kit consisting of a chert knife blade, two chert flakes, and two chert scrapers is near the right hand (Figs. 4, D198-D199; 6, D217; 31, D196-D197). Only three of the four flakes and scrapers are mentioned in the Dickson notes. A triangular chert arrowpoint was near the right shoulder (Fig. 7, D200).

Burials 116-118. Associated in a mass grave of three individuals directly south of No. 115 are two supine females and an infant (Fig. 45). The long axis of each is west-northwest to east-southeast with the head to the west. Number 117 is covered by Nos. 116 and 118 in that order. The compactness of the burial suggests that they were wrapped before interment. Their grave penetrated the original hill surface.

Number 116 is a female of 63 years. It is extended with the arms to the sides.

Number 117 is a female, age 47. The upper body is twisted to the left, lying partially on its side, and the arms are flexed with the hands toward the face. The legs are bent slightly left.

Number 118 is an infant of 6 months. Probably associated with the infant, and behind the heads of all three, is a small, loop-handled, shell-tempered plain jar (Fig. 22, D201). A small, plain bone bracelet was found "on the arm bone" of this burial — possibly the left arm since the remaining fragments were on the left side (Fig. 14, D413).

Burial 119. A 37-year-old male rests in a grave two feet above and behind the heads of these latter burials (Fig. 45). The long axis of the supine burial is north to south with the head to the south. The arms are to the sides and the head is turned left. The head also rests several inches over and above the head of No. 124. Either this burial was made when the body was partially disintegrated or it was disturbed shortly after its interment, for many ribs are missing and the spinal column is disarticulated. A Stage IV arthritic involvement affects the fifth lumbar vertebrae and the sacrum. To the left of the head is a black-polished, Spoon River Beaker with handle and pouring lip (Fig. 24, D210).

Burial 120. Lying parallel to but one foot below and to the right of No. 99 is a supine female of 65 years (Fig. 44). She is oriented north-northwest to south-southeast with the head to the northwest. The arms are to the sides with the right hand over the pelvis, presenting a general squeezed appearance suggestive of wrapping. This burial was intrusive and had disturbed nearly all of No. 121. To the left of the head is a shell-tempered, cordmarked jar (Fig. 24, D207). Two areas on this jar show evidence of repair by the Indians. A damaged area between the neck and shoulder was filled with a mixture of clay and some small bits of mussel shell; a small hole, approximately 13 mm. in diameter, near the base was repaired by a pottery (clay? and crushed mussel shell) rivet. Vitrification of the inside head of the rivet verges near the melting point while the outer head appears to have been exposed to a less extreme temperature. The outer rivet head can be seen on the edge of a large damaged area near the jar base in Fig. 24. Unfortunately, the rivet has recently been virtually destroyed by a rock thrown by a small visitor.

Burial 121. The only bones of this 41-year-old female that remain articulated are the lower legs, the rest of the burial having been disturbed by the intrusive grave of No. 120. They protrude from the profile to the left of the former burial (Fig. 44). The skull and its articulated mandible were placed with the other disturbed bones at the foot of the intrusive grave and covered by No. 120. Its original position was apparently oriented north-south, with the head to the south, in a grave cut into the original hill surface. No artifacts were exposed.

Burial 122. A male of 52(?) years (from bone condition) is positioned in a grave dug into the original hill surface to the south of No. 120. The body axis is north-northwest to south-southeast with the head to the northwest. The burial is extended with the arms to the sides and the feet missing. Its left lower arm was partially destroyed by a steel support post from the wall of the original excavation. Although only the legs of this burial were ever displayed, recent excavation revealed that the upper body had been excavated and reburied by the Dicksons. Five unnotched, triangular arrowpoints are clustered between the knees with the points toward the feet (Fig. 7, D202-D206).

Burial 123. The supine burial of a 9-year-old child lies behind the head of No. 119 (Fig. 45). The grave for this burial penetrated the original hill surface. It is oriented west-northwest to east-southeast with the head to the northwest. Near the right hand is the only Ramey or "Cahokia" knife in the excavation while a Dickson Trailed, loop-handled jar remains *in situ* near its feet (Figs. 6, D209; 24, D208).

Burial 124. Positioned in a grave between the head of No. 119 and the upper portion of No. 126 (2 feet below) is the supine burial of a 3-year-old (calculated) child (Fig. 45). The long axis is west-northwest to east-southeast with the head to the west. The arms are to the sides, but parts of the burial were disturbed after excavation. No artifacts are exposed.

Burials 125 and 126. In a grave below the original hill surface to the south of Nos. 116-118, a female(?) of 11 years covers a 35-year-old female (Fig. 45). The burial is oriented west-northwest to east-southeast with the head to the west. The head of the adult is turned slightly to the right. Around the left ankle of the adult are 12 mussel-shell rattles (Fig. 12, D211), most of which remain *in situ*. None were apparently found on the right ankle.

Burial 127. The supine burial of a newborn infant partially covers the left side of Nos. 125 and 126 (Fig. 45). It is oriented east-northeast to west-southwest with the head to the northeast. The skull either slumped due to the deterioration of Nos. 116-118 or was disturbed by those burials; only scattered fragments remain. A miniature, shell-tempered plain jar rests near the head, and a necklace of 13 small marine-shell beads and one crude mussel(?)-shell pendant is located on the chest (Figs. 23, D212; 11, D215). One chert flake and one scraper were found in the fill nearby (Figs. 31, D214; 4, D213).

Burial 128. Resting between and above Nos. 115 and 108 is the supine burial of a large male, 37 years of age (Fig. 46). The long axis of the burial is west-northwest to east-southeast with the head to the south. A tool kit consisting of two chert scrapers, two chert flake knives, and one chert block is at the right hand (Figs. 4, D218 and D222; 5, D219 and D221; 31, D220) and a fragmentary, shell-tempered, cordmarked jar is to the right of the head (Fig. 24, D216).

Burial 129. The supine burial of an 8-year-old child lies below the level of the original hill surface near the south side of the excavation (Fig. 47). The burial orientation is west-northwest to east-southeast with the head to the west. The lower half of the burial is covered by No. 131 and has not been exposed. No artifacts are exposed.

Burial 130. On the same level to the right of No. 129 is another child (female?) 6 years of age (Fig. 47). The long axis is apparently west-northwest to east-southeast with the head to the northwest, but only a small portion of the burial has been exposed. No grave goods are exposed.

Burials 131-146 and173-174. Centered on the southern limits of the excavation are at least six superimposed graves containing some 20 exposed individuals (Fig. 47). Burials 145, 146, and possibly 130 were the earliest interments and were later superimposed by Nos. 131-132, possibly No. 129, and by a mass grave containing at least 12 individuals. The graves for Nos. 131-132 and the mass group apparently disturbed existing burials since the remaining fill is littered with bone fragments and both graves have partially redeposited burials (Nos. 133 and 144) in association. It is possible that the mass grave was the latest addition to the area, redisturbing the bone pile (No. 144 and 133) which was placed in the grave of Nos. 131-132. The lower burials of the group rest well below the original hill surface. Each individual in the group is oriented generally east to west or west-northwest to east-southeast, and (with the exception of Nos. 142 and 146 which have the heads to the east) all heads are to the west.

Number 131, a female of 38 years, and No. 132, a newborn infant, rest near the right edge of the group. The legs of the adult are partially covered by the reburial of No. 144, and its upper section is slumped due to the disintegration of No. 129. The compactness of the burial suggests wrapping. The infant lies with its head over the pelvic area and it extends between the legs of No. 131. Neither burial has associated furniture.

Number 133 is probably a disturbed burial of a 25-year-old female. The articulated skull and mandible are under No. 134, but the remainder of the burial may be mixed in with the nearby reburial No. 144. Two chert flakes remain *in situ* along the right side of the jaw. They are not pictured. These flakes were not mentioned in the Dickson notes.

Number 134 is an infant of 2 years. A disc bead of marine shell appears on its chest (Fig. 11, D223).

Number 135, a 7-month fetus, situated between Nos. 134 and 136, has no associated artifacts.

Number 136 is supine, a child of 8 years, which is sandwiched between Nos. 146 and 140. Only the upper part of the individual has been exposed and much of it is disturbed. Apparently no artifacts are in association.

Numbers 137-138 and 173 and 174 cover Nos. 136 and 140, each separated by a few inches of earth. Of the six, only No. 138 has associated burial furniture.

Number 137 is an 18-year-old male that is not fully exposed. The compactness of the remains may suggest wrapping, and the head is turned slightly left.

Number 138 is also a male, 20 years of age, which was apparently wrapped. Near the left hand is a large asymmetrical, double-pointed knife (Fig. 6, D225).

Number 139, a partially disarticulated fetus (9 fetal months), lies below and adjacent to the legs of No. 134. Two small marine-shell beads and a small *Olivella jaspidea* bead are located on the chest (Fig. 11, D227-D228). Possibly these were part of a necklace.

Number 140 is a newborn infant (according to cranial development) of which only the skull and the right arm are exposed. It is sandwiched between Nos. 136 and 137. Behind the head are a small, shell-tempered plain jar with flat-sided loop handles and a small, handled beaker (Fig. 23, D224 and D229). Both remain *in situ*.

Number 141, a child (female?) of 7 years, rests on the left edge of this mass group. The slump under its right side caused this dorsal burial to shift approximately 45 degrees laterally. Scattered over the burial are 54 large disc beads of marine shell (Fig. 11, D230). They were strung by the Dicksons and appear today in a general necklace pattern.

Number 142 is a partially disarticulated (from slumping?) infant. A small disc bead of mussel shell is located on the chest (Fig. 11, D231).

Number 143, a fetus (6½ fetal months), is situated between Nos. 137 and 141. There is no associated burial furniture.

Number 144, a disturbed burial of a 30-year-old male, is centered mainly over the lower legs of No. 131. Parts of No. 133 may be intermingled with this reburial. Both were probably disturbed by the intrusion of the mass group. No grave offerings are in association. Recent cleaning of this burial has revealed at least three more skulls. They have not been considered here.

Number 145 is an extended 6-year-old child. Its upper body is covered by No. 144 several inches above. The lower body has only recently been excavated, although the head and upper extremities had originally been exposed by tunneling. No artifacts were found. Its grave extended well into the original hill surface.

Number 145 is an extended burial of a 6-year-old child. Its upper body is covered by No. 144 several inches above. The lower body has only recently been excavated, although the head and upper extremities had originally been exposed by tunneling. No artifacts were found. Its grave extended well into the original hill surface.
to 140, 174, 137, 138 and 173; thus only the tibias of No. 146 can be seen on Fig. 47.

Number 173, represented by a partial skull and other body parts of a 6-month fetus, is partially under the left leg of No. 137.

Number 174, a 1½-year-old infant, apparently lies between Nos. 137 and 138 and is only partially exposed.

Burials 147 and 148. A child of 7 years overlies a 51-year-old female in a grave cut into the original hill surface north of the mass group (Fig. 47). Both burials are oriented east to west with their heads to the east. The arms are to the sides with the hands of No. 148 over its pelvic area. This along with the squeezed appearance of the shoulders suggests wrapping. On the level of No. 148 and behind the heads are two small, shell-tempered plain jars which are similar in size and shape (Fig. 25, D232 and D234). Both contain shell spoons (probably *Lampsilis ventricosa*) (Fig. 16, D233 and D235). A large scraper is at the right hand of No. 148 (Fig. 4, D237).

Burial 149. A female of 27 years rests in a grave penetrating the original hill surface to the north of Nos. 147 and 148 (Fig. 50). The long axis of the burial is east to west with the head to the west. The arms are to the sides with the knees slightly flexed left and the head is also turned left. A scraper is near the right hand (Fig. 4, D238).

Burials 151 and 152. An infant of two years and a female of 18 years are placed side by side in a grave cut into the original hill surface behind and to the left of No. 149 (Figs. 48 and 50). Both are oriented east to west with the head to the west. The feet of No. 151 and the legs of No. 152

are covered by the upper part of No. 154. A mussel-shell pendant is on the chest of the infant (Fig. 12, D241). A marine-shell pendant *(Busycon spp.)* and a large, hemispherical bead of marine shell are on the chest of the female (Figs. 13, D242; 11, D245), and a small cordmarked jar (red-painted interior) containing an unaltered mussel-shell valve (spoon?) *(Lampsilis ventricosa)* is to the left of the head (Figs. 25, D243; 31, D244). A chert hoe fragment and a simple flake knife, possibly representing a tool kit, are at the right hand (Figs. 10, D246; 5, D247).

Burial 153. On a level below the original hill surface to the left of No. 152 is a male of 47 years (Fig. 48). The long axis of this supine burial is north to south with the head to the north. It has no burial furniture.

Burial 154. In a grave disturbing the legs and feet of Nos. 151 and 152 and covering the upper body of No. 157 is the loosely flexed burial of a 46-year-old female (Fig. 50) lying on its right side facing east. The limbs were partially disarticulated at the elbow and knee at burial. The upper arms extend downward, the right arm flexed with the hand on the chest. The disarticulated and fragmentary left forearm was laid in front of the face. The upper legs were still articulated but were angled to the right while the bones of the lower legs were piled on the upper body. The left hand and both feet are missing. A shell-tempered plain jar with multiple projections on an everted rim is near the lower back (Fig. 25, D248).

Burials 155 and 156. Surrounded by Nos. 149, 154 and 157 and separated by a 2- to 3-inch layer of earth, two females (55 and 19 years) are buried one on top of the other, in a grave cutting into the original hill surface (Fig. 50). Both are in an extended position, with No. 155 above, and oriented east to west with the head to the west. The compactness of No. 155 suggests wrapping and its head is slumped slightly to the left and down. At least 12 small Mucket(?)-shell rattles *(Actinonaias carinata)* remain *in situ* around the ankles (Fig. 12, D250), and a scraper appears near the right hand (Fig. 4, D249). A fragmentary, shell-tempered plain jar was found behind the head of No. 155 (Fig. 26, D251).

Burial 157. Partially covered by Nos. 154 and 158, a female of 60 years lies parallel to the left of Nos. 155 and 156, in a grave cutting into the original hill surface (Fig. 50). The long axis of the burial is west-northwest to east-southeast with the head to the northwest. The arms are to the sides with the left hand over the pelvis. There are no grave offerings.

Burial 158. An infant of 20 months covers the right leg of No. 157, in a grave cutting through the mound and into the original hill surface (Fig. 50). It is oriented east to west with the head to the west. It rests partially on its right side with its head turned right. The feet and the left lower leg are missing. No grave offerings are associated.

Burial 159. Protruding from the profile to the right of No. 161 and directly below a *Busycon* spp. shell (D352) are a few bones of either a disturbed burial or a secondary burial, a female of 30 years (Fig. 52). It is only partially exposed and cannot be related to other burials or grave offerings.

Burial 160. The partially excavated burial of a 50-year-old male lies in the southeast corner of the excavation in a grave cut into the original hill surface (Fig. 51). It is oriented north to south with the head to the south. The removal of a tree in 1925 probably disturbed the lower legs. No grave offerings are present.

Burial 161. Twenty-four inches above the legs of No. 163 is the supine burial of a 6-month-old infant (Fig. 52). The long axis of the infant is east to west with the head to the west. The head of the burial is disturbed. At the back of the head is a (originally) black-polished, lobed jar (Fig. 24, D252), and piled on the neck and chest area are at least 103 (Dickson estimate, 200) *Olivella jaspidea* shell beads (Fig. 11, D265). A small, notched, triangular arrowpoint was apparently on the chest below the beads, but it is no longer present. The entire area around this burial is littered with debris which includes nine sandstone, diorite and granite rocks, one small clinker and several sherds from at least two shell-tempered plain and one angular-shouldered vessels (Figs. 31, D255-263, D266; 33, D254 and D407). One of the sandstone pieces (D261) is a fragment of a slot abrader. None of this debris is mentioned in the Dickson notes.

Burials 162, 164, 165 and 182. Three supine adults and one child are in a mass grave one foot below and to the left of No. 163 (Fig. 52). Each burial axis is oriented west-northwest to east-southeast with the head to the west. Numbers 162 and 165 are covered by Nos. 164 and 182. The humus line in the adjacent profiles implies that these burials are nearly two feet below the level of the original hill surface. However, because the earth has been removed to the level of the lower burials, all evidence of intrusion is obliterated except for two areas. The grave outline is still evident in the wall profiles near the head of No. 165 and at the feet of the group.

Number 162 is a male of 47 years. Only the skull and the upper right side of the body is exposed. No grave goods are associated.

Number 164 is a female, 20 years of age. On the chest are at least 19 small marine-shell disc beads (Fig. 11, D344). The Dickson notes do not indicate a necklace in this instance, and it is possible that the beads were worn on the clothing or perhaps were accidently included with the fill.

Number 165, a 42-year-old male, was apparently partially disarticulated at the time of burial. The left arm (minus the radius and some bones of the hand) is somewhat out of position at the side. Two bone fishhooks appear near the right shoulder (Fig. 30, D267 and D268).

Number 182 is a child (female?) of 2 years. Near or on the left arm bones is a fragment of an engraved bone bracelet (Fig. 14, D343), and at the back of the head is a small, shell-tempered plain, loop-handled jar (Fig. 24, D342).

Burial 163. The supine burial of a 42-year-old male partially covers Nos. 162 and 164 (Fig. 52). It appears to be in a grave and is oriented west-northwest to east-southeast with the head to the west. The shoulders are pulled in with the arms to the sides and the hands over the pelvis. Although the legs are not completely exposed, the angle of the femurs suggests that the feet were either drawn together or crossed, suggesting that this burial was wrapped. Its legs are covered by Nos. 161 and 232. No artifacts were found with this male, but the left mastoid process and mandible are heavily stained by copper suggesting that some copper object may have accompanied this burial. Artifacts may have been previously removed as the burial is partially disturbed.

Burial 166. Three feet above and behind the head of No. 165 and partially covered by No. 167 is a supine(?) burial of a 36-year-old female (Fig. 53). The long axis of the burial is north-northeast to south-southwest with the head to the north. The lower legs were destroyed by previous excavations. This burial, which may have been wrapped, has its head turned left: its torso is also twisted left, covering the arm. By the right side is a large, dark-slipped, shell-tempered effigy bowl possibly depicting a common crow *(Corvus brachyrhynchos)* (Fig. 22, D113). At the left hand are three mussel-shell spoons and a large, fragmentary chert flake knife (Figs. 16, D272-D274; 5, D269). Two of the spoons are probably Pocketbooks *(Lampsilis ventricosa)* while the third is a Pink Heel-Splitter *(Proptera alata).*

Burials 167, 196, 197 and 198. Four burials lie above and behind the head of No. 166 (Fig. 53). Number 167 is a male of 50 years whose upper portion is greatly slumped due to the decomposure of No. 166. The long axis of the burial is east to west with the head to the west. A bundle burial, No. 196, is situated on its feet. The bones of two individuals, a female, 19 years of age, and a child of 5 years are associated in this bundle (which may actually represent a disturbed burial rather than a prepared secondary interment). Since the leg bones of No. 196 and the upper part of No. 197 nearby are both of females the same age, they may be parts of the same individual which was disturbed by another grave (No. 195?). A chert flake is located to the left of the head of No. 167 (Fig. 31, D276).

Number 197 is an intrusive interment of an extended female of 19 years. The long axis of the burial is north-northeast to south-southwest with the head to the south. The arms are to the sides; but the burial has been disturbed from the lower chest area down. Its grave disturbed the left forearm, pelvic region and the left femur of No. 167 and probably the burial of a 2½-year-old child, No. 198. The fragmentary remains of the child are in the fill near the head of No. 197. An unworked piece of hematite and another of limestone are over the chest area of No. 197 (Fig. 31, D364-D365). Neither of these latter pieces is mentioned in the Dickson notes. In fact, D365 may actually be a piece of "whiterock" from the parking lot once located near the excavation.

Burial 168. The flexed burial of a 49-year-old male is situated below the original hill surface below and to the left of No. 167 (Fig. 53). It is oriented north-northeast to south-southwest with the head to the south. Loosely flexed, the burial rests on its right side facing east. Many extra bones in the fill around this individual suggest that a previous burial(s) may have been disturbed by its placement. To the left of the head is a shallow, shell-tempered plain, animal effigy bowl containing a mussel-shell spoon (probably *Lampsilis ventricosa*) (Figs. 26, D270; 16, D271).

Burial 169. Sandwiched between Nos. 172 and 170 is a child of 6 years (Fig. 49). It appears to be below the level of the original hill surface. The long axis of the burial is north to south with the head to the south. Only the upper one-third of the burial is excavated. No burial furniture is exposed.

Burial 170. The partially excavated burial of a 46-year-old male covers the lower section of No. 169 (Fig. 49). The long axis of the burial is east-northeast to west-southwest with the head to the southwest. Its head is turned slightly to the left. This burial was apparently placed in a grave cut through the mound and into the original hill surface. An area from the pelvis to the ankles is unexcavated since it is covered by Nos. 171 and 183 one and one-half feet above. A large tool kit is still *in situ* near the feet. Included in this are 1 chert hoe (Fig. 10, D278), 2 shell arm rattles or clackers (Fig. 12, D279-D280), 1 antler flaker (Fig. 9, D281), 1 drill (Fig. 8, D284), 10 scrapers (Fig. 4, D283, D285-D289, D291, D293, and D311), 1 fragmentary triangular arrowpoint (Fig. 7, D290), and 20 chert flakes (Fig. 31, D292, D294-D310 and D398-D399). A few specimens are not completely excavated and are shown completed in broken lines. A fragment of a mussel-shell spoon on the chest of this burial may or may not have been associated since it is not mentioned in the Dickson notes (Fig. 16, D277). There is also the possibility that the tool kit was associated with some other burial, now destroyed, since it is positioned in the fill several inches above the level of No. 170. Excavation around the feet of No. 170 would undoubtedly produce additional artifacts.

Burials 171 and 183. Scattered bones of two burials rest approximately 18 inches above the pelvic area of No. 170 (Fig. 49). The long axis of the only undisturbed part of the adult burial is generally east to west with the head to the west. Both are close to the mound surface and have been greatly disturbed.

Number 171 is a female of 40 years. Only five vertebrae, several ribs and the left arm are still in articulation. Most of these show traces of burning (recent?). Below and touching this burial are scattered bones and bone fragments of No. 183, an infant of 2 years. This burial may have been disturbed by the placement of No. 171, but this is not definite since it has not been completely exposed. There are no associated artifacts.

Burial 172. A few inches below No. 169 and resting below the original hill surface is a 54-year-old male (Fig. 49). It is oriented north-northeast to south-southwest with the head to the south. The upper right side and the skull have been disturbed by previous excavation. Although the upper skeleton is in an extended position with the arms to the sides, the legs are semiflexed downward and to the right. No burial furniture is associated.

Burial 177. On the same level behind the head of No. 36 is a bone pile representing a 45-year-old male (Fig. 38). It appears to be disturbed by previous excavation, but only a portion of the burial has been exposed. No grave offerings are evident.

Burials 179 and 180. In a grave cutting into the hill surface to the left of Nos. 65 and 66 are the supine burials of a 3-year-old child and a male of 27 (Fig. 39). The child overlies the left side of the adult. The orientation of each is east to west with the head to the east. Over the right hip and hand of the child is a tool kit comprised of three deer-antler flakers (Fig. 9, D139, D141, D315), 2 smooth pieces of sandstone (Fig. 31, D316 and D400), 1 broken tip of a heavy knife (Fig. 6, D317), 18 chert flakes (Fig. 31, D320-D321, D323-D324, D327-D334, D336-D340), 4 flake knives (Fig. 5, D322, D325-D326, and D335), and 1 scraper (Fig. 4, D318). One piece (Fig. 8, D319) may be a crude drill. Two crude, triangular arrowpoints were also included in this tool kit, but they are now missing along with two(?) chert flakes. The mandible of No. 180 was stolen during a break-in in 1968.

Burial 181. The fragmentary proximal end of a left femur of a 53-year-old male protrudes from the profile one foot below and to the left of the head of No. 180 (Fig. 39). No other bones are exposed. It is oriented generally north-northeast to south-southwest. It was probably in a grave since it is well below the level of the original hill surface.

Burials 185 and 186. In a grave penetrating the original hill surface in the southeast corner of the excavation is the extended burial of a female of 49 years (Fig. 51). The burial orientation is north to south with the head to the south. The head is turned to the left. Portions of the upper region, pelvis, and right leg are not exposed. Number 186 is assigned to the ribs of a child lying under No. 185. The Dickson notes indicate that no more of the burial was exposed although it was believed that the entire skeleton was there. *In situ* to the left of the head of No. 185 are two pottery vessels — a black-polished beaker with an effigy handle (arm and fist or paw) and a smoothed-over cordmarked, everted-rim jar (Fig. 27, D345-D346). Although the jar contains a mussel-shell spoon, it has not been completely exposed (Fig. 51, D347). The jar also has a perforation (8 mm. in diameter), just above center in one side, made when the clay was still plastic.

Burial 187. The disturbed burial of a 60-year-old female lies in a grave two feet above the right leg of No. 185 (Fig. 51). The long axis of the burial is north to south with the head to the north. The upper region is missing — probably due to previous excavation. The legs crossed (left over right) may indicate the body was wrapped. There are no associated grave offerings.

Burial 188. A few inches above the left side of No. 187 is a male of 38 years (Fig. 51). It is oriented north to south with the head to the south. Only the left leg is exposed, but the rest of the burial appears to have been destroyed by previous excavation. A mussel-shell spoon (probably *Lampsilis ventricosa*) is situated near the feet (Fig. 16, D348) although association is doubtful since it was not mentioned in the Dickson notes.

Burial 189. Protruding from the profile to the right of No. 190 is the back of the skull of a 22-year-old female (Fig. 52), the only exposure of this burial.

Burials 190, 191 and 232. These burials are situated behind the head of No. 189 in an area disturbed by farming(?) activities (Fig. 52).

Number 190 is a male of 13 years. The long axis of the burial is north-northeast to south-southwest with the head to the south. The upper region was cut by the grave of No. 232. The head is moved out of position to the south, the left ribs and arm are disturbed and the left femur is missing. Near the head are a fragmentary, dark-slipped, shell-tempered jar (Fig. 27, D351), a mussel-shell spoon, and a rough piece of sandstone (Fig. 16, D349 and D403). The latter pieces are only partially exposed.

Number 191 is an infant of 6 months oriented east to west with the head to the west. Several sherds of pottery, fragmentary shells and bits of rock are in the fill around the remnants of this infant. Among these is a fragmentary spoon made from a Pink Heel-Splitter *(Proptera alata)* (Fig. 16, D350), a large shell pendant(?) *(Busycon* spp.*)* (Fig. 13, D352), and two shell-tempered sherds (Fig. 33, D408-D409). One (D408) is similar to Chamberlain Incised Shoulder ware (Mill Creek pottery from northwestern Iowa) except that it is shell-tempered. No notation by the Dicksons is made of this debris in their burial descriptions although one piece, D352, is mentioned in a separate set of notes.

Number 232 is a fetus, 7 fetal months of age. The long axis of this intrusive burial is east to west with the head to the west, but few bones remain in articulation. Its grave apparently disturbed the upper portion of No. 190. A chert flake and a right valve of a Three-Horned Warty-Back *(Obliquaria reflexa)* near this infant may have been included in the fill (Fig. 31, D357 and D356), while a fragmentary shell spoon (Fragile Paper Shell, *Leptodea fragilis*) may be a grave offering (Fig. 16, D355). Also associated is a heavy, miniature, shell-tempered plain jar that contains a small shell pendant *(Busycon* spp.*)* (Fig. 26, D353-D354). These pieces remain *in situ*, the vessel in the ground and the pendant imbedded in the earth within it.

Burials 192-195. Three superimposed graves containing two adults, a child, and an infant cut through the mound and into the original hill surface along the western limits of the excavation (Fig. 53). The long axes of the extended burials are west-northwest to east-southeast with the heads to the west. The lowest burial, No. 195, is covered on at least the upper legs by an associated secondary(?) burial, No. 194, which is only partially excavated. Burial 193 was then superimposed over No. 194, and No. 192 was later added, probably partially disturbing No. 193. One or more of these graves probably disturbed the legs and part of the upper body of nearby No. 197 and possibly destroyed the feet of No. 167. The leg bones of No. 197 may have been piled on the lower legs of No. 167 along with the bones of a second individual. A pottery vessel, possibly associated with one of the disturbed burials, is in the grave fill midway between Nos. 197 and 195.

Number 192 is an infant, 6 months of age. It is somewhat disarticulated, but it is oriented generally east to west with the head to the west. Probably behind the head was found a miniature, shell-tempered plain, owl effigy, hooded bottle with a bail handle (Fig. 29, D389).

Number 193 is the partially excavated secondary burial of an 11- to 12-year-old female. A large chert scraper or knife was associated with this burial (Fig. 4, D361).

Number 194, also only partially excavated, is a male of 55 years.

Number 195 is an extended female, 46 years of age. Behind the head are two matched shell-tempered plain vessels, a Dickson Plain jar and a handled beaker (Fig. 28, D358 and D360). A shell spoon (probably *Lampsilis ventricosa*) with a notched handle is inside the jar (Fig. 16, D359). Neither of the pottery pieces are completely excavated. In the earth profile approximately one foot above the face is a shell-tempered, cord-marked, loop-handled jar (Fig. 27, D362). A partially exposed mussel-shell spoon remains *in situ* inside the vessel (Fig. 53, D363). Only a slight discoloration on the left maxillary and right clavicle remains of two copper-covered wood ornaments originally thought to have been associated with this person (Fig. 15, D404, D405). These pieces were stolen from an exhibit case in the aftermath of the tornado of 1933. They are apparently those ornaments mentioned on page 28 of "Dickson Mound Builders Tomb" (Dickson, n.d.) but no mention of them is made in the Dickson field notes. Their association with this burial is unverified.

Burials 199-207. Ten secondary or disarticulated burials are situated on or below the original hill surface directly below the lower regions of Nos. 77 and 79 (Fig. 41). Only the edge of this group is excavated; other unexposed burials are probably associated. Without further exposure, it is impossible to determine what this group represents in terms of mortuary practices. Near the head of No. 206 is a beaker with double pouring lips (Fig. 26, D366). No other artifacts are exposed.

The age and sex of each burial is listed below:
Number 199 . . . Male . . . . 40 years
Number 200 . . . Female . . . . 41 years
Number 201 . . . Female . . . . 58 years
Number 202 . . . Female . . . . 45 years
Number 203 . . . Female . . . . 15(?) years
Number 204 . . . Child . . . . 6 years
Number 205 . . . Child . . . . 5 years
Number 206 . . . Female . . . . 40 years
Number 207 . . . Fetus . . . . . . 8½ lunar months
                  Fetus . . . . 9 lunar months

Burials 208 and 209. Behind the head of No. 67 are the remains of two extended infants, neonate and one-year-old (Fig. 39). The remains are somewhat disturbed. The long axis of each is east to west with the head to the east. Both are in a grave that apparently disturbed the head and upper body of No. 67.

Burial 210. Three feet above and to the right of No. 54 is the supine burial of a 2-year-old infant (Fig. 55). The long axis of the burial is north-northeast to south-southwest with the head to the south. It is approximately one foot higher than No. 211 to the right. No artifacts are associated.

Burial 211. The burial of a 22-month-old infant lies in a grave cutting into the hillslope approximately 9 inches above and to the left of the head of No. 212 (Fig. 55). The long axis of the infant is north-northeast to south-southwest with the head to the south. Only the head and upper portion is exposed, but most of the burial appears to be disturbed by farming and tree roots. Still *in situ* to the right of this child's head are two marine-shell beads, two shell pendants(?) (*Busycon* spp.), a plain jar with rounded-strap handles, and a flake knife (Figs. 11, D373-D374; 13, D369-D370; 29, D372; 5, D371).

Burial 212. A male of 48 years lies in a grave penetrating the original hill surface that is partially covered by Nos. 211, 213, 214, and 215 (Fig. 55). The long axis of this extended burial is north-northeast to south-southwest with the head to the south. No grave offerings are exposed. The right humerus shows a well-healed fracture.

Burial 213. Almost completely destroyed by farming or previous excavation, this burial of a 6-year-old child is situated with its head 2½ feet above the pelvic region of No. 212 (Fig. 55). The body may have been oriented west-northwest to east-southeast with the head to the southeast. No artifacts are associated.

Burials 214 and 215. Three individuals are situated approximately two feet above the lower legs of No. 212 (Fig. 54). Each is oriented north to south with the head of No. 214 to the south and the heads of the two fetuses (No. 215) possibly to the north (all but the skull fragments have been disturbed). Number 214, a child (female?) of 8 years, is in an extended position with its arms to the sides and the hands on the pelvis. To its left are two fetuses (both 7 fetal months) that have apparently been disturbed by farming. The feet of No. 214 are across and touching the ankles of No. 217. A fragmentary, handled beaker is situated to the left of the legs of No. 214 (Fig. 28, D375), while six small marine-shell beads were near the skull of No. 215. Five of these remain (Fig. 11, D376).

Burial 216. In a grave dug into the original hill surface and partially covered by the legs of No. 217 is the flexed burial of a 35-year-old female (Fig. 54). It was superimposed over the grave containing Nos. 218-220 and 224. The long axis is north-northeast to south-southwest with the head to the southwest. Its legs are flexed right. No burial furniture is in association. Many bones of this burial are affected with an acute inflammatory condition probably associated with multiple fractures of the right arm and ribs.

Burial 217. A 50-year-old female (Fig. 54), oriented east to west with the head to the east, lies at a right angle to Nos. 214-216. Only the legs and part of the pelvis are excavated, but the upper region is destroyed by previous excavation. The area of the pelvis and femurs is slumped nearly eight inches lower than the feet. Apparently Nos. 214, 215, 216, and 217 were interred within a relatively short time span, for those above are affected by the slump caused by the deterioration of the lower, No. 216.

Burials 218-220 and 224. Three extended burials and a secondary burial are included in a mass grave which is partially covered by Nos. 221-223 three to four feet above and by No. 216 several inches above (Fig. 54). The group is probably in a grave below the original hill surface, and only the back of the skull and the pelvic area to the knees of Nos. 218-220 have been exposed. The burials are oriented west-northwest to east-southeast with the heads to the west. Number 218 (female, 19 years) and 220 (female, 20 years) are resting side by side with Nos. 219 (male, 28 years) and 224 (secondary burial of a 43-year-old male) covering them. Around the left wrist of No. 219 were 30 spheroidal beads of marine shell ''about the size of a pea.'' These were stolen while being exhibited elsewhere. The Dickson notes attribute them to No. 218, but the only wrist exposed in the group is No. 219.

Burials 221 and 222. A male of 17 years and a 7-month-old infant on its chest are the uppermost burials in the area (Fig. 54). The long axis of each burial is north to south with the head to the south. Both were apparently in an extended position with the arms to the sides; but they have been badly disturbed by recent farming or previous excavation. Suggestive of wrapping, the shoulders of the male are pulled in with the arms to the sides and the left hand under the pelvis. Nine fragments of sandstone and conglomeratic sand rock and one angular-shouldered sherd were included in the fill near the head (Figs. 31, D378-D386; 33, D377). None of this material is mentioned in the Dickson notes.

Burial 223. A child of 3 years is positioned between Nos. 221 and 228, with only its head and upper right arm exposed (Fig. 54). The long axis of the burial appears to be north to south with the head to the south. A fragmentary plain jar with rounded-strap handles is located near the right arm (Fig. 27, D387). It may have contained a mussel-shell spoon (probably a Pocketbook, *Lampsilis ventricosa*) (Fig. 16, D388). Included in the fill are two fragmentary bird bones and a red-slipped, shell-tempered pottery sherd. Only the jar was mentioned in the Dickson notes.

Burials 225 and 226. Two feet above the right side of No. 228 are the remains of two individuals, a 6-month fetus and a 22-month infant (Fig. 54). The larger child, No. 226, is below with the remains (right femur and left humerus) of No. 225 resting between its femurs. The long axis of No. 226 is north to south with the head to the south. Both have been disturbed by recent farming activities.

Burial 227. Its head partially covered by No. 228 and its legs extending into the east profile wall of the excavation, a 30-year-old male lies in a grave cut through the mound and into the hill surface below and to the right of Nos. 225 and 226 (Fig. 54). It is oriented west-northwest to east-southeast with the head to the west. Much of the exposed burial appears to be destroyed (previous excavation?). A fragmentary, shell-tempered plain deep bowl (slight traces of red-filmed interior) with two broken lugs or pouring lips and a fragmentary, unclassified, angular-shouldered jar with crosshatched incising rest near the right shoulder (Fig. 29, D390 and D392). A mussel-shell spoon (probably a Pocketbook, *Lampsilis ventricosa*) was found among the fragments of D390 (Fig. 16, D391).

Burial 228. A 46-year-old female is in a grave originating in the mound and cutting into the hillslope which is partially covered by Nos. 225 and 226 (Fig. 54). It is oriented north to south with the head to the south. The head and upper right arm were apparently destroyed by previous excavation. The upper right side is also slumped due to the deterioration of No. 227. No grave goods are exposed.

Burial 229. Protruding from the east profile of the excavation two feet above the femurs of No. 227 is the burial of a 45-year-old male which has been disturbed by previous excavation (Fig. 54).

Burial 230. A 6-year-old child lies behind and approximately one foot above the mass grave of Nos. 6-9 (Fig. 35). The long axis of the burial is west-northwest to east-southeast with the head to the northwest. The area from the elbows to the head was destroyed by previous excavation. A small, black-slipped (the slip is now nearly destroyed by repeated firing) jar is near the right side (Fig. 29, D393). The depth of the burial suggests employment of a prepared grave.

Burial 234. Behind the head of No. 124 is the disturbed burial of a newborn infant (Fig. 45). The skeleton may have been articulated but disturbed in excavation. No burial furniture is associated.

SUMMARY OF BURIALS

It is suspected that most of the burials were placed in dug graves, since some 79 percent of the undisturbed burial population could definitely be associated with that practice. Seventy-three of these graves contain only 1 burial each; 20 contain 2 individuals; 6 have 3 individuals each; 4 have 4 associated burials; 2 have 8, 1 has 10, and 1 has 12 individuals all placed within a relatively short time span. Because of their locations higher up in the mound fill, graves could not be determined for 49 individuals representing 33 separate interments. Twenty-two of these interments contain 1 burial; 7 have 2 associated burials; 3 have 3; and 1 has 4 individuals. Some 13 other burials were completely disturbed, either by previous excavation or by aboriginal grave-digging activities. Eleven of these appear to have been single interments while two others have the bones of two individuals represented.

The above figures imply that nearly four of every five burials were actually intrusive into the mounds represented in the Dickson excavation. The presence of so many intrusive graves poses an interesting question: If most of the burials were placed in pits, how were the mounds created? Since it has become obvious that most, if not all, of the burials in the Dickson excavation were placed in dug graves, it is probable that individual mounds were built and then filled with graves as has been demonstrated elsewhere in the cemetery (Conrad 1972).

SUPINE BURIALS

The most popular burial position was the supine or extended dorsal placement; 82 percent of the 248 excavated burials are so buried. The arms of extended burials are often at the sides and the legs extended, but frequently the body was so tightly wrapped at the time of burial that the arms are drawn either across or under the body with the hands either over the pelvis or under the hips, the shoulders pulled nearly to the face, and the legs crossed. A more detailed discussion of wrapping is forthcoming. Two extended burials, Nos. 61 and 89, and one flexed burial, No. 37, are in a prone position. All three of these are probably female. Recent cleaning revealed a fourth prone burial, No. 17, an infant. While the face-down interment may be indicative of punish-

ment or banishment, it probably was not intentional. At least one prone burial has associated artifacts; and two are included in mass groups — modes which seem to suggest reasonably normal interments.

Occasionally the head of an extended burial will be turned either right or left. This is apparently not intentional and seems to have no correlation with either age or sex, the placement of burial furniture, or the placement of other burials (except in instances where many individuals are packed into the same group).

FLEXED BURIALS

Two tightly flexed and six semiflexed burials are present. Two (Nos. 154 and 168) have Mississippian ceramics in association, and three others (Nos. 9, 37, and 216) are associated with or cover Mississippian burials. The remainder (Nos. 10, 23, and 172) are situated in graves extending below the mound and could conceivably represent burials of Woodland people. Two others (Nos. 48 and 149) have the knees slightly bent, but the position of the legs of No. 48 is probably due to a pathological condition. The flexed burials are not usually associated with other burials. Exceptions are No. 9 (a child) and No. 37 (which is face down).

Infants, children or adolescents are rarely in a flexed burial position (the only child to be even semiflexed is No. 9). Age or sex does not seem to be a factor since both young and old (24 to 54 years) males and females are represented. However, the following trait is shared by all members of the flexed group. Although these burials are scattered over the mounds on different levels, the long axis of each body is on a general north-south axis with the head to the south. The limbs are always flexed to the right and the head is usually facing east. Data are somewhat limited by the small number of flexed bodies on which to base conclusions; but this particular variation of burial may have been status-oriented toward the distinction of a specific group of individuals.

SECONDARY BURIALS

Seventeen groups or bundles of bones are present as well as a single, partially exposed grave containing the piled remains of 10 individuals. The preparators of the bodies often included the bones of more than one person in a secondary burial; so the 26 burial numbers actually represent 31 individuals (This figure does not include the extra burials recently recorded in bundle No. 144). Of those listed as being secondary burials, at least 5 (representing 7 individuals) probably are bones which were disturbed by aboriginal grave-digging and reinterred in the new grave.

Probably due to wrapping, the prepared bundles are usually quite compact. Their girth is usually dependent upon the number of bodies included; but the bundle length, determined by the length of the long bones, varies little. Although there are several bundles in which most of the bones are present (many of them still articulated), generally only the long bones and occasional ribs and vertebrae are represented. The skull is usually present with female burials, but it is absent in secondary burials of males. The bones of the hands and feet may or may not be included in secondary burials of either males, females or children. While this may appear to have some social significance (e.g., saving these parts for mementos or for social ritual), these bones, among the smallest skeletal parts, simply may not have been recovered by the preparator of the bundle — especially if nothing but the loose bones of the individual remained. The basis for this assumption is the fact that bones of the hands and feet are still present in the five secondary burials which were only partially decayed at the time of their interment.

Bundles occur most frequently as separate interments (9 instances, including the group of 10 individuals); but they are also placed on the legs of extended adults in 7 instances and appear in single instances at the side and at the head.

Artifacts are associated with only two secondary burials. A chert scraper appears with No. 193 and a beaker may be associated with No. 206.

In many instances, the bundle probably represents a reburial, secondary burial, or possibly even the remains of an individual who died away from his home area and whose bones were not soon recovered. However, in several instances, bundles seem to represent remnants of bodies disturbed by grave-digging and reinterred with the fill.

The presence of a bundle of bones does not necessarily imply that the person involved was originally placed on a scaffold or any other above-ground device. Sheltered open pit and surface burials, known historically for the Illinois, Sauk, Fox, Potawatomi, Menominee, Ioway, and Winnebago (Hall 1962: Vol. 1, 29), are practices that often precede the second stage of collecting and gathering bones for reinterment. Exposure in charnel houses might also be a possibility.

CREMATED BURIALS

One possible (although doubtful) clue suggesting cremation is present. Unfortunately, the burial involved has been almost completely disturbed (Burial 171, female, 40 years). Only five vertebrae, several ribs and the left arm are still in articulation. Limited areas on these bones show exposure to uneven heat. Charring of the bone surface which fluctuates between deep blackening and light charring is evident on the bones of the left arm and ribs while the bones of the vertebral column have been more evenly fired. None of the undisturbed bones have evidence of firing on their under surfaces suggesting that the burning was made *in situ*. Supporting this position are a few bones of No. 183 (directly below No. 171) which also exhibit light charring.

It is probable that the burning is of recent origin. Several points support this position: (1) the burial is less than one foot below the original mound surface; (2) it has been recently disturbed; (3) the uneven charring of the bones and the lack of baked or burned soil is not characteristic of the thoroughness of firing usually associated with aboriginal cremations; and (4) other modern ''pothunter'' pits containing burned bones were found elsewhere in the burial area during the recent excavations.

MASS GRAVES

Individuals included in mass graves (single burials of two or more persons) equal nearly 60 percent of the total burial population. This seems rather significant and may be evidence of a variety of mundane occurrences. Possibly it resulted from collecting bodies and having single communal interments at a designated time. Supporting this theory are the many secondary burials associated with the mass graves which may represent earlier deaths. Only four of the extended burials in the mass graves are even partially disarticulated, however, suggesting that most of the bodies were probably not saved for any length of time (at least during the warmer months). If individuals in mass burials actually prove to be related in some way, the occasional associated bundles could conceivably represent deceased relatives who had previously been buried or exposed at some other location.

The upper burials in each mass group usually show evidence of posthumous shifting, indicating that most members of the group were buried at one time and that enough flesh was present at the time of interment to later cause a definite slump as the lower burials disintegrated. These persons could have been victims of disease or pestilence, disasters, etc., who died at about the same time or they could represent spring burials of the "frozen" winter dead.

The same consideration given an individual burial was apparently paid to members of a mass grave. Burial furniture, both utilitarian and ornamental, occurs nearly as frequently with individuals in mass groups as with the single burials.

COMPLETENESS OF BURIALS

Discounting secondary burials, burials only partially exposed (children excluded because their hand and foot bones are small and easily missed in excavating), and disturbed burials, about 57 whole adult burials remain. Only six percent of this number can be termed complete — and even this is allowing for the occasional absence of a phalange or two. Bones most often missing are from the hands and feet. It was first assumed that these smaller bones were simply missed in the original excavation or in later cleaning (which is probably the case when an occasional bone or two is missing from a hand or foot); but a closer examination often revealed that the same phalanges of a given hand or foot (e.g., all of the middle and distal phalanges) are missing and that the entire foot or hand is sometimes absent. Although the loss of these bones may well be recent, their absence might imply that the preinterment history of certain people was characterized by either loss or extraction of some skeletal parts. It seems unlikely that these parts would become lost because the rest of the burial was not disarticulated. Even if the

body had deteriorated badly prior to burial, the feet and hands would have had a tendency to dehydrate rather than to rot because they are not especially fleshy.

A conjectural postulation is that the Indian may have removed these body parts prior to interment to serve as mementos or for their use in social ritual. Such practices may have been present in other parts of Illinois (Binford 1962:94). No artificial scratches are evident on any of the remaining phalanges, distal ends of the radii and ulnae, or the distal ends of the tibiae and fibulae to suggest removal by cutting. If it was intentional removal, no age or sex distinction was apparently made.

One rather disturbing aspect concerning this study is the current absence of some body parts, primarily hands and feet, recently discovered to have been present and photographed during the early years of the excavation. Although aboriginal removal of body parts cannot be entirely ruled out, it is becoming increasingly more plausible that a majority of the missing body parts in the Dickson excavation were lost during the original excavation or have since become misplaced during cleaning and handling of the exhibit.

The inconsistencies of burial practices, such as these which have been presented in this section, would probably be common among many prehistoric cultures. There were undoubtedly many different traditional methods of disposing of the dead recognized by the Spoon River variant people. It was not uncommon for the burial areas of several historic Plains manifestations to contain small mounds, graves, and scaffolds. If used during the winter months, tree burials commonly accompanied these. However, all members of a family or clan would not necessarily embrace the same burial method. Concerning the Hidatsa, Bowers (1965:170) states: "In some instances all members of some households would be placed on scaffolds, while all members of other households would be buried in the ground. In other instances a household might practice both scaffold disposal and interment."

CONJECTURAL INTRAGROUP
RELATIONSHIPS

It has become increasingly evident that, in addition to the few children usually represented in each of the mass groups, there were occasionally young males and females present. Rather prematurely, this writer expected to find some associated male-female burials that were reasonably close in age and young adult females with nursing-age children who had either starved or were put to death when no relative or member of the village could adopt them after the death of the mother. While both sexes and all ages are often noted in the same mass grave, rarely do they seem to be associated in a manner that would be indicative of a nuclear family relationship. Males and females nearly the same age are often included in the same mass grave, but rarely are they together in such a manner as to suggest mates. The difference in their ages is often an obstacle when attempting to determine relationship. Males in a given group tend to average up to 35 years older than females, but females are sometimes much older than the accompanying males. However, in some polygamous societies a first wife will often be 10 to 30 years older than her husband and occasionally the husband will be many years her senior.

While the wide range of individual ages and the presence of both sexes in each mass group may be indicative of nuclear or extended family relationships or extended kin ties, such determinations for a majority of the group burials are still premature. One may speculate that, because of the obvious care these people have shown the dead in other ways, it seems reasonable to assume that they would also have kept members of a deceased family together, providing they expired at about the same time. While people in some mass groups may be unrelated victims of natural phenomena such as sickness, childbirth, accidents, etc., most groups are probably comprised of members of extended families or moieties. In the event of an extended family situation, one could accept the often associated bundle burial as representing a previously deceased relative.

Six possible cases of blood-relationship were noted. Four females (Nos. 152, 126, 82 and 164 — 18, 35, 48 and 20 years of age) have burials of children in direct association (Nos. 151, 125, 83 and 182 — 2, 11, 13 and 2 years of age). One woman, No. 54, may have died in childbirth complicated by infection and disease.

Fetuses about the same age are included in the same grave in four instances, Nos. 87, 105, 207, and 215 (e.g., No. 87 contains parts of three babies, all seven fetal months of age). The small bodies in each of these burials are usually found closely associated in a small heap and may represent multiple births.

Numbers 2 and 3, interred in a mass grave with two small children, could be brothers. They are about the same age, and their physical characteristics are nearly identical. This is especially noticeable in the striking similarity of the facial structure of the bones. Both are affected with arthritis and have about the same degree of involvement on the same joints.

Another instance of possible relationship centers around two associated babies (Nos. 73 and 74) also of similar age. It is difficult to determine much from physical characteristics (except that No. 74 is slightly larger), but their artifacts suggest a close association. Each has a single bead on its chest, and the inverted placement of one pottery vessel within the other is also unique for the Dickson Site, conveying the theme of unity. These occurrences coupled with the particular variation of burial may suggest a close mundane relationship.

WRAPPING

Although no tangible evidence of cloth, hides, or similar substances remains today, many (if not most) of the burials appear to have been originally wrapped. Discounting bundle burials (which were nearly always wrapped), partially exposed burials, disturbed burials, and flexed burials, at least 41 of the remaining 174 extended burials were probably tightly bound prior to interment. Since many of this number are children (it is virtually impossible to detect the effects of wrapping on a body as small as that of a child), these figures are somewhat misleading. Actually 41 of 80 adults, or about 51 percent, have been bound tightly enough to retain a squeezed appearance. This percentage would probably be much higher had it not been for the fact that 60 percent of all adults are included in mass graves. The upper burials in these graves are often so slumped out of position that it is impossible to detect evidence of wrapping.

The most common evidences of wrapping are: the shoulders pressed in, sometimes nearly to the face; the arms over the chest area or tight to or slightly under the sides with the hands under the pelvis; and the feet often crossed. When in the latter position, the legs are nearly always crossed left over right. In only two instances is the reverse true. Possibly the final position of the legs is another indication of right-handedness among these people. (The right-handedness of this group is demonstrated elsewhere in this report by a study of their shell spoons.) In preparing the body, the legs could best be maneuvered by a person situated at the feet, facing the corpse. A heavy object such as a lifeless limb could be most easily moved by pulling it rather than by pushing it away; a right-handed person facing the body in this manner would naturally grasp the left leg and pull it across.

ORIENTATION OF BURIALS

In viewing the *in situ* excavation, certain patterns of burial orientation are recognized. Burials often appear to be oriented to each other. The orientation of individuals in mass graves is most obvious. Interred at the same time, all share about the same axis and usually touch one another. Secondly, patterns of single burials sharing a common axis (not members of mass graves but individual interments roughly grouped on the same level) are also noted. Only occasionally does one find a single burial which is not accompanied by a corresponding burial(s) with a similar axis on the same general level nearby.

These small concentrations of fresh burials were apparently attractive spots for later interments. The upper burials in one of these concentrated burial areas will often show the effects of the lower bodies. So short was the span of time that separated these interments that, as the lower bodies decayed, a definite shifting resulted which allowed parts of the upper burials to slump and fall away. With so many burial groups affected in this manner, the false impression is given that a high percentage of the burials in the excavation was placed within a relatively short space of time. Actually the horizontal expansion of the many similarly constructed groups has resulted in slumped burials on roughly corresponding levels.

Burials seem to be intentionally oriented in four main directions, N-S, E-W, WNW-ESE, NNE-SSW, and two minor directions, NNW-SSE and ENE-WSW (See Fig. 57 and Tables 2-5). It was observed before taking compass readings that many burials would probably cluster around the N-S and E-W points and that

some would be oriented toward the direction of the winter solstice and others at right angles to these. Binford (1966) found a similar situation with Late Woodland and Mississippian structures and Mississippian burials at the Carlyle Reservoir, and the data so far collected at Dickson offer support for his position.

Burials oriented E-W appear on either side of due E, about 24 percent of the total oriented between 80 and 90 degrees E, the remainder clustering between 92 degrees E and a point midway between sunrise at the equinox and the winter solstice.

About 73 percent of those burials oriented N-S are grouped between true N and a point midway to the direct right angle to sunrise at the winter solstice while 27 percent are similarly grouped within 11 degrees between true S and a point midway to the direct right angle to sunrise at the summer solstice.

A close grouping was evident with those burials oriented WNW-ESE on an angle corresponding to sunrise at the winter solstice (about 121° 20′E). All of these clustered between 115 and 137 degrees E, 40 percent to the north and 60 percent to the south of the solstice point.

The least variation found with any of the four major burial orientations was with those burials oriented NNE-SSW on a direct right angle to sunrise at the winter solstice. The group ranged between 22 and 42 degrees E, with the majority (about 78 percent) between 30 and 42 degrees E.

Four burials were in the general area of sunrise at the summer solstice (about 57° 20′E), and they are sole occupants of the entire area between 42 and 76 degrees E.

Nine burials, grouped between 146 and 158 degrees E., are intersected by the direct right angle to sunrise at the summer solstice.

The two orientations involving the summer solstice were apparently not popular in this part of the Dickson Mounds Cemetery. Few burials appeared in the general area of sunrise at the summer solstice although a small number did cluster at a right angle to that point. The total number of burials in the four major burial orientations is about equally divided, and their division is equally as uniform when a comparison of individual interments is made (see Table 5). Under the heading of "individual interments" would come single burials and all members of mass groups who were interred together (e.g., since all four were buried together at one time,

TABLE 2
Burial Orientation

North to South			East to West		
Burial No.	Measured Orientation	Head Loci	Burial No.	Measured Orientation	Head Loci
11	7°	S	2	105°	E
16	14°	S	3	105°	E
17	14°	S	4	105°	E
19	11°	S	15	76°	E
20	7°	S	33	107°	E
21	9°	S	52	87°	E
22	7°	S	61	104°	E
31	15°	S	62	106°	E
32	16°	S	64	107°	E
73	11°	S	65	101°	E
74	13°	S	66	105°	E
85	170°	S	67	93°	E
88	174°	S	68	99°	E
89	168°	N	100	94°	W
90	173°	S	106	92°	W
94	176°	N	110	87°	E
95	173°	N	114	90°	*
96	1°	S	114	90°	*
97	11°	S	131	103°	W
101	168°	S	132	102°	W
103	5°	S	135	104°	W
119	172°	S	136	104°	W
153	14°	N	137	102°	W
154	9°	S	138	107°	W
160	8°	S	140	92°	W
169	10°	S	141	105°	W
175	16°	S	142	107°	E
185	9°	S	143	103°	W
187	178°	N	145	108°	W
188	3°	S	146	98°	W
203	2°	*	146	97°	E
214	14°	S	147	101°	E
221	15°	S	148	104°	E
222	15°	S	149	104°	W
223	16°	S	151	96°	W
226	177°	S	152	95°	W
228	8°	S	155	103°	W
			156	102°	W
			158	104°	W
			161	98°	W
			167	80°	W
			171	89°	W
			174	85°	W
			178	107°	*
			179	106°	E
			180	106°	E
			191	85°	W
			208	84°	E
			209	87°	E
			217	83°	E

*Secondary burial

TABLE 3
Burial Orientation

Burial No.	West-Northwest to East-Southeast (Winter Solstice Angle 121° 19′) Measured Orientation	Head Loci	Burial No.	North-Northeast to South-Southwest (Right Angle to Winter Solstice 31° 19′) Measured Orientation	Head Loci
1	118°	NW	6	40°	SW
5	118°	SE	7	42°	SW
24	117°	SE	8	39°	SW
25	119°	SE	9	42°	SW
26	115°	NW	27	32°	SW
46	123°	SE	28	29°	SW
47	127°	SE	29	25°	SW
48	124°	SE	35	38°	SW
49	123°	SE	37	35°	SW
50	130°	NW	38	37°	SW
51	132°	NW	39	33°	SW
56	122°	*	40	36°	SW
57	117°	SE	41	41°	SW
58	121°	SE	42	37°	SW
59	120°	SE	43	36°	*
60	118°	SE	44	39°	SW
63	116°	SE	45	35°	NE
82	122°	NW	53	39°	SW
83	123°	NW	54	39°	SW
98	119°	NW	55	38°	SW
98	119°	NW	69	37°	SW
108	137°	NW	70	36°	SW
109	136°	NW	71	34°	SW
112	127°	NW	75	38°	SW
113	119°	NW	76	26°	SW
115	136°	NW	78	22°	SW
116	130°	NW	79	24°	SW
117	128°	NW	80	39°	SW
118	129°	NW	81	23°	NE
123	137°	NW	84	27°	*
124	124°	NW	86	25°	NE
125	125°	NW	87	37°	SW
126	127°	NW	87	35°	SW
128	136°	SE	87	34°	SW
129	126°	NW	91	29°	*
130	119°	NW	91	27°	*
134	120°	NW	91	28°	*
139	120°	NW	92	28°	SW
157	116°	NW	93	33°	SW
162	125°	NW	111	41°	SW
163	122°	NW	166	32°	NE
164	119°	NW	168	37°	SW
165	128°	NW	172	39°	SW
182	120°	NW	190	39°	SW
192	120°	NW	197	41°	SW
193	129°	*	199	31°	*
194	125°	*	200	35°	*
195	126°	NW	201	35°	*
218	134°	NW	202	31°	*
219	132°	NW	204	34°	*
220	134°	NW	207	36°	*
224	123°	*	207	36°	*
227	122°	NW	210	33°	SW
230	124°	NW	211	35°	SW
			212	37°	SW
*Secondary burial			216	24°	SW

TABLE 4

Burial Orientation

East-Northeast to West-Southwest (Summer Solstice Angle 57° 20′)			North-Northwest to South-Southeast (Right Angle to Summer Solstice 147° 20′)		
Burial No.	Measured Orientation	Head Loci	Burial No.	Measured Orientation	Head Loci
72	64°	NE	10	146°	SE
77	54°	SW	14	143°	SE
127	62°	NE	23	158°	SE
170	47°	SW	36	148°	SE
			99	147°	NW
			102	147°	SE
			120	146°	NW
			122	151°	NW
*Secondary burial			150	155°	*

Nos. 2, 3, 4, and 30 would be considered an individual interment).

It should also be pointed out that some Spoon River variant mounds and cemeteries in the area have burials oriented toward more than one direction (Dickson, Keeler, Weaver, Fiedler, Rose, and Crable) while others have an almost exclusive N-S orientation of bodies (Morton and Emmons). It is feasible that the former type of burial area may represent a common burial place for more than one village or moiety group within the community while the latter type of burial mound, with nearly all bodies sharing a common axis, may represent the burial ground used by a single moiety of the local community. Symbolisms and distinctions such as those were undoubtedly present among Mississippian people. It is highly probable that prehistoric people had, as did the later historic Indians, factions or divisions within their communities which were manifested by descent or marriage. It is difficult to imagine a large group of people who did not recognize family or clan distinctions or have lineal or affined affiliations.

In observing settlement patterns at sites closely related to Dickson, we find almost identical situations concerning the orientations of structures and features. The only house excavated at the Myer Site (FV33) has its longitudinal axis angled WNW-ESE, the same general orientation as the WNW-ESE oriented burials in the Dickson Mounds Cemetery (Caldwell, personal communication). An identical situation is evident at the Larson Site FV1109 (Harn 1966). Forty-eight excavated houses have their longitudinal axes oriented between 120 and 130 degrees E of N. At least five houses have an opposite orientation, the longitudinal axis being about 35 degrees E of N. This orientation would nearly center the group of NNE-SSW oriented burials at Dickson. All other features at Larson (the house rows, the plaza, and the temple mound) are oriented the same as the previously mentioned houses. These same orientations are also noticed with the excavated Mississippian structures at the Weaver Site, FV237 (Wray and MacNeish, n.d.). The houses at the Fouts Site (FV664) are oriented ENE-WSW at angles close to sunrise at the summer solstice (Cole and Deuel 1937:113), and the excavated structures at the Eveland Site, FV900 (Caldwell, manuscript on file at the Illinois State Museum), have their longitudinal axes either N-S or E-W. The house at the Fiedler Site is oriented NNE-SSW at approximately 29 degrees E, and the burials in three associated mounds have orientations similar to the burials at Dickson (Morse, Schoenbeck, and Morse 1953:Figs. 11, 17, 18, and 19). The same is true of Emmons (Emmons, Munson, and Caldwell 1960), Shyrock and Kingston Lake (Wray n.d.:a,b), Buckeye Bend (Cantwell and Harn n.d.), and other excavated Mississippian sites in the area (Harn 1980).

TABLE 5

Interments Represented By The Six Orientations

	N-S	E-W	WNW-ESE	NNE-SSW	NNW-SSE	ENE-WSW
Total Interments (including extended, flexed, and secondary burials)	37	50	54	56	9	4
Individual Interments	27	23	29	30	9	4
Orientation of Extended and Flexed Burials (excluding secondary burials)	36 Head S: 31 Head N: 5	47 Head E: 23 Head W: 24	50 Head SE: 13 Head NW: 37	44 Head SW: 40 Head NE: 4	8 Head SE: 5 Head NW: 3	4 Head SW: 2 Head NE: 2

There is no known instance of a Mississippian site in the Spoon River area that does not conform closely to the orientation pattern evident at Dickson. Burials and structures are nearly always oriented N-S, E-W, NNE-SSW, and WNW-ESE, or occasionally NNW-SSE or ENE-WSW; rarely do a majority of their longitudinal axes lie at points between these directions. Such orientation of features may not be an exclusive Mississippian trait, however. A study of several excavated Red Ocher and Middle Woodland sites in the Spoon River area suggests that orientation with respect to solar phenomena may have been present at a much earlier date (Cole and Deuel 1937:Figs. 17, 32, & 36).

It may be a coincidence that the orientations of features at these sites are so similar to each other and that the burials in their associated cemeteries and burial mounds are oriented at similar angles. However, most features and burials have longitudinal axes that closely correspond with or are at right angles to sunrise at the time of the winter and summer solstices and the equinoxes. The close coincidence between the actual burial and house angles and the expected angles is convincing. A very small percentage of the aboriginal features varies from the expected angles, but most are within 10 degrees of azimuth points. Considering the possible variations in the time of measurement or observation of the sun (e.g., an observation made when the sun first breaks the horizon at the winter solstice

would be several degrees north of an observation made only minutes later when the sun was completely clear of that level), the short sighting plane involved in aligning a human body or the side of a structure to a distant point, and allowing for errors in engineering calculations and crude instruments in the hands of these people, the orientations of most features would certainly fall within the acceptable limits of variation, if one views these features as being placed with respect to solar phenomena.

It is becoming apparent that most Mississippian people and their close cultural relatives, from the Southeast to the headwaters of the Mississippi River, had a great awareness of solar phenomena (Binford 1962, 1966; Wittry 1964). Probably the erection of structures, the "village plan," and the orientation of burials were based on solar phenomena as well as on other events in their social organization which we do not now recognize. Among these postulated entities might be: (1) that an orientation was attached to each child at birth (possibly the same orientation as the mother's family); (2) that he was identified with this direction throughout his life; (3) that this orientation encompassed all members of the same clan; (4) that these six orientations at Dickson actually represent distinct divisions within the community that were based on solar phenomena; (5) that solstices and equinoxes were important annual events.

ANTHROPOMETRIC STUDIES

Much of this section is the result of comprehensive studies undertaken by the late Dr. Georg K. Neumann of Indiana University in the forty-one years he was closely associated with Dickson Mounds. His notes were relied on entirely for the segments on *Life Span, Stature* and *Crania.* Neumann's observations were also used in the *Arthritis* section, although it is largely a summation of Chapman's (1962) discussion with revisions and minor corrections by the writer.

The 248 excavated burials, along with the many burials that were salvaged when the Dicksons erected the museum building, constitute an unusually large sample which facilitates the study of the various phenomena of bone. In this large population, we are able to view the formation of patterns and characteristics which allows for several internal comparative studies. These can often be related to external factors in such a manner as to present a rather graphic portrait of the secular existence of the Spoon River variant people.

In the following comparative analysis, only those burials whose age and sex have been definitely established will be used. Those in which the sex is not definite or the age is estimated or otherwise questionable have been disregarded.

LIFE SPAN

Using the above criteria, some 269 individuals remain; 78 are male, 85 are female, 75 are children under 13 years of age, and 31 are fetuses. The 163 males and females are of interest when a comparative review of their ages is made. The average age at the time of death of this group (13 years of age or older) is listed below.

Males	42.0 years
Females	35.4 years
Males, including children	29.7 years
Females, including children	25.6 years

One will readily note that the average Dickson male could expect to live approximately 4.1 years longer than an average female, a situation that is completely reversed today. One factor probably involved was childbirth and its hazards without today's conveniences. Almost as soon as sex can be determined, we see a marked increase in the death rate among females in comparison to the very gradual increase among males. This rate of death among women is very high in the late teens and tapers only slightly before it declines sharply in the late twenties, suggesting a child-bearing period of no more than twenty years. From age 13 to 28, 38 of 85 females (nearly 45 percent) died. In the same length of time, only 11 of the 78 males (about 14 percent) met a similar fate. The majority of the survivors of both sexes perished between the ages of 30 and 55, the highest rate occurring about midway between these ages. A similar correlation is noticed after age 55. As old age approaches, the number of survivors is nearly equal; the death rate steadily declines, accounting for all persons by the 75th year (see Fig. 58). The fetal death rate was noticeably high during the sixth to seventh month and expectantly high at the time of birth. A high death rate was noticed among all children up to 12 years between the first month and the third year: 44 out of 75 — or over 58 percent of the total — died during that short span. This rate is especially high from 1.5 to 2.5 years and may reflect the inability of infants to adjust to solid foods at weaning. Female children had a tendency to live longer than did male children, and there is no appreciable gap with either sex in which no deaths occurred.

Of the 269 individuals present, only 31 (about 11 percent) are fetuses or newborns. This figure appears too low. It is possible that this is a section of the cemetery in which a normal number of infant mortality victims from a short time period (e.g., one or two years) were swamped by an abnormally large number of adults, adolescents, and children who had been annihilated by disease or disaster. Such a situation would allow for the presence of the normal number of infant mortalities and explain the high ratio of adult-adolescent-children to fetus-newborn burials. On the other hand, the Spoon River variant people may have practiced infanticide, in which case the body of the infant might not normally have been interred.

TABLE 6
Cranial Measurements and Indices (after Neumann*)

Measurements

No.	Notation	Mean
1.	Glabella-opisthocranion	181.8
5.	Nasion-basion length	105.6
8.	Maximum breadth	140.3
9.	Minimum frontal breadth	95.9
17.	Basion-bregma height	145.3
40.	Basion-prosthion length	102.9
44.	Biorbital breadth	101.8
45.	Bizygomatic breadth	140.6
47.	Facial height, nasion-gnathion	121.6
48.	Upper facial height, nasion-alveolar point	75.1
49.	Posterior interorbital breadth	25.8
50.	Anterior interorbital breadth	20.8
51R.	Orbital breadth, right	44.1
51L.	Orbital breadth, left	43.6
52R.	Orbital height, right	34.1
52L.	Orbital height, left	34.2
54.	Nasal breadth	26.3
55.	Nasal height	53.3
60.	Maxillo-alveolar length	57.0
61.	Maxillo-alveolar breadth	67.2
62.	Palatal length	47.1
63.	Palatal breadth	39.8
66.	Greatest width of mandible at angles	102.8
72.	Facial profile angle	82°.8

Indices

	Mean
(8) 100/(1). Cranial index	77.25
(17) 100/(1). Length-height index	80.43
(17) 100/(8). Breadth-height index	104.16
(9) 100/(8). Transverse fronto-parietal index	68.36
(47) 100/(45). Total facial index	86.37
(48) 100/(45). Superior facial index	53.16
(52) 100/(51). Orbital index (mean)	78.12
(54) 100/(55). Nasal index	49.30
(61) 100/(60). Maxillo-alveolar index	115.94
(63) 100/(62). Palatal index	76.55
(45) 100/(8). Transverse cranio-facial index	99.94
(9) 100/(45). Zygomatico-frontal index	67.83

*Neumann, Georg: Appendix IV in *Rediscovering Illinois* by Fay-Cooper Cole and Thorne Deuel 1937, p. 260.

STATURE

The stature of the people has been computed mainly by using measurements of the lower limbs when available. Pearson's interracial formula listed below was felt to give the most consistent results for a population of medium stature such as the Middle Mississippian people when compared to stature measurements in the grave (Neumann, personal communication).

Pearson: Male — 71.272 + 1.159
        (Femur   cm. + Tibia   cm.)

        Female — 69.154 + 1.126
        (Femur   cm. + Tibia   cm.)

Since all skeletal material remains *in situ*, exacting measurements of many specimens are often difficult or impossible to obtain. This is especially true in the case of secondary burials. For this and other reasons, only 41 adult males and 37 adult females are readily available for a detailed analysis of stature. There are no extremes in height. The shortest adult male measured was over five feet tall; and, had it not been for an arthritic condition at the time of his death, the tallest male would have stood over 5 feet 9 inches in height. For brevity, a detailed listing of the 78 separate heights is not presented; rather, the average of each sex is given:

Average height of Dickson males: 5 ft. 6 in.
Average height of Dickson females: 5 ft. 2 in.

CRANIA

In a study of the crania, only undeformed adult male skulls were considered. After eliminating skulls of females, adolescents, children and senile individuals, skulls which exhibited cradleboard flattening or posthumous deformation, and skulls which were fragmentary or incomplete, only seventeen remained. Individual measurements and indices of these crania are not listed here (see Cole and Deuel 1937:264); but the mean measurements and indices of all crania are listed in Table 6. Observations and summary of the crania made by Neumann (Cole and Deuel 1937:252) which cannot be altered or improved by the writer, appear below in their entirety.

OBSERVATIONS

The external occipital protuberance is very small and the occipital bone medium-bombed. The sagittal section presents a well-rounded contour, with the vertex in the middle of the parietal arc, and little if any praelambdoidal flattening. The parietal eminences are medium, the superior surfaces of the parietals slightly flattened and crested. From the norma occipitals the brain case exhibits a rounded-out pentagonal form. The forehead is retreating, the frontal eminences being only very slightly developed; the supraorbital ridges medium and of the type in which the ridge forms part of the superior medial edge of the orbit; the glabella is medium high, the fronto-nasal junction a bit beetling, and the nasion region relatively high. Mastoid processes are medium, the palate is paraboloid, the nasals medium large and convex with a double curve, the nasal margins are variable (five have the infantile form, two a fossa praenasalis, five the anthropine form, and four the sulcus praenasalis), as is the nasal spine, which ranges from submedium to large. Some of the faces are very large and coarse, but most are not especially flat. The mandible is rather heavy and massive, with a square chin.

SUMMARY

The seventeen undeformed adult male crania of this series are rather intermediate when one glances at the indices. The cranial index ranges from 71.81 to 81.92, most of the indices falling between 75 and 79, with a mean of 77.25 (mesocranial). The skull can further be described as high, all being uniformly hypsicranial and acrocranial (means 80.43 and 104.16), with a forehead medium in breadth in relation to the brain case (metriometopic 68.36) and very narrow in relation to the bizygomatic width (zygomatico-frontal index 67.83). The face again is intermediate in width (mesoprosopic 86.37 and mesene 53.16), the orbits medium (mesoconch 78.12), the nasal proportions medium (mesorrhine 49.30), and the palate variable (brachyuranic 115.94, on the border of mesurany, and leptostaphyline 76.55). The series as a whole is rather uniform, showing fairly low variability, although there are perhaps two skulls among them that may show admixture from a strain somewhat Australoid in appearance. There is a medium amount of prognathism (mesognathous, facial profile angle of 82°.8), a retreating forehead, medium-developed parietal eminences, medium supraorbital ridges, and a face that is only slightly flat.

The crania from the Dickson Mounds Cemetery compare favorably with skulls from other Spoon River variant mounds in the area. Mound F⁰14 of the Morton group (Cole and Deuel 1937:246) produced a good sample of adult and middle-aged undeformed male skulls as did the Rose Mound group (Baker *et al.* 1941:80). Generally, the skulls from both the Dickson Mounds and the other two previously mentioned Mississippian manifestations seem to vary more toward the Mongoloid in measurement.

TABLE 7
Artificial Cranial Deformity

Burial No.	Age	Degree of Deformity
MALES		
1 (Male?)	24	Moderate
3	46	Slight
24	65	Slight
45	32	Pronounced
106	40	Slight
110	41	Moderate
119	37	Moderate
138	20	Slight
FEMALES		
31	28	Pronounced
37	46	Moderate
46	20	Pronounced
60	17	Pronounced
81	28	Pronounced
82	48	Moderate
83	13	Moderate
84	22	Moderate
100	20	Pronounced
111	19	Extreme
125	11	Slight to Moderate
126	35	Slight
149	27	Pronounced
152	18	Slight
164	20	Slight
193	12	Pronounced
195	46	Slight
CHILDREN		
14	5 (Female?)	Pronounced
96	6	Pronounced
151	2	Moderate
179	3	Moderate
214	8 (Female?)	Pronounced

While the crania of Maples Mills (Late Woodland) sites in the area — Gooden Mounds F⁰85-86 (Cole and Deuel 1937:260) and the Hagan Mound (Baker *et al.* 1941:80) — also compare favorably with each other, the measurements and indices are markedly different from those of the Spoon River variant skulls from the same area. In comparison, Neumann states that "those of the Woodland group vary a little more toward the Caucasoid side without forgetting that both represent races of the general yellow-brown Asiatic variety of man."

One skull in the Dickson excavation, F⁰34-109, a 35-year-old male, most nearly approaches the mean for the Spoon River variant people in many of the measurements (Fig. 56, A-C).

ARTIFICIAL DEFORMATION OF THE CRANIA

Partially due to the great weight of the overburden of soil that originally rested above the burials, many distorted bones were noticed. This unintentional deformation was frequently noticed in the more pliable bones, especially the parietal bones of the skull. The thin skulls of the children are most susceptible to this type of warping, and they are of little value for use in a comparative analysis of artificial deformity (only a few skulls of children have survived either complete crushing or distortion by the weight of the soil). Consequently, only the adult crania, plus the crania of a few children, could be studied. Material left *in situ* and not completely exposed further hampered this study; and this, along with occasional warping, reduced the available total of crania by nearly two-thirds.

The artificial deformation of the Dickson skulls may have resulted from the accidental application of pressure to the cranium stemming from the widespread use of the cradleboard. The deformation is usually restricted to the occipital region and is square with the skull, rather than angling toward the crown. Of the available adult crania, 33 percent have been deformed in this manner. The degree of deformation is usually not great (Fig. 56, D-E), but one extreme case is present (Fig. 56, F). In many of its measurements, the skull of this person (No. 111, a 19-year-old female) could qualify to be placed into a "binding" category. The maximum glabellar length is only 125 mm. while the average length of other 19-year-old females is around 163 mm. Even though No. 111 is small statured, the breadth of the face and the basibregmatic height of the skull is greater than that of other females the same age. So pronounced is the deformity that the skull is pressed into a laterally thin form with a high, almost nonsloping forehead, and a broad, flat face.

A glance at Table 7 reveals that occipital flattening is far more prevalent in adult female crania — a ratio of 2:1 over those of Dickson males. The female skulls also show a greater degree of flattening: About 76 percent have moderate to pronounced occipital flattening in contrast to male skulls which are not deformed to that degree. The deformed male crania are usually only slightly flattened, but three cases of moderate flattening are present.

It is possible that the practice of artificial deformation of the crania was an intentional modification rather than resulting from accidental pressure applied by the cradleboard. If such a practice were linked to socially defined status positions, these positions were apparently not attainable by all members of the same family or clan. Assuming that individuals in mass graves are in some way related, we see that occipital flattening is never evident with a majority of the group. No more than one or two persons in any of the larger mass graves shows artificial skull deformity. Of the five instances where isolated burials of females with children were noticed, we find a much better correlation. The three females with children that could be examined showed that both individuals of each pair had occipital flattening (Table 8).

None of the six examples of possible blood-relationship were available for a thorough examination. Four of these examples were of associated fetuses which would not show evidence of artificial deformation of the crania and, in one other case (Nos. 73 and 74), the skulls were fragmentary and not completely exposed. The skull of one of the two burials in the sixth example (No. 3) has occipital flattening, but the skull of its possible relative (No. 2) is somewhat fragmentary and is not completely excavated. The only exposed area on its left occipital does appear to be moderately flattened.

TEETH

Since teeth sometimes preserve evidence of an earlier period of malnutrition or disease (providing the person was sufficiently young that dental calcification was incomplete), they can often be used as a standard for judging previous dietary conditions or diseases. Aside from a few chronic abscesses, little dental pathology is noticed in the Dickson series. Normal variations — such as the lack of a third molar, the presence of supernumerary teeth, and impacted third molars — are occasionally noticed. One burial (No. 5) has an everted right lateral incisor growing upward through the nasal cavity; another has hypoplastic tooth enamel (No. 111, a 19-year-old female). Involvement in the latter instance is slight and appears to be limited to the incisors and cuspid teeth, suggesting that the cause of their underdevelopment occurred prior to age four. No pathology was indicated elsewhere in

TABLE 8

Cranial Deformity in Related(?) Individuals

Burial No.	Sex	Age	Occipital Flattening
53	—	Neonate	—
54	F	38	None
82	F	48	Present
83	F	13	Present
125	F	11	Present
126	F	35	Present
151	Child	2	Present
152	F	18	Present
164	F	20	Present
182	F(?)	2	Occipital region not exposed

the skeletal remains; but there is pronounced artificial deformation of the skull.

Shovel-shaped teeth are present with many of the Dickson burials. This condition is particularly evident in the median incisors but also affects the lateral incisors of some individuals as well. Often any evidence of concavities on the back sides of adult teeth have been worn away as a result of advanced attrition. Of the children, adolescents, and young adults examined, nearly 73 percent have shovel-shaped teeth.

Because of the presence of many young adults, adolescents, and children, general tooth conditions of the Dickson population are excellent. Except for the fact that attrition is severe in all older individuals, strong and well-formed teeth, almost devoid of any calculus, persist. Caries is almost completely lacking in the younger people and are not commonly present until attrition has exposed the primary dentine. Some adults show a great loss of molars with pronounced resorption of the alveolar ridge. Periodontal disease (pyorrhea) was apparently fairly common and this, coupled with caries, has produced several chronic dental abscesses.

Dental Attrition

Probably directly attributable to their diets and cultural traits, dental attrition is very evident among these people. The use of attrition as an aid in determining the age of individuals can be somewhat beneficial to the archaeologist, but one must bear in mind that it is only an aid and should not be used as an end in itself. Many factors are involved in a study of this sort. There are undoubtedly differences in wear among individuals for physical and cultural reasons and a slight difference in the rate of dental wear between sexes. Some women seem to show a slightly greater degree of attrition than do men of the same age. Degrees of dental attrition can be roughly grouped into the four stages shown on Fig. 59.

The average burial in the Dickson excavation adheres closely to these patterns comparing age versus tooth wear. In fact, there is a very low variability among the 150 + adults that were examined. Barring extreme differences in the dietary conditions, the calculations listed on Fig. 59 would probably be representative for most late-prehistoric manifestations in the Central Illinois River Valley area.

Filed Teeth

One instance of artificial tooth mutilation is found in the Dickson Cemetery. Although not common, similar evidences of tooth filing have been noticed elsewhere in Illinois (Stewart and Titterington 1944:317-321) more commonly in the Cahokia area and occasionally in the southern states. All filing seems to be associated with Mississippian people.

No tooth filing was noticed in the Dickson excavation, but one young female(?) skull with the two upper median incisors filed was found elsewhere in the mound around 1900. (Unfortunately, the mandible was not recovered for study.) These incisors are crossed by a single horizontal groove cut back from the incisal edge about one-third the length of the exposed enamel. A sharp filing instrument was apparently used to make a continuous sweep across both teeth. Horizontal notching such as this is less common than vertical notches along the incisal edges. The filed teeth at Cahokia are predominately vertically notched.

The writer is well aware that any horizontal indentation or "band" on the enamel of a tooth surface immediately suggests hypoplasia. However, hypoplastic enamel ordinarily appears in all tooth crowns undergoing development at the same time the disturbance (e.g., a vitamin D deficiency) in enamel formation took place. Other teeth (lateral incisors, cuspids, and premolars) would normally have been affected had this been pathological instead of artificial.

BONE DISEASES

Many diseases do not involve changes in the skeleton, but those which do are of great value in assessing the health of prehistoric people. Although the frequency of some of the following diseases is low, they will be mentioned. The importance of the study of all prehistoric diseases is unquestioned, although sufficient space is seldom devoted to this aspect in studies of prehistoric people. Brothwell (1963) states: "Paleopathology not only enables various modern ailments to be traced back into history and pre-history, but may also provide new information concerning the manner in which they can manifest themselves."

ARTHRITIS

Osteoarthritis is the most prevalent of the bone diseases that are represented with the skeletal remains. The causes of arthritis are numerous and varied and have been aired so often that no detailed discussion will ensue. The major causes of osteoarthritis are attrition, infectious agents via the blood stream, and trauma (both mechanical and toxic); even severe working conditions may have been a contributing agent. Age is definitely a factor and the origin of many instances of arthritis could probably be traced to increasing body weight and faulty spine movement gradually wearing on the joints over the years. The larger joints are more commonly affected; but except in the spine, anklyosis is rare.

Other pathological types are rheumatoid arthritis and spondylitis deformans. These differ from osteoarthritis by a general absence of osteophytic lipping and by a type of ankylosis which may eventually produce a "poker spine" — complete spinal rigidity usually combined with a deformity caused by a kyphotic curvature. However, the joints of the hands and feet are most commonly affected.

Authorities seem to differ widely on the nomenclature and the number of divisions to be used in a classification of this degenerative joint disease. In the limited study presented here, Chapman's (1962:60) scale was used to determine the incidence and stage of osteoarthritis present with individuals in the excavation:

Stage I — is characterized by slight lipping at the superior and inferior margins of the bodies of the vertebrae, or other joints,
Stage II — exhibits a more pronounced degree of lipping,
Stage III — is characterized by extensive lipping often resembling a mushroom-like condition,
Stage IV — exhibits bony spurs or bridges with an increased mushroom-like outgrowth,
Stage V — presents actual ankylosis or bony union between two or more vertebrae, or other bones.

Since all skeletal material remains *in situ* and since many burials have not been completely exposed, this situation occasionally presented a formidable barrier when an examination of all areas of arthritic involvement on an individual was attempted. In such instances and where possible, the estimates of Neumann (personal communication), Chapman (1962), and the author were made from the only available criteria such as the exposed articular surfaces of joints.

Of the 56 males aged 21 and over, 47 cases of osteoarthritis were noticed. The incidence was 100 percent after age 47 was reached; and these cases were more advanced in proportion to the number surviving. However, Burial 119 (37 years), has a Stage IV involvement, and No. 170 (46 years) has one of the two Stage V involvements in the excavation. The youngest person with moderate involvement was No. 39 (24 years), and the oldest person to show involvement was No. 48 (75 years). This male had an extensive Stage IV condition that was probably rheumatoid arthritis.

Of the 47 females aged 21 and over, 31 cases of osteoarthritis were noticed. After 45 years of age, 100 percent of the women were arthritic, but females had fewer advanced cases than did males. Two had Stage III, one had Stage IV, and one (No. 58, 34 years) had Stage V involvements. All women exhibited minor arthritic changes prior to the mid-thirties, at which time Stage III lipping commonly appeared. This high percentage of involvement at an earlier age may reflect somewhat on the rigors of childbirth. Knaggs (1926:158-159) suggests that infections connected with birth injuries may serve as an ex-

planation for the greater occurrence of osteoarthritis in women of child-bearing age than in men of the same period.

Hooton (1930) found a similar parallel on high occurrence of arthritis among younger females as compared to males in his study of the skeletal remains of the Indians of Pecos Pueblo. Nearly half of the adults and subadults examined showed some arthritic involvement. Of the female cases (only two were young adults), 57.14 percent were middle-aged. This was in contrast to only 15.38 percent of the middle-aged males. The remaining males (84.62 percent) were over 50.

OSTEOMYELITIS AND OSTEOPOROSIS

Osteomyelitis, an inflammation of the inner (cancellous) bone tissue, accompanied a healed fracture of the right ulna of Burial 58, a 34-year-old female.

Possibly the osteomyelitis developed as a result of bacteria introduced directly into the bone at the time of the fracture (as it may have been compound), although it could have developed through infection that spread from some other area of the body to the injury. The inflammation seems confined to the area of the fracture where some bone destruction and a healed sinus area(s?) accompany a rounded sinus aperture. Since the burial remains *in situ* and has only the right lateral and the posterior surfaces of the ulna exposed, it is impossible to determine the full extent of the involvement (although it does not appear to be great).

Number 54, a 38-year-old female with a full-term baby in a breech(?) position, is affected by acute osteomyelitis in at least the first and second metacarpals of the left hand and moderate involvement of the third. Unfortunately, the hand is not completely exposed and few of the phalanges could be examined. Medullary abscesses with healed sinus areas and sinus apertures are evident on the first and second metacarpals. No other exposed bones show evidence of inflammation, but most bones available for study are extremely light in weight, suggesting severe osteoporosis. The combination of pregnancy and the aforementioned infection may well have produced the osteoporitic condition.

Burial 216, a 35-year-old female, is also affected with an acute inflammatory condition probably associated with multiple fractures of the right arm and ribs. The right humerus reveals evidence of deformity of the upper shaft, neck and tuberosities, suggesting an old, solidly healed fracture. The changes involving the neck and tuberosities are indicative of chronic infection with evidence both of bone destruction and repair occurring simultaneously. This condition suggests a longstanding inflammatory process, probably a pyogenic infection related to the previous fracture if the fracture resulted from some sort of penetrating wound.

The adjacent scapula reveals similar destructive and reparative changes which have resulted in alteration of the gross contours, particularly in the area of the acromion process. The outer end of the right clavicle shows similar thickening and irregularity suggesting bony overgrowth associated with inflammation. There also appears to be chronic sinus formation within the clavicle. The general inflammatory process appears to have extended up to the clavicle so that the process was rather extensive in its involvement about the shoulder. There was a similar, although less severe, involvement of the left clavicle as well.

The right elbow joint shows a minimal amount of osteoarthritis. The shafts of the right radius and ulna exhibit slight deformation, this being more pronounced in the ulna. The bone is thickened but smooth, indicating solidly healed fractures.

The manubrium and sternum both show evidence of bone destruction and bone proliferation with irregular sinus formation. The xiphoid process was not recovered. These changes also indicate chronic infection with sinus tract formation which probably resulted from either a penetrating wound or possibly from hematogenous infection.

Right ribs 8 through 12 also appear to have been fractured. Associated chronic infection is indicated by irregular sinus formations, and all show destructive and reparative changes which frequently resulted in gross alteration of the rib contours. The left ribs are not exposed.

INJURIES

Eight individuals were located which had a total of 17 injuries. All were simple fractures of bones although one may have been a compressed injury to the skull (Table 9).

With the exception of Nos. 48, 58, and 216, all fractures are well healed, exhibit only slight angulation, and suggest no deformity or residual disability. The possible fracture in No. 48 may have resulted in the generalized rheumatoid arthritis present. The left tibia and fibula are fused at their distal ends and are fused to the tarsal bones (which are also fused to each other) to form one bony mass. The bone boundaries are not distinguishable. The foot has a 30-degree extension deformity. The fractures with Nos. 58 and 216, although well healed, have accompanying osteomyelitic conditions.

The possible injury to the skull of No. 106 may have caused eventual death since only questionable healing has occurred. There is some evidence to suggest that this involvement may instead be a bone tumor, but exact determination is not possible at this time because the skull has been partially restored with plaster of Paris and there is much postmortem disturbance to the area in question.

Six of eight individuals with fractures are males. This high incidence is probably socially related and, while it may be attributed to the more rigorous upbringing of males in general, it may well reflect developing social stresses during late prehistory. None of the males having injuries is less than 40 years old while both females are in their mid-thirties.

TABLE 9

Bone Fractures and Injuries

Burial No.	Sex	Age	Location	Type
7	M	47	Rib	Healed fracture
21	M	44	Tibia	Healed fracture
25	M	67	Humerus	Healed fracture
48	M	75	Foot	Possible healed fracture
58	F	34	Ulna	Healed fracture
106	M	40	Clavicle	Healed fracture
			Rib	Healed fracture
			Skull	Compressed injury with questionable healing
212	M	48	Humerus	Healed fracture
216	F	35	Humerus	Healed fracture
			Ulna	Healed fracture
			Radius	Healed fracture(?)
			Ribs (8-12)	Healed fractures

CONCLUSIONS

The 30-by-60-foot Dickson excavation represents approximately one-tenth of the total area covered by the cemetery complex. At least 248 individual burials are present. Since overall burial density has been severely reduced by previous excavators and since there are undoubtedly a number of unexposed burials present, the original population of the excavation area may have exceeded 300. If this density is representative of the remainder of the cemetery, more than 3,000 individuals may have been present prior to modern exploration.

Three habitation sites are associated with the Dickson mortuary activity, Eveland F^V900, Myer F^V33, and Dickson Camp F^V35 (Fig. 60). The Eveland Site is small, perhaps covering less than three acres, and is situated on a toe-slope terrace at the bluff base 250 yards southwest of Dickson Mounds. It is highly probable that the Myer and Dickson Camp sites represent parts of the same extended habitation area; therefore, that site area hereinafter will be referred to as the *Myer/Dickson* Site. Myer/Dickson covers 20-plus acres of the blufftop behind and to the west of the burial area.

The large burial population at Dickson reflects a variety of causal factors. The cemetery was used for parts of four centuries, during which time there was considerable fluctuation in the number and size of the contributing populations. As is discussed later, there are two Spoon River cultural phases (Eveland and Larson) represented in the Dickson excavation, the Eveland Phase comprising only about seven percent of the burial population. Fortunately, the living areas associated with these two populations (the Eveland Site and the Myer/Dickson Site) are separate (Caldwell 1967:139-142), allowing some correlations to be drawn between habitation site size and associated mortuary population numbers. No detailed demographic studies have been completed for either habitation area aside from a projected maximum population estimate of 440 individuals for the Larson Phase occupation of the Myer/Dickson Site (Harn 1980: Table 4). Certainly the earlier Eveland Phase population was substantially smaller, judging by the small size of the Eveland Site. This size ratio is reflected in the Dickson excavation although the comparison is admittedly artificial. Had the Dickson excavation been carried out to the north

of its present location, a higher percentage of Eveland Phase burials would have been exposed along with several Late Woodland interments.

Burials in the Dickson excavation conform closely to the basic patterns regarding mortuary practice and burial furnishings which were introduced with the Middle Mississippian movement (Harn 1975b). Interment practices are relatively uniform within the excavation area and are quite comparable to other Spoon River burial sites, although on a somewhat larger scale.

In common with most local Spoon River burial sites, the cemetery at Dickson was placed on the bluff edge adjacent to a primary habitation area and contained graves dug into the original hill surface prior to any mound construction. Low, conical mounds were added later, increasing the height of the hill by an additional few feet. Intrusive graves were commonly dug into these mounds. A large pit resulting from repeated borrowing activities during mound construction is also present.

Most articulated burials are dorsally extended, although both prone and semiflexed burials are also present. A majority of the latter are probably associated with the early amalgamated Late Woodland-Early Mississippian population. Many bundles of bones and partially disarticulated bodies accompany mass graves, suggesting that the remains of some people were either treated differently than others prior to interment or were exposed for some time before burial. These bodies may have been placed in predesignated locations (a charnel house?) at death and their flesh allowed to decay, or they may represent reexcavated burials or persons who died away from the immediate area. It is supposed that the osseous remains were later collected and interred.

The skulls of males were rarely included in secondary burials whereas both long bones and the skull were usually present with female bundles. It is not known whether the bones of males were treated differently than those of females prior to interment, but some sort of differentiation was apparently made. Binford (1962) recorded a similar situation at Galley Pond and presented interesting speculations in constructing a related sociological model for the Mississippian people of that area. Possibly, at Dickson, as evidenced at Galley Pond, the importance of the creation of bundles may have been associated more with those bones of important individuals — although the near lack of burial furniture fails to support this position.

There are no recognized local antecedents for a majority of the religious/political paraphernalia and shell-tempered ceramic forms which appeared in the Central Illinois Valley during the two centuries following A.D. 1050. Only one ceramic form, the grit-tempered conoidal jar with fabric-marked, cordmarked, and smoothed-over cordmarked surface finishes, has been recognized in pre-Mississippian, terminal Late Woodland contexts. Type names for these vessels include Bauer Branch (Green 1977:25-43), Maples Mills or Canton ware (Cole and Deuel 1937:48; Fowler 1955), and Sepo Smoothed-over Cordmarked (Caldwell 1967:139; Harn n.d.). The recent excavations at Dickson Mounds produced substantial quantities of Sepo ware and minor quantities of Canton ware.

The major pottery sequence, discounting local variations, is very similar to the Cahokia ceramic sequence and suggests close affiliations with that region. However, distinctive angular-shouldered "Mississippian" jars appear quite early in the Spoon River area and may be the result of acculturation between migrant Mississippian people and the indigenous Late Woodland groups. Some early shell-tempered vessels are similar and often identical in form to local Late Woodland types; and some otherwise classic Powell Plain-shaped jars are grit-tempered. It presently is not clear which cultural influence inspired which ware.

At Cahokia, the shoulder-to-neck angle of Early Mississippian (Powell Plain and Ramey Incised) jars is approximately 45 degrees, but similar jars in the Central Illinois Valley frequently have extreme angles — the shoulder-to-neck angle sometimes approaching horizontal. Early Mississippian jars at Cahokia usually have rounded bases while bases of local Early Mississippian vessels often vary toward the more traditional Late Woodland conoidal form (cf., Fig. 18, D32).

The origin of the single or double decorative nodes on some jar handles is not known, but many Spoon River vessels are adorned in this manner. Bifurcated handles also appear with some frequency in many Mississippian contexts outside the region. Several shallow bowls and jars have equally spaced projections or lips on the rim edges, although such decorations are not as commonly seen outside this area. Possibly these were adapted Woodland decorative techniques, since raised rim projections and lugs are characteristic of many local Late Woodland jars. The high shoulders and conoidal bases of the early Mississippian jars were modified somewhat with the passage of time, but lips on bowl and jar rims and nodes on handles appear throughout the entire Spoon River and Spoon River-Oneota sequences in the Central Illinois River Valley.

Nearly one-half of all burials, including those in mass graves, have associated nonperishable grave goods. The range of material traits represented is typical of other Spoon River variant burial sites recorded in the area. With the exception of the Crable Site (McDonald 1950; Morse 1960, 1969; Smith 1951), which is chronologically later than Dickson, close compatibility is evidenced between mortuary and material traits at Dickson and other Spoon River sites such as Berry (Conrad n.d., a); Crabtree (Snyder 1908:33-42); Emmons (Griffin and Morse 1961; Morse et al. 1961); Fiedler (Morse et al. 1953); Frederick (Young 1960); Kingston Lake (Simpson 1952; Wray n.d., a); Morton (Cole and Deuel 1937); Rose (Baker et al. 1941:22-28); Shyrock (Wray n.d., b); and Weaver (Wray and MacNeish n.d.). With the exception of the period following the arrival of Oneota traditions into the area, it is evident that burial at Dickson Mounds continued throughout the entire local Mississippian sequence.

Burial furniture in the Dickson excavation is largely utilitarian with no exotic paraphernalia being present. Although some ceramics are quite well made, no special funerary vessels were apparently manufactured expressly for inclusion with the dead. All vessels are comparable to those found in excavations of habitation areas. One jar (Fig. 20, D117, with No. 96) has a very rough appearance and is tempered with large, irregular pieces of shell. Unsmoothed and asymmetrical, it may represent a newly or hurriedly made funerary vessel.

All other pottery, as a group, usually exhibits indication of use. Appendages such as effigy heads, pouring lips, handles, etc., have often been broken off prior to interment, and in one instance (Fig. 24, D207, with No. 120), a hole in a jar has been repaired by means of a plug. The black-polished slips on jars were usually deteriorated or destroyed by repeated firings, but the slips on the beakers were still intact, indicating that they were not exposed to extreme or prolonged periods of heat. Most of the shallow bowls and jars show evidences of reheating; and carbon deposits on their bases and lower side surfaces suggest frequent use or firing prior to interment.

Our earlier proposal (Harn 1971b:71) that more than one temporal period was represented in the Dickson excavation was supported by the subsequent excavation and analysis of over 800 additional Dickson Mounds burials between 1966 and 1968 (Conrad 1972; Harn n.d.), although some revision to the proposed burial sequence is made in light of these recent investigations. A much larger sample of local Mississippian sites has now been excavated and preliminarily analyzed, including such major Spoon River ceremonial centers as Orendorf (cf. Stephens 1976) and Larson (cf. Harn 1966, 1980). These excavations have provided substantial data toward clarifying the complex Spoon River social organization that was only beginning to become apparent a decade ago.

It is now generally recognized that the material and social differences existing between members of the proposed Larson and Dickson phases of the Spoon River variant are not as defined as was originally seen. An earlier overview of local Mississippian cultural development (Conrad and Harn 1972) recently has been revised and updated, providing the basis for dividing the Spoon River variant into five phases: Eveland, Orendorf, Larson, Crable, and Sleeth (Conrad n.d. b). While changes in material items do occur temporally in the Dickson excavation, it is now apparent that a majority of these changes were taking place within one phase, Larson. What was seen as a shift from Larson to Dickson Phase at Dickson mounds (Harn 1971b:71) is now regarded as a transition from early to late Larson Phase — the Dickson Phase as defined by Conrad and Harn (1972) having been omitted from the proposed cultural scheme (Conrad n.d., b).

Other cultural phases also may be represented in the Dickson excavation. One semiflexed burial (No. 172) may have been affiliated with a premound cemetery; but unfortunately, it has no associated burial furniture. Two other semiflexed burials (Nos. 10 and 23), probably associated with Mound E, also lack burial furniture.

Parts of two, and possibly three, burial mounds are represented in the Dickson excavation. Twelve burials (Nos. 1, 10, 11, 14-17, and 19-23) in the northeastern excavation corner are associated with Mound E (Harn n.d.), a structure that was built early in the burial sequence. Excavations of other sections of that mound produced both extended and semiflexed burials with a variety of associated Early Mississippian Eveland Phase and Late Woodland Sepo Phase burial offerings. Diagnostic Eveland Phase pottery vessels included Ramey Incised, Powell Plain, and a miniature water bottle. Late Woodland ceramics included Sepo Smoothed-over Cordmarked and Sepo Plain jars. This mound was of further interest because of the high incidence of elite regalia present. Included were bead ensembles, bracelets, necklaces, a beaded sash, and rattles. Unfortunately, much of Mound E was found to have been largely destroyed by uncontrolled digging outside the Dickson excavation.

Both extended and semiflexed burials appear in the portion of Mound E excavated by the Dickson family, but neither of the possible Late Woodland burials has associated grave goods exposed. Ceramics occurring with the extended Eveland Phase burials include Powell Plain jars, shell-tempered plain jars with pronounced shoulders and moderately conoidal bases, and an effigy bowl.

At least the southwestern portion of Mound E was overlain by Mound I, but definite dimensions of the mound could not be established because of the vast destruction by previous excavators.

The remainder of the burials in the Dickson excavation were probably contained within Mound I, the largest burial unit within the cemetery complex. Their excavation covers approximately 51 percent of the original Mound I area. Mound I is superimposed over the southwestern edge of Mound E and also appears to be superimposed over Mound B along its northern edge (Harn n.d.).

Although most of the burials in the Dickson excavation outside Mound E were probably associated with Mound I, precise verification was not possible for some 25 percent of the burial population because of disturbances by later aboriginal graves, uncontrolled digging by relic collectors, and by the Dicksons' excavation method of removing all overburden to the level of the lowest burials leaving few good earthen profiles. Burials probably associated with Mound I are Nos.: 2-9, 12, 13, 26, 28-35, 37-42, 45, 46, 50, 51, 53-55, 67, 68, 72-84, 86, 89, 90, 92-106, 108-113, 115-121, 123-128, 131, 132, 134-143, 146-148, 150-152, 154-156, 158-171, 174, 178-180, 182, 185, 187, 188, 190-197, 199-217, 221-228, 230-232, and 234.

Analysis of Mound I ceramics suggests that only Larson Phase burials are represented, but there is such a stylistic range of wares present that an extended period of burial activity is implied. Although no rolled-rim jars occur in the assemblage to suggest an Eveland Phase presence, the shoulder-sharpness of many jars is reminiscent of vessel shoulders of the earlier Powell and Ramey series (See vessels D23, D95, D181, D183, D201, D208, D358, D362, and D390). These vessels appear early in the Larson series, with the Dickson Trailed jars becoming a hallmark of the fully developed Larson Phase by the end of the 13th century A.D. (Harn 1980). Their gradual disappearance and the transformation to globular jars are among the attributes that characterize the later Larson Phase occupation that appears to be represented in Mound J (Harn n.d.) and in other regional Mississippian centers such as Lawrenz Gun Club and Walsh (Harn 1980).

Figure 61 reveals that the majority of the Mound I burials are concentrated in a somewhat circular pattern in the southern 60 percent of the Dickson excavation and that burials are more randomly dispersed in the northern 40 percent. While this pattern may be attributable to more intense pothunting activities in the northern portion (for which there is ample evidence), there is a distinct possibility that two separate burial units are involved. It is certainly feasible that the circular southern burial concentration was originally contained within a separate mound.

Analysis of ceramics from the two groups sheds little light on the matter, partly because of the small pottery sample included with the northern group. Only nine vessels are present with the 30 burials. Associated pottery is comprised of cordmarked and plain globular jars with everted rims, Tippits and Spoon River beakers, a lobed jar, an effigy bowl, and one moderatly angular-shouldered jar found with Burial 9. Interestingly enough, Burial 9 was placed with another burial having a classic Cahokia Cordmarked jar in association, suggesting that at least this particular jar type extended well into the Larson Phase period.

Pottery of the southern burial group contains eight of the previously discussed earlier Larson Phase jar forms, three of which have trailed designs on the shoulders. The remainder of the assemblage is similar to that of the northern group except that more bowls are represented and black-polishing of vessel surfaces is more common. If burial superimposition is involved, the moderately angular-shouldered jars are always the earlier jar forms.

The burial sequence in Mound I was certainly extended, probably continuing for several decades. It can be proposed that the burial area was expanded northward during this time in light of the apparent separate concentrations of burials and the paucity of earlier jar styles with the northern burial group. A northern burial progression may also be supported by the presence of the late Larson Phase Mound J which was subsequently constructed to the north of Mound I (Harn n.d.).

The proposed lateral expansion of Mound I may have been similar to that documented for Mound J (Harn n.d.), although certainly of longer duration. Unfortunately, precise determination of the Mound I burial sequence will probably never be possible because of the absence of good earthen profiles in the Dickson excavation and the immense disturbance to the small remaining portion of the mound.

Dickson Mounds and its associated habitation areas, the Eveland and Myer/Dickson sites, were a part of a larger integrated network of Mississippian sites which were present in the Central Illinois River Valley. Over 150 habitation sites of the Spoon River variant are presently recorded within the region. It has been proposed that a majority of the later Mississippian sites are separated into somewhat self-contained communities positioned at regular intervals along a 100-mile riverfront between the present-day towns of Peoria and Meredosia, Illinois. Large towns apparently served as nuclear community centers for related hamlets, farmsteads, camps, and day-activity stations positioned nearby. The settlement pattern seems to have been influenced by access to favorable biotic zones, water sources, landforms, and soil types, with political organization playing only a minor role (Harn 1980).

Little contemporaneity apparently existed between a majority of the town sites, the settlement pattern instead representing a continuum of occupation as populations shifted into new areas from the late twelfth to the middle fifteenth centuries A.D. No town and no defined community has been found to exist during the initial Early Mississippian Eveland Phase occupation of the Spoon River area. Sites of this period are small in size and are widely dispersed. The Eveland Site is the only Eveland Phase habitation known in the immediate area. It is to this small living area that the earliest Mississippian burials in the Dickson Mounds are probably attributable (Caldwell 1967:139). At least 12 burials in the Dickson excavation are associated with this occupation.

The major period of Mississippian occupation of the Dickson Mounds area was during the Larson Phase, which was apparently begun by the middle of the thirteenth century A.D. with the erection of a major town at the Larson Site about one mile to the southwest. This occupation probably represented a substantial population intrusion into the area coming in the wake of the abandonment of the Orendorf Site area by early Larson Phase people.

The majority of the Dickson excavation burials are associated with the Larson Phase occupation, most individuals probably having died at the nearby Myer/Dickson Site. Myer/Dickson appears to have functioned as a secondary center or hamlet of the local Larson Phase occupation. Although no statistics are yet available for Myer/Dickson, comparison of Dickson Mounds Larson Phase ceramics with those of the Larson Site (Harn 1980:Table 3) suggests close contemporaneity.

External influences on the Dickson Mound population are much in evidence and appear to have resulted from both trade and personal contact as well as by indirect acculturation. Cultural exchange appears to have been carried out along two opposing avenues. Secular exchange of items and innovations reflective of daily living was undertaken in a basic east-to-west pattern between the Spoon River population and peoples of the Western Prairie and Eastern Plains while religious expressions were received in a south-to-north pattern from the Cahokia and Caddoan areas (Harn 1975b:430).

Pottery influences are presently the most easily recognized of the external evidences of contact. Most obvious are those attributable to the Cahokia region. The trailed decorations of the Dickson Ceramic series may be indicative of interaction between Spoon River tradition people and such Upper Mississippian and Oneota affiliates as the Silvernale and Orr foci of the northeastern plains, the Over Focus, and the Big and Little Sioux phases of the Middle Missouri Tradition. Whether these influences began in the Spoon River area and spread to those regions is not known. Perhaps more important than precise determination of this sequence is the recognition that all of these decorative elements probably evolved from a common ancestor, Ramey Incised.

Pottery with definite Mill Creek (northwestern Iowa) influences is occasionally found in the Dickson Mounds area. Several such sherds have been recovered by surface collecting and one Chamberlain Incised Shoulder-like sherd (shell-tempered, however) was associated with No. 232 in the Dickson excavation. A fragmentary Forman Series-like jar (also shell-tempered) was recovered by Arthur and Ernest Dickson "in a firepit" approximately 350 yards east of the Dickson Mounds (Harn 1975b: Fig. 2, h), and several Chamberlain Incised sherds were recovered during recent excavations of the Eveland Site (Illinois State Museum collections).

The bone bracelets from the Dickson excavation, as well as a number of others found during recent excavations at Dickson (cf. Conrad 1972: Plate 16, a-c) are similar to those found on coeval sites of the Eastern Plains (cf. Fugle 1962: Fig. 11, r; Fig. 24, e-f; Fig. 35, m-n).

With possible influences from the northern Illinois, northwestern Iowa, and southeastern Minnesota areas appearing in the Central Illinois Valley, one is not so limited in searching for a people from which other influences could have arisen. Instead of viewing Cahokia as the point of origin of all artifactual and cultural change, it has become advantageous to search the regions of the Great Lakes and Prairie Peninsula for possible relationships.

Three other items of extraneous origin are evident in the Dickson excavation: *Busycon* spp. shell, chert, and possibly catlinite. Objects of marine shell — large bowls or dippers, pendants, and beads — were found at Dickson; and gorgets and masks of marine shell have also been found at Dickson and in other local Mississippian mounds (cf. Harn 1975 a). Marine shell seems to appear more commonly during the Mississippian Period than during all preceding periods combined. Burials in Middle Woodland mounds in the Spoon River area occasionally have large *Busycon* shells in association, but their main function appears to have been as bowls or dippers. The use of marine shell in any quantity by other pre-Mississippian groups is virtually absent. Due to the probable lack of well-established trade routes which connected the Central Illinois Valley to the Gulf region, marine shells were probably one of the more prized items of the earlier groups, their ownership somewhat restricted to the social elite. It is suspected that the network of Mississippian centers stretching from the Upper Mississippi Valley to the Gulf made marine shell more easily obtainable in late prehistory and resulted in a general deflation of its value.

Chert sources are the most easily traced of the extraneous items. One Ramey knife (Fig. 6, D209, with No. 123) was made of Mill Creek chert from Southern Illinois. This chert is associated primarily with hoes and large blades which were supplied in finished form to the Spoon River area. Other artifacts in the excavation are manufactured from cherts from at least three sources: Dongola chert from Southern Illinois, represented by a single lamellar flake knife; glacial and unidentified chert, used for approximately six percent of the chert artifacts; and Avon chert, accounting for about 92 percent of all chert present. The Avon chert outcroppings occur over the Burlington limestone in the Mississippian formations along Cedar Creek, a tributary of the Spoon River north of Avon, Illinois. This distinctive chert was relied on heavily by all prehistoric people in the Central Illinois Valley. Large quantities of cores, waste flakes, blanks, and completed and unfinished artifacts cover much of the terrace adjacent to the main quarry site.

The use of catlinite from the vicinity of Pipestone, Minnesota, is unique in the Dickson Mounds area. One pipe (Fig. 30, D48, with No. 35) was apparently manufactured from low-grade Minnesota pipestone, but it has since been stolen without the source material having been positively identified.

The ratio of one class of artifacts, hoes, to other artifact classes in the Dickson excavation is disproportionately high and probably does not accurately reflect local subsistence activities. Substantial differences apparently existed between subsistence patterns of the Spoon River area and the areas of larger populations such as

Cahokia. While similar ratios of some artifact classes exist between the two regions, wide differences exist between others. A comparison of the frequency of arrowpoints, knives, scrapers, and horticultural equipment from both areas supports this proposition.

It is evident that while great numbers of arrowpoints are commonly recovered on Mississippian sites in the Spoon River area, a paucity of similar artifacts is evident on Mississippian sites in the region of Cahokia. In an earlier survey of Mississippian sites in the American Bottom, arrowpoints were an occasional and sometimes rare find (Porter 1962:34-35, and Harn 1971a:37-38). The same was true of knives and scrapers.

Surface surveys of Mississippian sites in the Dickson Mounds area produced more than 2,000 lithic artifacts. Of this number, possibly only three were horticultural tools; most were arrowpoints, knives and scrapers. The ratio of hoe fragments to general chert debitage is equally low. Only three of the 2,873 pieces of chert debitage from the Larson Site were polished from use. Two samples collected on the Buckeye Bend Site produced 687 and 378 flakes. Only one chip with a minute polished area was recovered. These sites were chosen primarily because chert hoes and spades are known to have been found there.

In contrast, the situation in Southern Illinois is somewhat reversed. Highway salvage excavations at the Mitchell Site produced a large number of spades, hoes, and hoe fragments; and the percentage was high in comparison to the total of all other lithic artifacts cataloged (Porter 1960:5). These data were supported by the writer's survey of 23 other Mississippian sites in that area. During this survey, a relatively high ratio of horticultural implements and polished chert hoe fragments was also noted (Harn 1971a:37-38).

These proportional differences of artifact frequencies between the Central Illinois Valley and the American Bottom suggest two different economies that probably stemmed from differing cultural and environmental conditions. The rapid depletion of natural food resources by the heavy permanent population occupying Cahokia probably resulted in a certain dependence upon horticulture in that region. Since hunting and gathering would have become secondary, a lower ratio of hunting and processing equipment would be expected. The subsistence pattern in the Central Illinois Valley may have been based primarily on the exploitation of abundant game and foraging with secondary emphasis on horticulture. An annual planting-hunting-gathering cycle may have been established and a general trend toward Primary Forest Efficiency (Caldwell 1958) more noticeable. Supporting this position is the greater frequency of arrowpoints for hunting and knives and scrapers for processing opposed by the paucity of horticultural implements.

Burial activity at the Dickson Mounds Cemetery appears to have begun by A.D. 1000 and terminated by the middle of the fourteenth century A.D. The related habitation areas, Eveland and Myer/Dickson, were apparently occupied for relatively short periods of time, since superimposed structures and storage/refuse pits are not numerous and neither has an apparent occupational stratum. Other excavated Spoon River variant sites in the area also suggest occupations of less than 100 years (Bender et al. 1975:122-125). Indications are that a light-to-moderate population was usually contributing to the burial population, perhaps, in part, on a seasonal basis (Harn 1980).

Dickson Mounds may have been used fairly steadily for the greater part of four centuries, but each of the Late Woodland and Mississippian phases may have buried for relatively short intervals. It appears that small Late Woodland Sepo and/or Maples Mills populations were burying at Dickson by A.D. 1000, with Mississippian use of the cemetery not beginning until the appearance of the Eveland Phase sometime after A.D. 1050. The Eveland Phase dead were interred together with those of the Sepo and Maples Mills populations until Late Woodland acculturation to the Mississippian movement was complete sometime during the late twelfth century A.D. (Harn 1975b; n.d.). The appearance of the Larson Phase brought an increase in the burial population by A.D. 1250 which lasted for the greater part of the next century. It is doubtful that any burials were made at Dickson much after A.D. 1350, since no evidence of Oneota influence is present.

The end of burial activity at Dickson Mounds also seems to coincide with the decline of Cahokia and may well be related. While the decline may reflect religious-political change or such forced situations as warfare or a major climatic shift, the Mississippian expression simply may have become so diluted by the various host populations that it was no longer effective.

Another possibility is that there were large population declines resulting from disease. There is some question whether or not an adequate population, sufficiently distributed, existed to maintain a communicable disease. However, pestilence would have been far more devastating to large populations than war, domestic upheaval, or a climatic shift, and the large market-metropolitan center of Cahokia would have represented the ultimate nucleus from which disease could have developed and been spread. It may be significant that the last mounds to be used for burial at Dickson had unusually high proportions of mass graves and ironic that Cahokia, which had offered so much to the Spoon River variant, may have made its final contribution so engulfing and permanent that it extinguished much of the Mississippian fluorescence in the Central Illinois River Valley.

In searching for close cultural relatives of the Dickson Mounds people, one does not have to leave the Central Illinois Valley proper. Although it is chronologically later, pottery similar to that in the Dickson excavation is evidenced in the Illinois Valley from the vicinity of the mouth of the Sangamon River southward for some 30 miles. It has been proposed that Mississippian abandonment of the Dickson Mounds area took place before A.D. 1350, with the displaced population settling at either or both of the Mississippian towns of Lawrenz Gun Club or Walsh (Harn 1980). The subsequent abandonment of the Lawrenz Gun Club and Walsh Site areas appears to have been followed by major occupations of the Illinois Valley in the Crable Site area, midway between the Spoon and Sangamon rivers, and later in the Sleeth Site area 20 miles upstream along the Illinois.

The appearance of Oneota traditions at this time marked the beginning of the final Spoon River cultural transformation. Oneota appears to represent a population intrusion, arriving in classic form at the C.W. Cooper Site four miles upriver from Dickson Mounds during the late fourteenth century A.D. (Bender et al. 1975:124). It is quite possible that an Upper Mississippian or Oneota-like culture may have been in an emergent stage prior to A.D. 1400 in the Central Illinois Valley; but because of close sociopolitical affiliations with Cahokia, it was not as readily adopted as in the Western Prairie-

Eastern Plains and Great Lakes regions where there was no direct Mississippian influence to intervene. When the radiation of cultural influences from Cahokia began to decline and eventually wane sometime during the late fourteenth century A.D., the long grasp Cahokia had held over the Central Illinois River Valley apparently began to loosen. In this void, the Spoon River variant people appear to have gradually slipped from a Middle Mississippian-like culture and embraced Oneota traditions.

The Crable Site (Smith 1951) is a classic example of this adoption. Although apparently founded during the late Larson Phase, the site's greatest occupation was somewhat later in time. The majority of the available Spoon River materials at Crable (primarily ceramics) are slightly later than similar materials at Dickson, suggesting a late Larson to Crable Phase date for the former. A complete mixing of Spoon River tradition and classic Oneota elements was found in all areas of the site, and all of the excavated pottery types (excluding Maples Mills) "are apparently roughly contemporaneous, with no indication of a time difference" (Smith 1951:27).

Perhaps only three generations had passed since the last burials were made at Dickson Mounds before bearers of Oneota traditions arrived in the Illinois Valley and attracted the remnants of the Spoon River variant. In a few more generations Oneota was to be gone, and with it its new followers, leaving the Central Illinois River Valley in a cultural void.

REFERENCES CITED

Baker, Frank C.; James B. Griffin; Richard G. Morgan; Georg K. Neumann; and Jay L. B. Taylor
1941   Contributions to the Archaeology of the Illinois River Valley. *Transactions of the American Philosophical Society*, Vol. 32, Pt. 1, pp. 22-28.

Bender, Margaret M.; Reid A. Bryson; and David A. Baerreis
1975   University of Wisconsin Radiocarbon Dates XII. *Radiocarbon*, Vol. 17, No. 1.

Binford, Lewis R.
1962   Archaeological Investigations in the Carlyle Reservoir, Clinton County, Illinois. *Archaeological Salvage Report*, No. 17. Southern Illinois University Museum, Carbondale.

1966   Archaeology at Hatchery West, Carlyle, Illinois. *Archaeological Salvage Report*, No. 25. Southern Illinois University Museum, Carbondale.

Bowers, Alfred W.
1965   Hidatsa Social and Ceremonial Organization. *Bureau of American Ethnology Bulletin*, No. 194.

Brothwell, Don R.
1963   *Digging up Bones*. British Museum of Natural History, London.

Caldwell, Joseph R.
1958   Trend and Tradition in the Prehistory of the Eastern United States. *Illinois State Museum Scientific Papers*, Vol. X and *American Anthropological Association Memoir*, No. 88.

1967   New Discoveries at Dickson Mounds. *The Living Museum*, Vol. 29, No. 6, October. Illinois State Museum, Springfield.

Cantwell, Anne-Marie, and Alan D. Harn
n.d.   Untitled report in preparation concerning investigations at the Buckeye Bend Site (F^{V}1079) in Fulton County, Illinois.

Chapman, Florence H.
1962   Incidence of Arthritis in a Prehistoric Middle Mississippian Indian Population. *Proceedings of the Indiana Academy of Science*, Vol. 72, pp. 59-62.

Cole, Fay-Cooper, and Thorne Deuel
1937   *Rediscovering Illinois*. University of Chicago Press, Chicago.

Conrad, Lawrence A.
1972   1966 Excavation at the Dickson Mounds: A Sepo-Spoon River Burial Mound in the Central Illinois Valley. Unpublished Masters thesis on file at the University of Wisconsin.

n.d.,a   The Berry Site: A Multicomponent Site in the Central Illinois River Valley. Manuscript in preparation.

n.d.,b   The Spoon River Culture in the Central Illinois River Valley. Unpublished manuscript in possession of the author.

Conrad, Lawrence A., and Alan D. Harn
1972   The Spoon River Culture in the Central Illinois River Valley. Unpublished manuscript on file at the Dickson Mounds Museum, Lewistown, Illinois.

Crane, H. R., and James B. Griffin
1960   University of Michigan Radiocarbon Dates V. *American Journal of Science Radiocarbon Supplement*, Vol. 2, pp. 31-48.

Dickson, Don F.
n.d.   *Dicksons Mound Builders Tomb*. Guidebooklet written in the early 1930's.

Emmons, Merrill; Patrick J. Munson; and Joseph R. Caldwell
1960   A Prehistoric House from Fulton County, Illinois. *The Living Museum*, Vol. 22, No. 5, pp. 516-517. Illinois State Museum, Springfield.

Fowler, Melvin L.
1955   Ware Groupings and Decorations of Woodland Ceramics in Illinois. *American Antiquity*, Vol. 20, No. 3, pp. 213-225.

1962   American Bottoms Archaeology, July 1, 1961-June 30, 1962. *Illinois Archaeological Survey*, *First Annual Report*. University of Illinois, Urbana.

Fugle, Eugene
1962   Mill Creek Culture and Technology. *Journal of the Iowa Archaeological Society*, Vol. 11, No. 4 (edited by Marshall McKusick).

Green, William
1977   Final Report of Littleton Field Archaeological Survey, Schuyler County, Illinois. Upper Mississippi Valley Archaeological Research Foundation, *Reports on Archaeology* No. 1.

Griffin, James B.
1949   The Cahokia Ceramic Complexes. *Proceedings of the 5th Plains Conference*, edited by John L. Champe. University of Nebraska Laboratory of Anthropology, Notebook No. 1, pp. 44-57.

Griffin, James B., and Dan F. Morse
1961   The Short-Nosed God from the Emmons Site, Illinois. *American Antiquity*, Vol. 26, No. 4, pp. 560-563.

Hall, Robert L.
1962   *The Archeology of Caracjou Point, with an Interpretation of the Development of Oneota Culture in Wisconsin*, 2 vols. University of Wisconsin Press, Madison.

Harn, Alan D.
1964   Strip Mining and Archaeology in Fulton County,
        Illinois. Paper presented to the Committee for the
        Preservation of Archaeological and Historical
        Sites of the Illinois State Academy of Science.

1966   A Surface Survey and Salvage of the Larson Site
        in Fulton County, Illinois. Unpublished
        manuscript on file at the Dickson Mounds
        Museum, Lewistown, Illinois.

1967   Dickson Mounds: An Evaluation of the Amateur
        in Illinois Archaeology. *Earth Science*, Vol. 20, No.
        4, pp. 152-157.

1971a   An Archaeological Survey of the American Bot-
        toms in Madison and St. Clair Counties, Illinois.
        In Archaeological Surveys of the American Bot-
        toms and Adjacent Bluffs, Illinois. *Illinois State
        Museum Reports of Investigations* No. 21. Springfield.

1971b   The Prehistory of Dickson Mounds: A Pre-
        liminary Report. *Dickson Mounds Museum An-
        thropological Studies* No. 1. Illinois State Museum,
        Springfield.

1975a   Another Long-Nosed God Mask from Fulton
        County, Illinois. *The Wisconsin Archeologist*, Vol.
        56, No. 1, pp. 2-8.

1975b   Cahokia and the Mississippian Emergence in the
        Spoon River Area of Illinois. *Transactions of the Il-
        linois State Academy of Science*, Vol. 68, No. 4, pp.
        414-434.

1980.   Variation in Mississippian Settlement Pattern:
        The Larson Community in the Central Illinois
        River Valley. *In* Mississippian Site Archaeology
        in Illinois: II. *Illinois Archaeological Survey Bulletin*
        No. 11. Urbana.

n.d.   The Archaeology of Dickson Mounds. *In* Dickson
        Mounds: Cultural Change and Demographic
        Variation in the Life of a Late Woodland-Middle
        Mississippian Cemetery (edited by Alan D. Harn
        and George J. Armelagos). Mansucript on file at
        the Dickson Mounds Museum, Lewistown.

History of Fulton County, Illinois.
1879   Chapter XI. Charles C. Chapman and Co.,
        Peoria.

Hooton, Earnest A.
1930   *Indians of Pecos Pueblo, A Study of Their Skeletal Re-
        mains*. Yale University Press, New Haven.

Knaggs, R. Lawford
1926   *Diseases of the Bone*. William Wood and Co., New
        York.

McDonald, S. E.
1950   The Crable Site, Fulton County, Illinois. *Journal
        of the Illinois State Archaeological Society*, Vol. 7, No.
        4, pp. 16-18.

Moorehead, Warren K.
1930   Cultural Affinities and Differences in Illinois Ar-
        chaeology. *Transactions of the Illinois State Academy of
        Science*, Vol. XXII. Springfield.

Morse, Dan F.
1960   The Southern Cult: The Crable Site. *Central States
        Archaeological Journal*, Vol. 7, No. 4, pp. 124-135.

1969   The Crable Site. *In* Ancient Disease in the
        Midwest. *Illinois State Museum Reports of Investiga-
        tions*, No. 15, Appendix 2, pp. 63-68. Springfield.

Morse, Dan F.; Phyllis Morse; and Merrill Emmons
1961   The Southern Cult: The Emmons Site. *Central
        States Archaeological Journal*, Vol. 8, No. 4, pp.
        124-140.

Morse, Dan; George Schoenbeck; and Dan F. Morse
1953   Fiedler Site. *Journal of the Illinois State Archaeological
        Society*, Vol. 3, No. 2.

Munson, Patrick J., and Alan D. Harn
1966   Surface Collections from Three Sites in the Cen-
        tral Illinois River Valley. *The Wisconsin Ar-
        cheologist*, Vol. 47, No. 3, pp. 150-168.

Porter, James W.
1960   Report of Phase 3 Archaeological Salvage Excava-
        tion of a Portion of the Mitchell Site, 20B2-3. *Ar-
        chaeological Salvage Report*, No. 5. Southern Illinois
        University Museum, Carbondale.

1962   American Bottoms Archaeology, July 1,
        1961-June 30, 1962. *Illinois Archaeological Survey,
        First Annual Report*. Edited by Melvin L. Fowler.
        University of Illinois, Urbana.

1964   Thin Section Descriptions of Some Shell
        Tempered Prehistoric Ceramics from the
        American Bottoms. *Research Report*, No. 7.
        Southern Illinois University Museum, Carbon-
        dale.

Sauer, Jonathan D.
1950   The Grain Amaranths: A Survey of their History
        and Classification. *Missouri Botanical Garden Annals*,
        Vol. 37, pp. 561-632.

Savage, T. E.
1921   Geology and Mineral Resources of the Avon and
        Canton Quadrangles. *Illinois State Geological Survey
        Bulletin*, No. 38 (Extract). Urbana.

Simpson, A. M.
1952   The Kingston Village Site. *Journal of the Illinois Ar-
        chaeological Society*, Vol. 2, No. 1, pp. 63-79.

Smith, Hale G.
1951   The Crable Site, Fulton County, Illinois. *Universi-
        ty of Michigan Anthropological Papers*, No. 7.
        Museum of Anthropology, Ann Arbor.

Snyder, John Francis
    1908   The Brown County Ossuary. *Journal of the Illinois State Historical Society*, Vol. 1, Nos. 2-3, pp. 33-43.

Stephens, Jeanette E.
    1976   Mississippian Settlement Relocation at the Orendorf Site. Paper presented at the 21st Annual Meeting of the Midwest Archaeological Conference in Minneapolis, Minnesota, October 20-22, 1976. (Mimeographed)

Stewart, T. D., and P. F. Titterington
    1944   Filed Indian Teeth from Illinois. *Journal of the Washington Academy of Science*, Vol. 34, No. 10.

Thomas, Cyrus
    1894   Report on Mound Explorations of the Bureau of Ethnology. *Bureau of American Ethnology*, 12th Annual Report, pp. 117-120.

Wanless, Harold R.
    1957   Geology and Mineral Resources of the Beardstown, Glasford, Havana, and Vermont Quadrangles, Illinois. *Illinois State Geological Survey Bulletin*, No. 82. Urbana.

White, W. A.
    1962   Refractory Clay Resources of Illinois. *Illinois State Geological Survey Industrial Mineral Notes*, No. 16. Urbana.

Winters, Howard D.
    1969   The Riverton Culture. *Illinois State Museum Reports of Investigations*, No. 13. Springfield; Illinois Archaeological Survey, *Monograph* No. 1, Urbana.

Wittry, Warren L.
    1964   An American Woodhenge. *Cranbrook Institute of Science Newsletter*, Vol. 33, No. 9. Bloomfield Hills, Michigan.

Wray, Donald E.
    1952   Archaeology of the Illinois Valley: 1950. In *Archaeology of the Eastern United States*. Edited by James B. Griffin. University of Chicago Press, Chicago.

    n.d.,a   The Kingston Lake Sequence. Unpublished manuscript on file at the Illinois State Museum, Springfield.

    n.d.,b   The Shyrock Site — Fulton County, Illinois. Unpublished manuscript on file at the Illinois State Museum, Springfield.

Wray, Donald E., and Richard S. MacNeish
    n.d.   The Weaver Site: Twenty Centuries of Illinois Prehistory. Unpublished manuscript on file at the Illinois State Museum, Springfield.

Young, Philip D.
    1960   The Frederick Site — Sc-11. *Illinois Archaeological Survey Bulletin* No. 2, pp. 71-79.

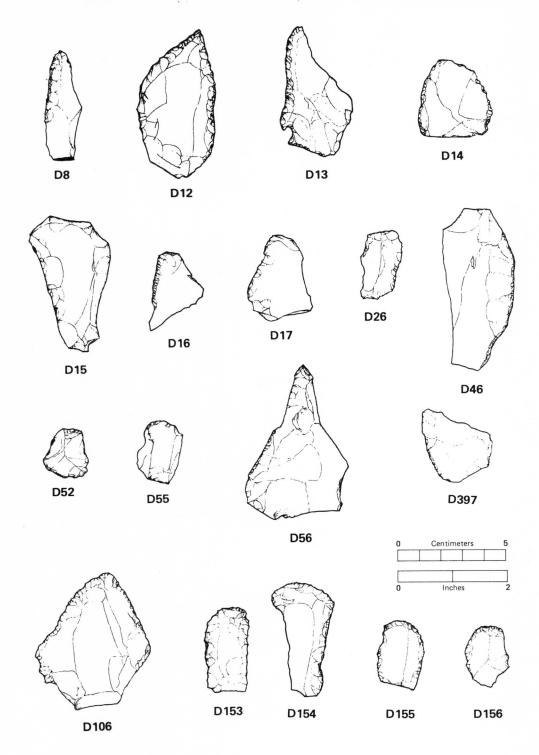

Figure 3. General utility tools: Chert scrapers.

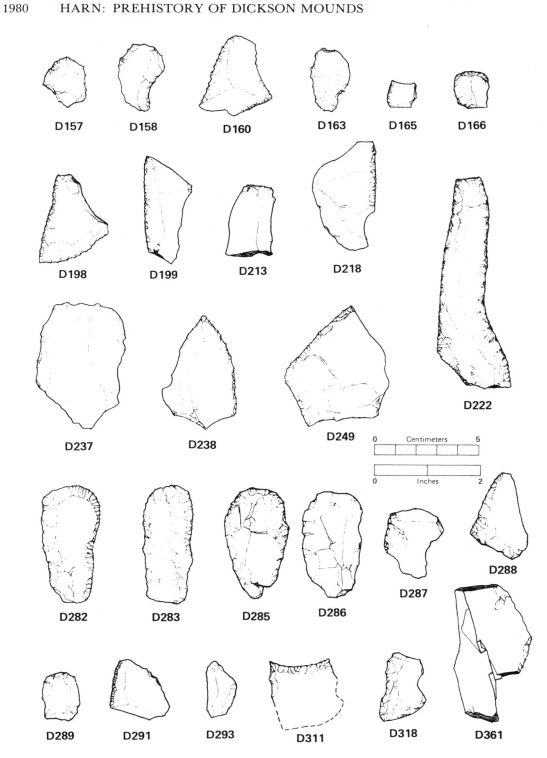

Figure 4. General utility tools: Chert scrapers.

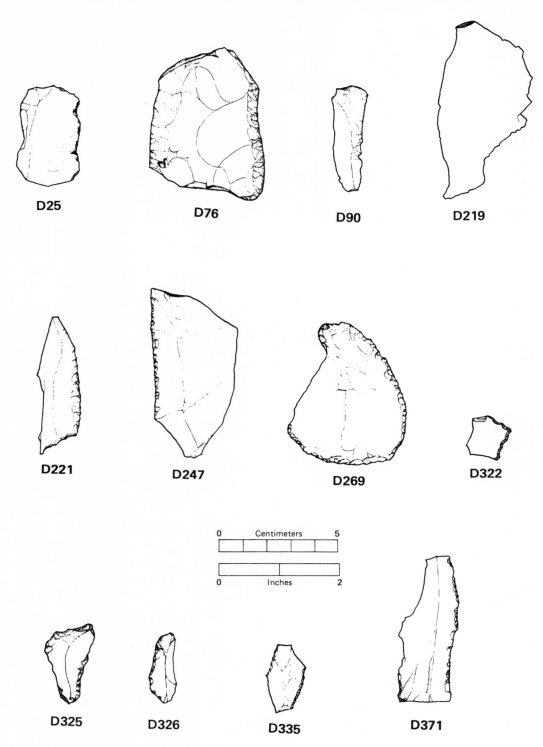

Figure 5. General utility tools: Flake blades.

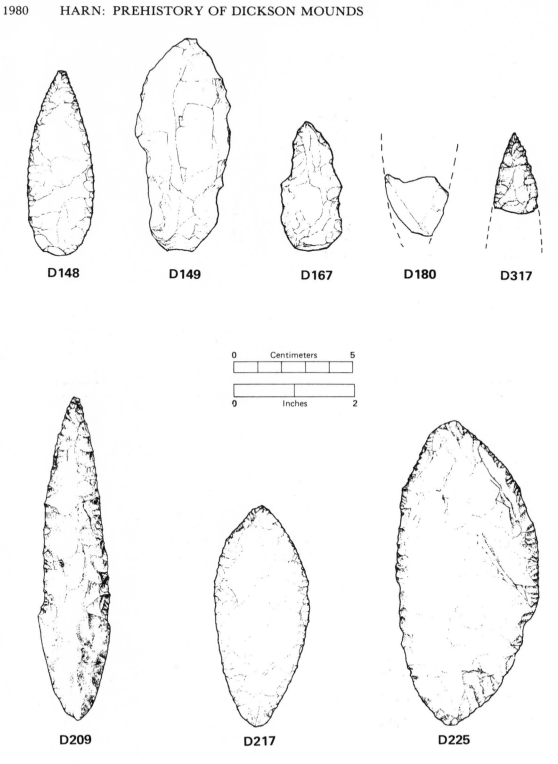

Figure 6. General utility tools: Knives.

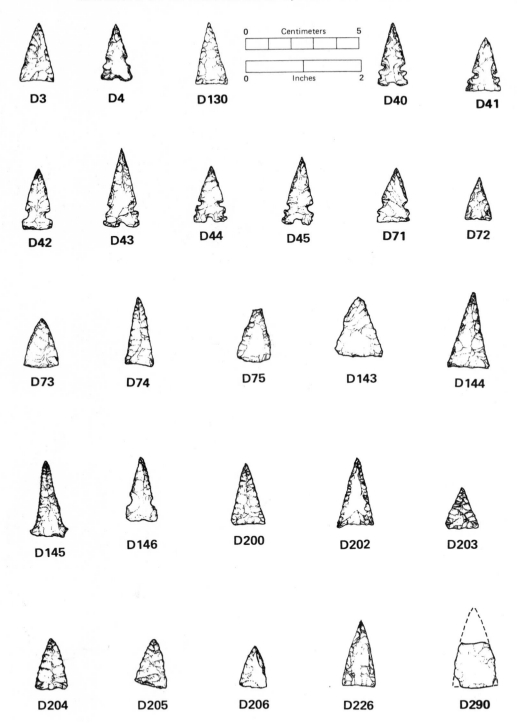

Figure 7. Weapons: Arrowpoints.

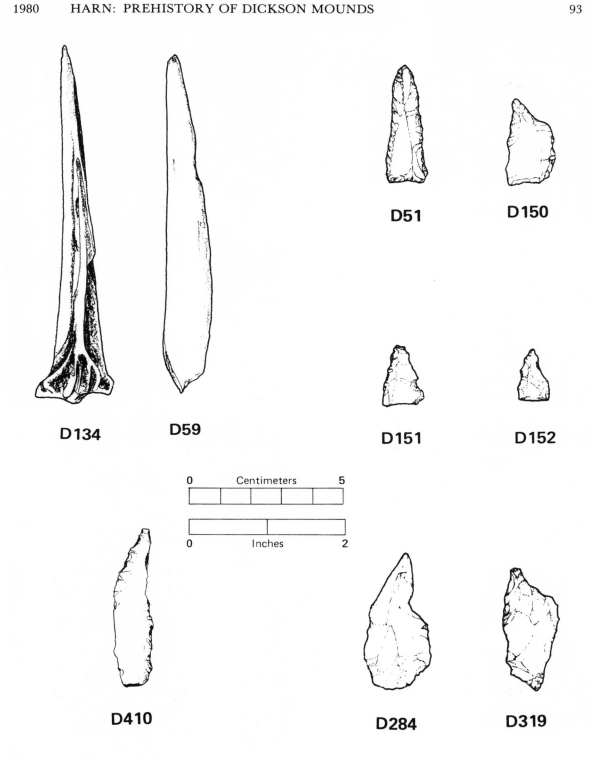

Figure 8. Fabricating and processing tools: Bone awl, bone weaving tool, and chert drills.

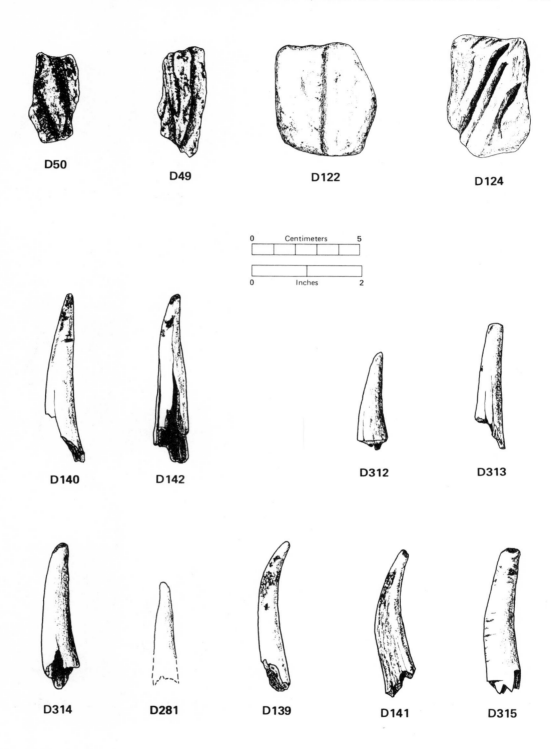

Figure 9. Fabricating and processing tools: Sandstone abraders and antler flakers.

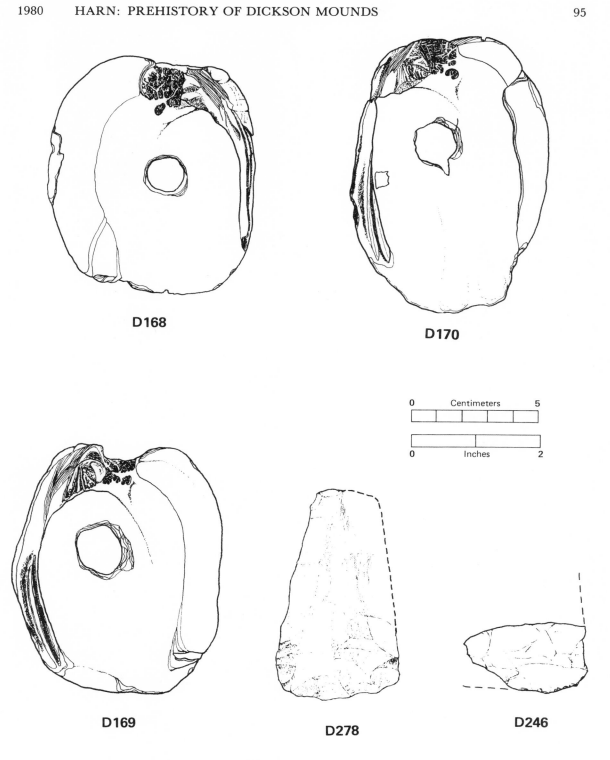

Figure 10. Digging or agricultural tools: Shell and chert hoes.

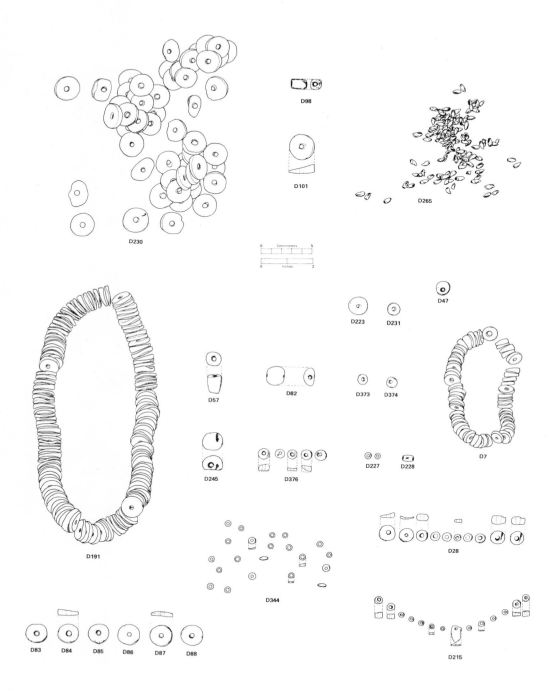

Figure 11. Ornaments: Necklaces, bracelets, and single beads.

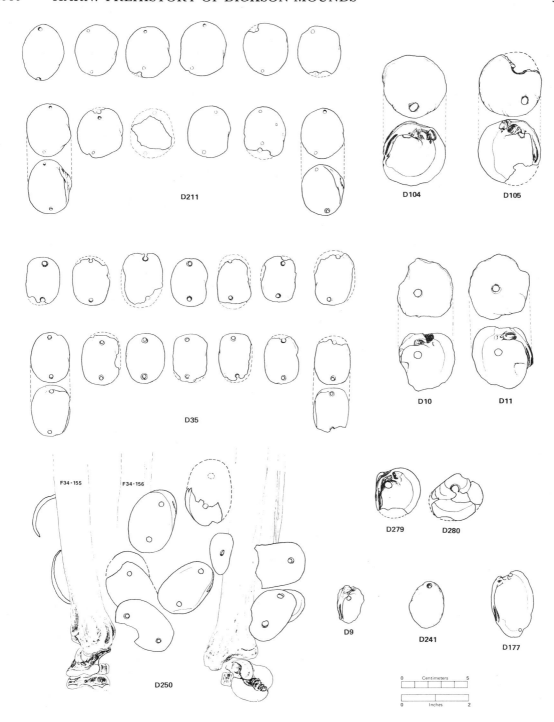

Figure 12. Ornaments: Mussel-shell ankle rattles, pendants, and arm rattles or clackers.

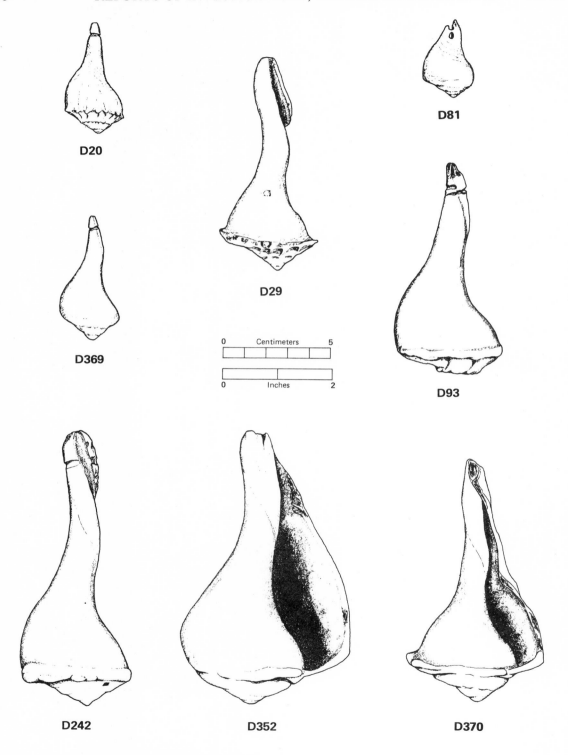

Figure 13. Ornaments: Marine-shell pendants.

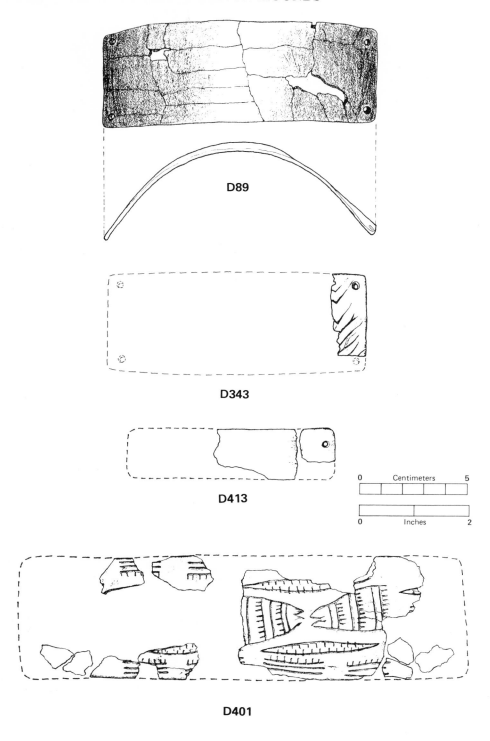

Figure 14. Ornaments: Bone bracelets.

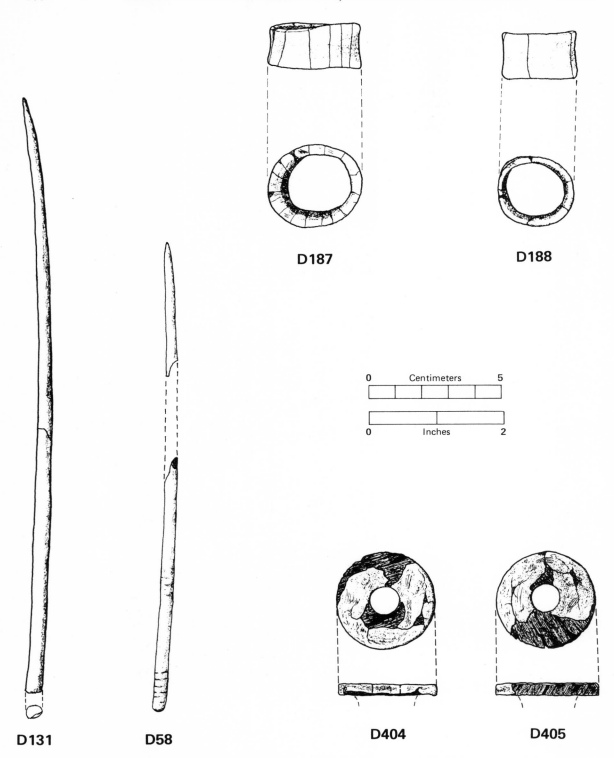

Figure 15. Ornaments: Bone hairpins, antler rings, and copper-covered wood ornaments.

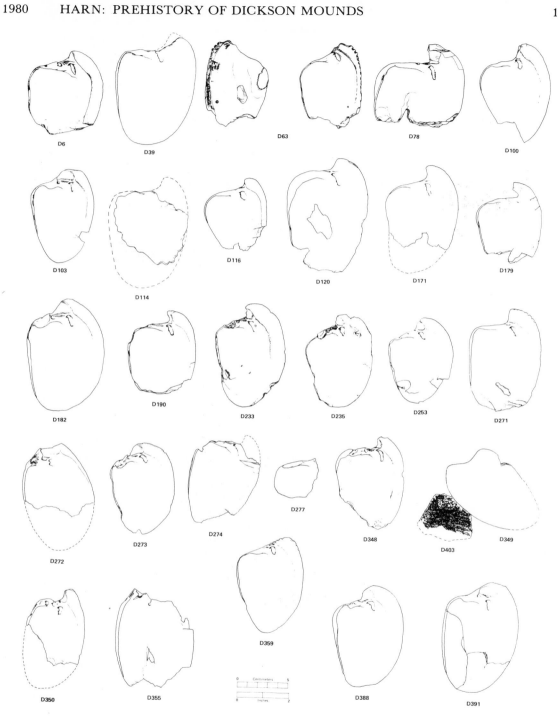

Figure 16. Domestic: Mussel-shell spoons.

Figure 17. Jars associated with Burials 1, 2, and 7.

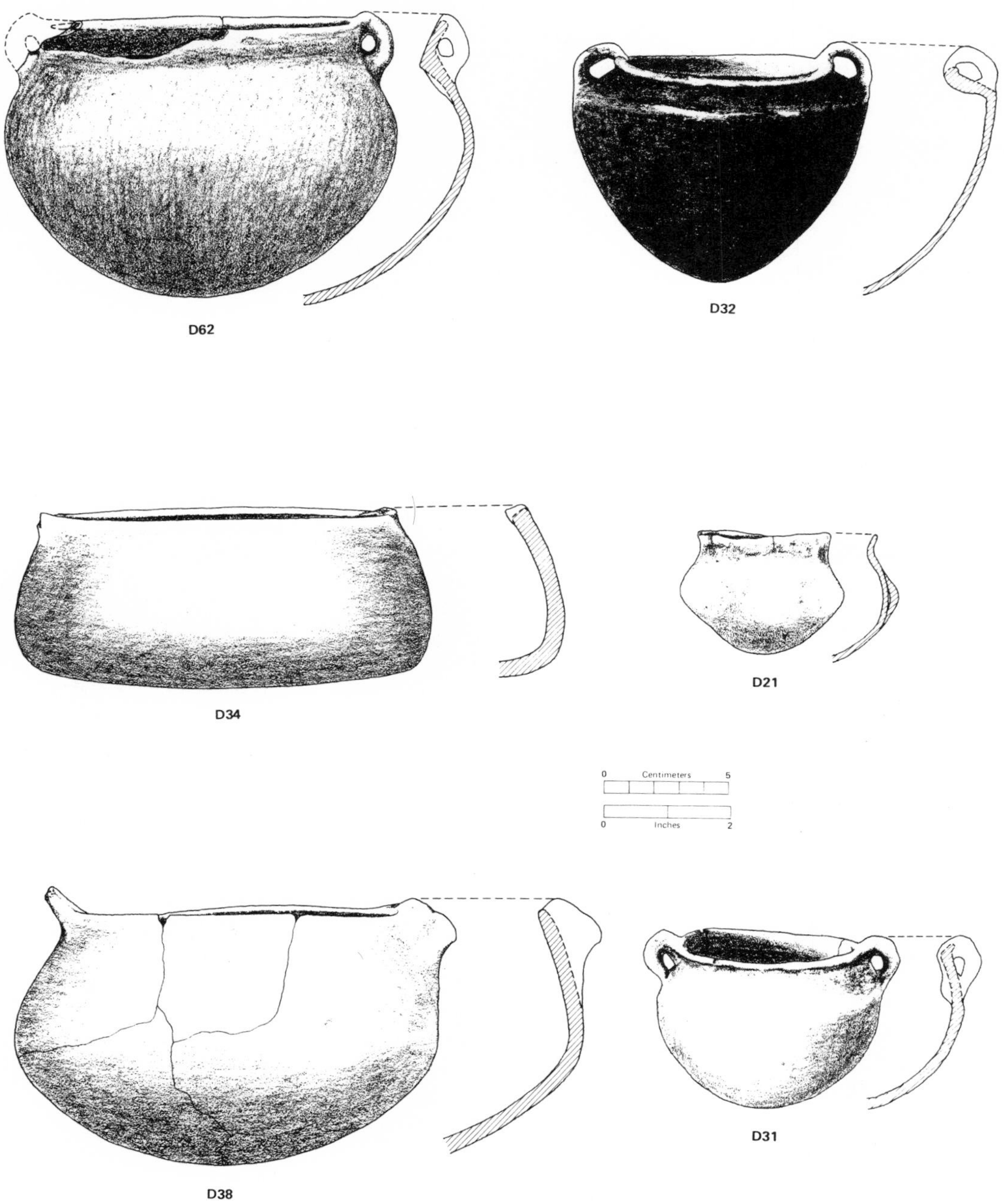

Figure 18. Jars and effigy bowls associated with Burials 38, 19, 21, 14, 31, and 17.

Figure 19. Jars, Spoon River Beaker, and shallow bowl associated with Burials 9, 100, 14, 47, 74, and 73.

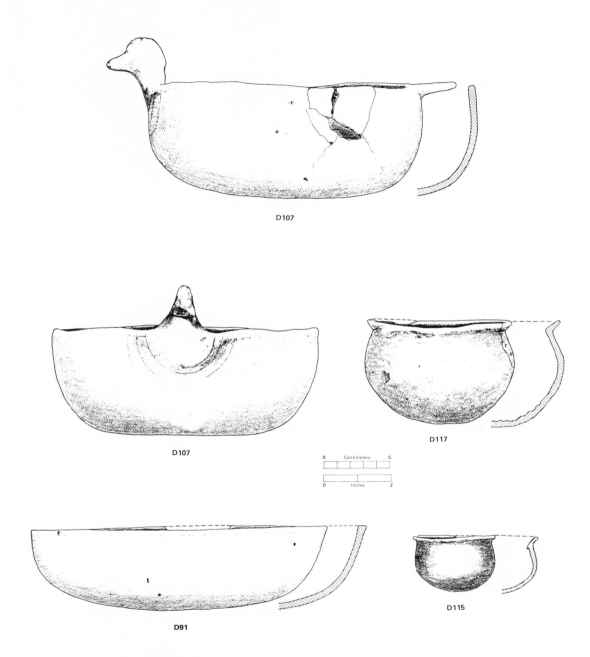

Figure 20. Effigy bowl, shallow bowl, and jars associated with Burials 79, 96, 54, and 87.

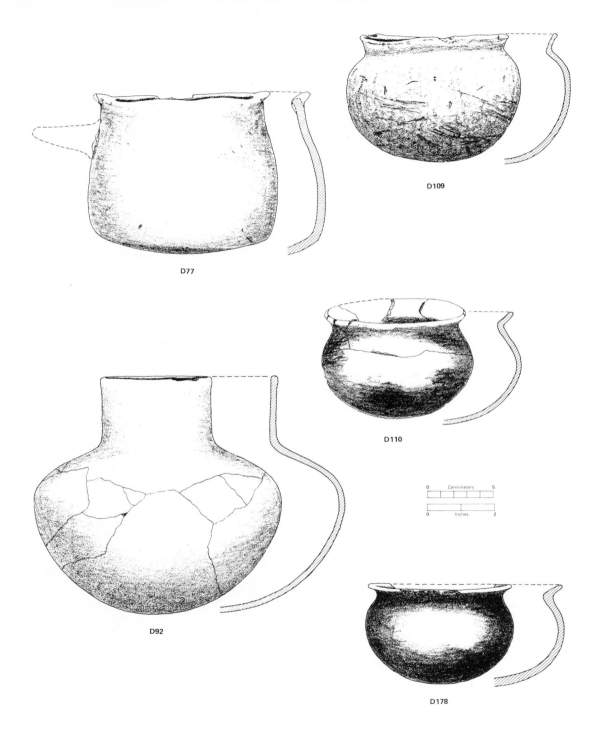

Figure 21. Water bottle, beaker, and jars associated with Burials 55, 85, 45, 86, and 88.

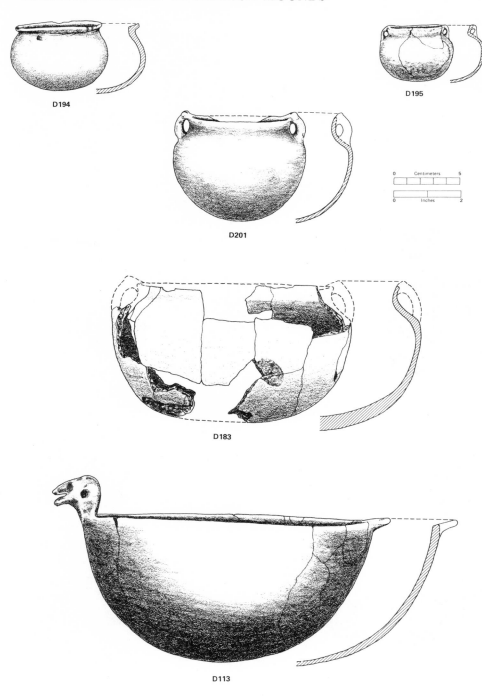

Figure 22. Effigy bowl and jars associated with Burials 105, 103, 166, 89, and 118.

Figure 23. Bowls, beakers, and jars associated with Burials 99, 98, 90, 140, 81, 140, and 127.

Figure 24. Jars, Dickson Trailed jar, and Spoon River Beaker associated with Burials 120, 128, 123, 182, 119, and 161.

Figure 25. Jars associated with Burials 94, 154, 148, 147, and 152.

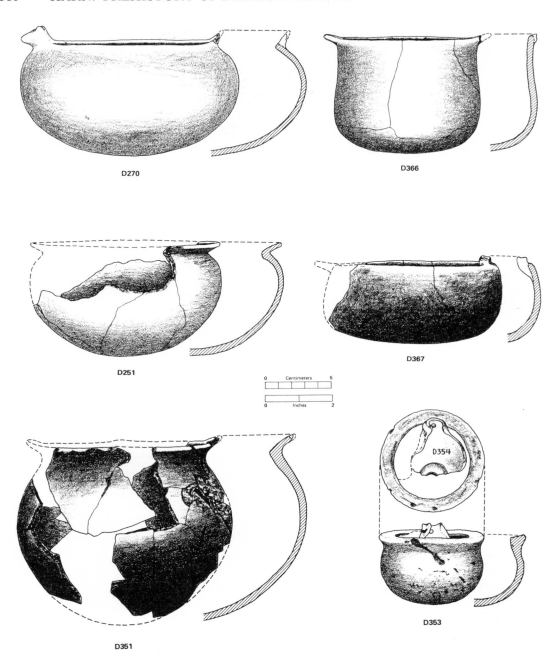

Figure 26. Effigy bowls, beaker, and jars associated with Burials 168, 206, 156, 67, 190, and 232.

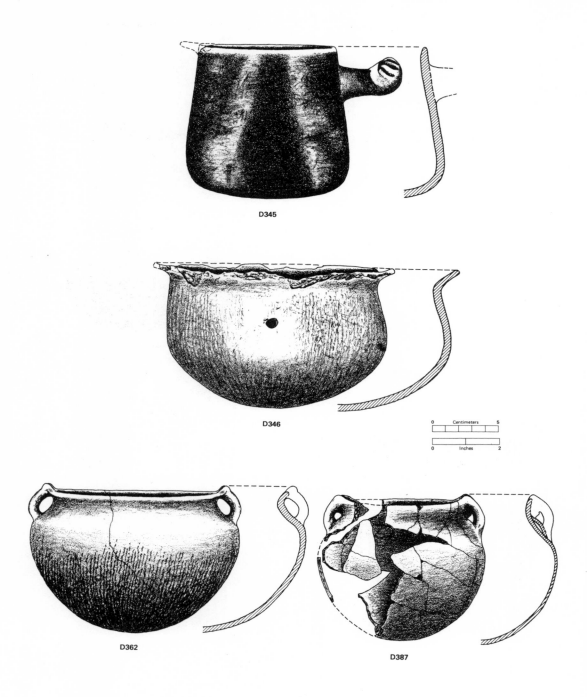

Figure 27. Beaker and jars associated with Burials 185, 195, and 223.

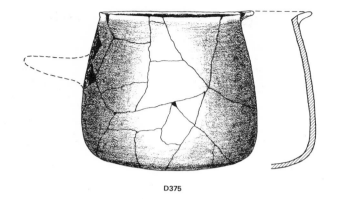

Figure 28. Beakers and jar associated with Burials 214 and 195.

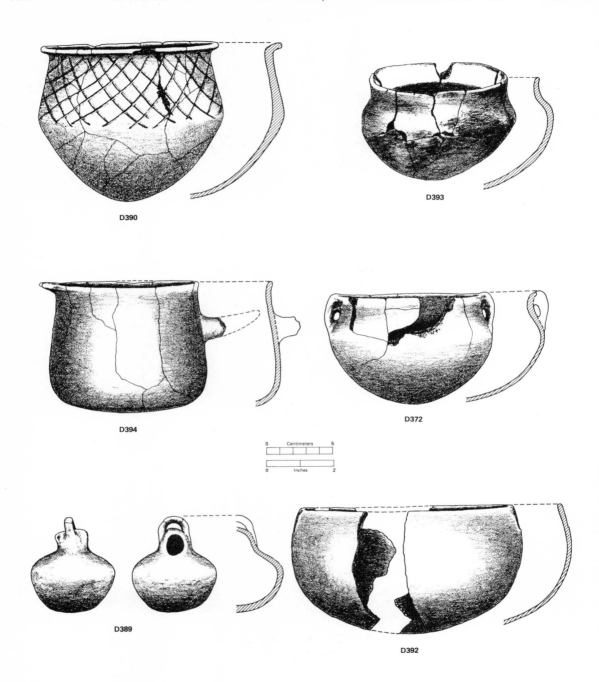

Figure 29. Jars, beaker, hooded water bottle and bowl associated with Burials 227, 230, 88, 211, 192, and 227.

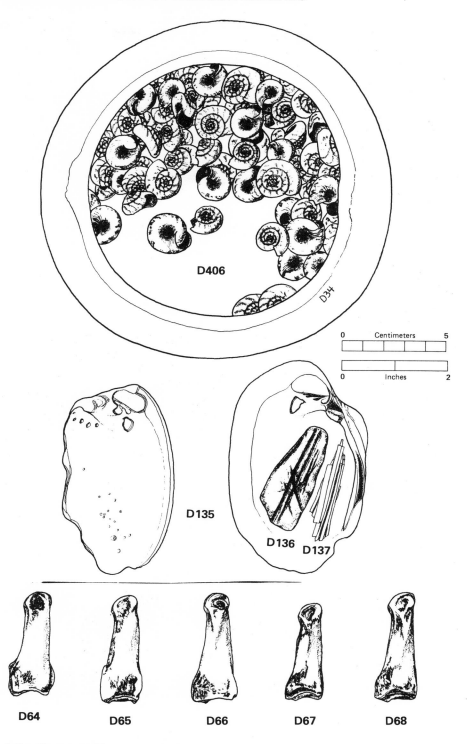

Figure 32. Miscellaneous: Terrestrial snail shells, "sewing" or scarification kit, and unaltered deer phalanges.

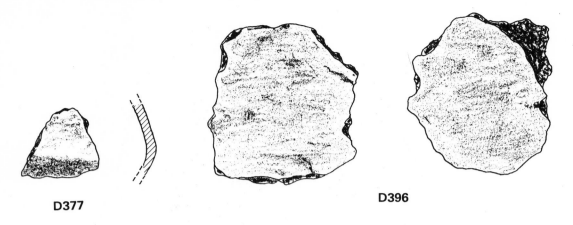

D377   D396

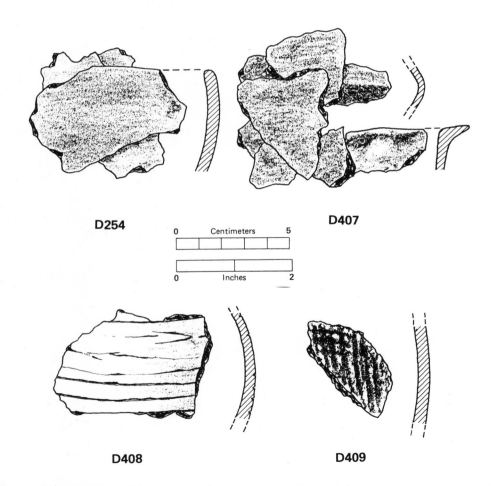

D254   D407

Figure 33. Pottery sherds associated with Burials 221, 101, 161, and 191.

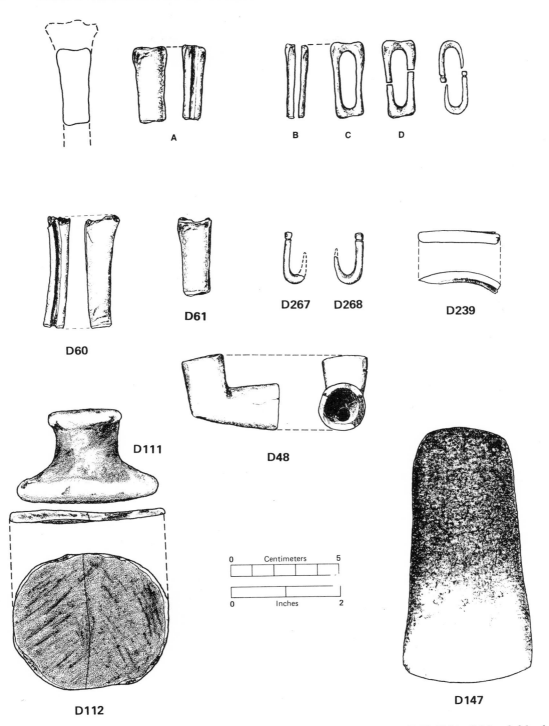

Figure 30. Miscellaneous: *Fishing*: A-D, method of fishhook manufacture; D60-D61, fishhook blanks; D267-D268, bone fishhooks. *Woodworking*: Beaver incisor chisel(?); celt. *Ceremonial*: Stone pipe. *Domestic*: Potter's trowel and spatula(?).

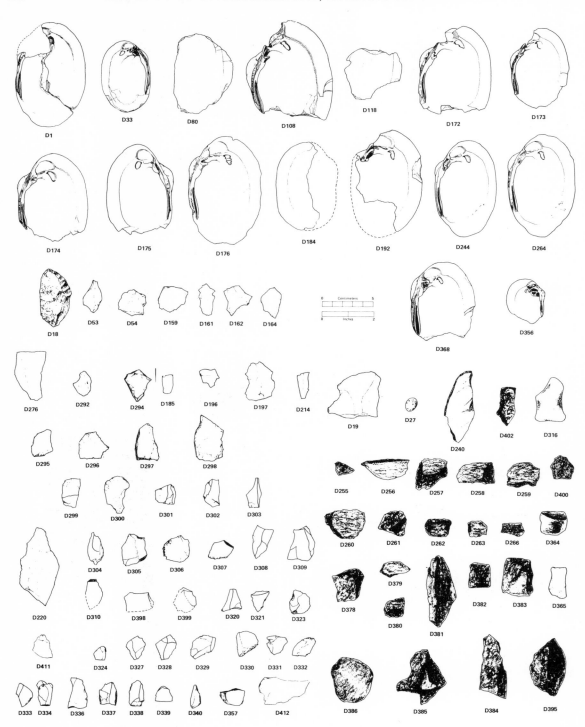

Figure 31. Miscellaneous: Unaltered valves of common mussel shell (some may be spoons); broken rock; and unretouched chert flakes.

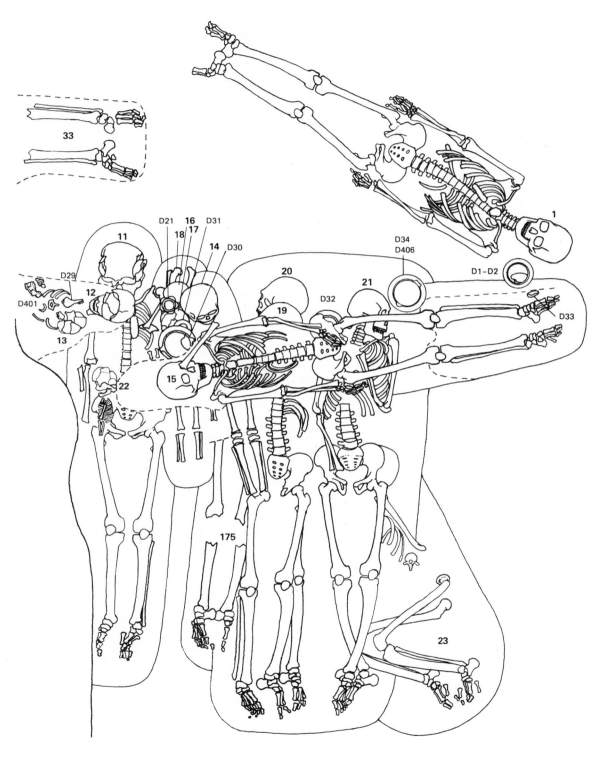

Figure 34.

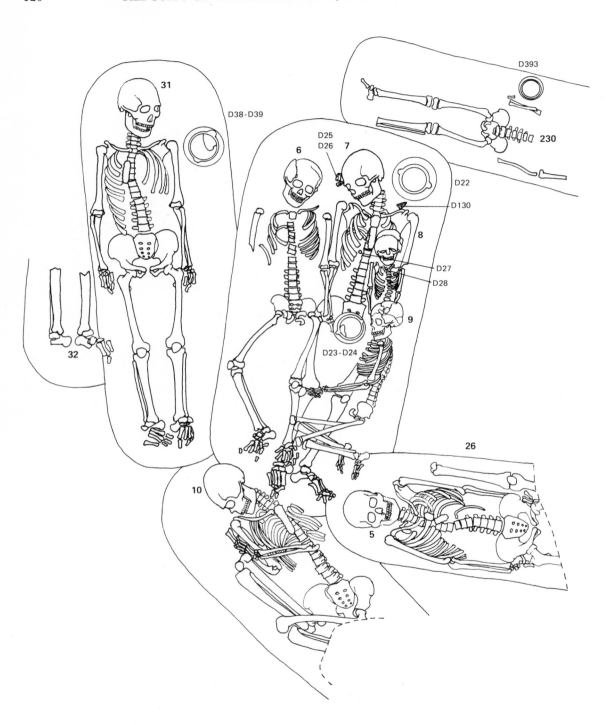

Figure

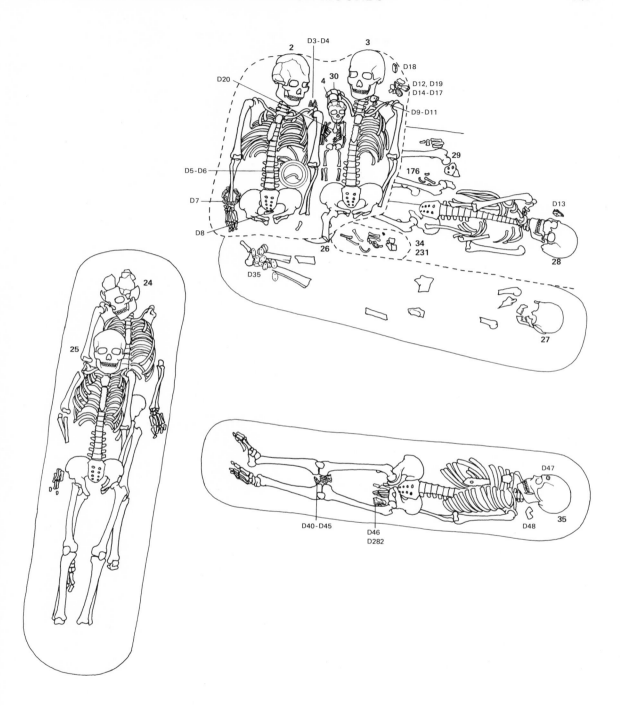

Figure 36.

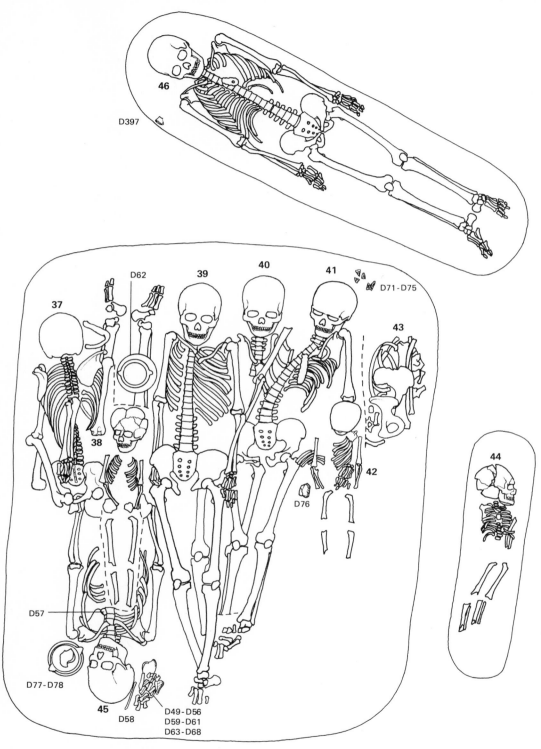

Figure 37.

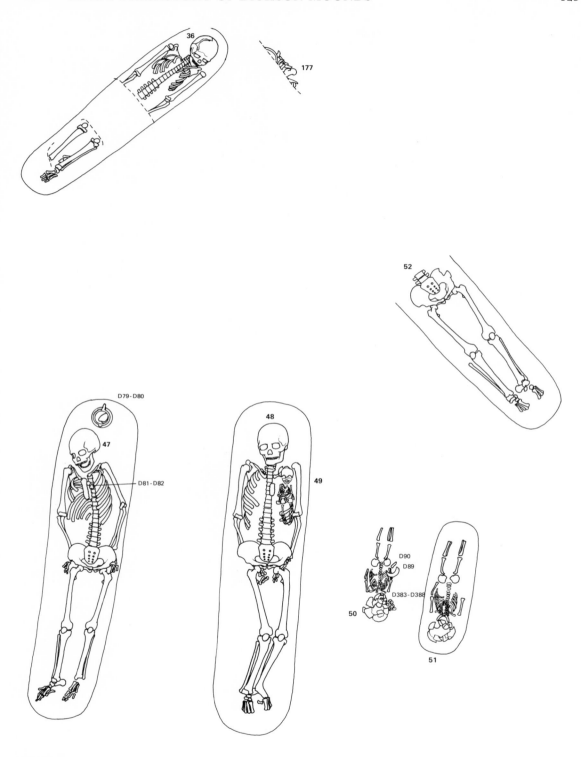

Figure 38.

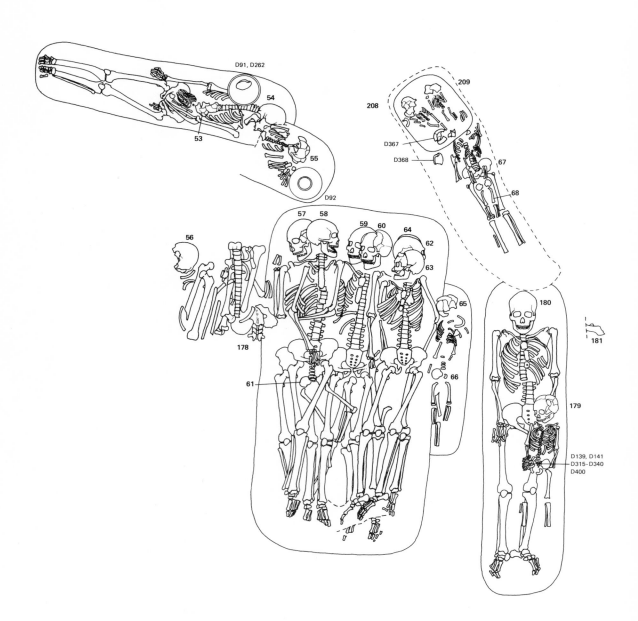

Figure 39.

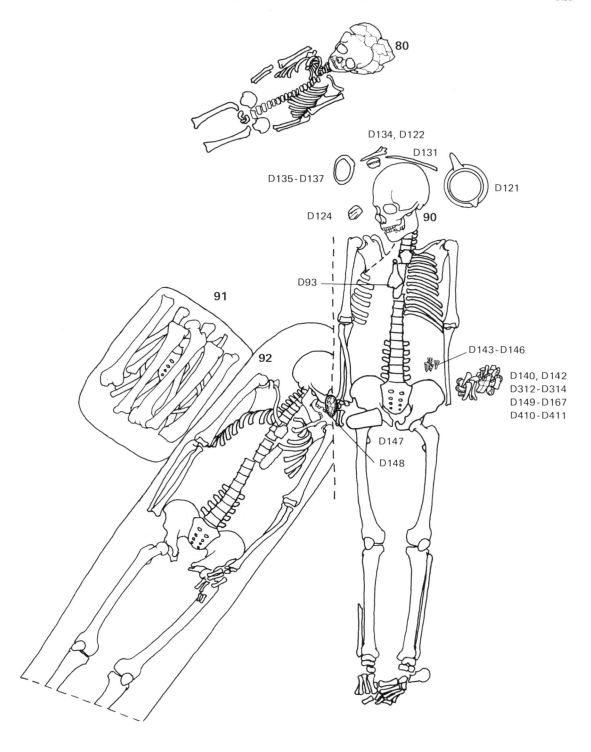

Figure 40.

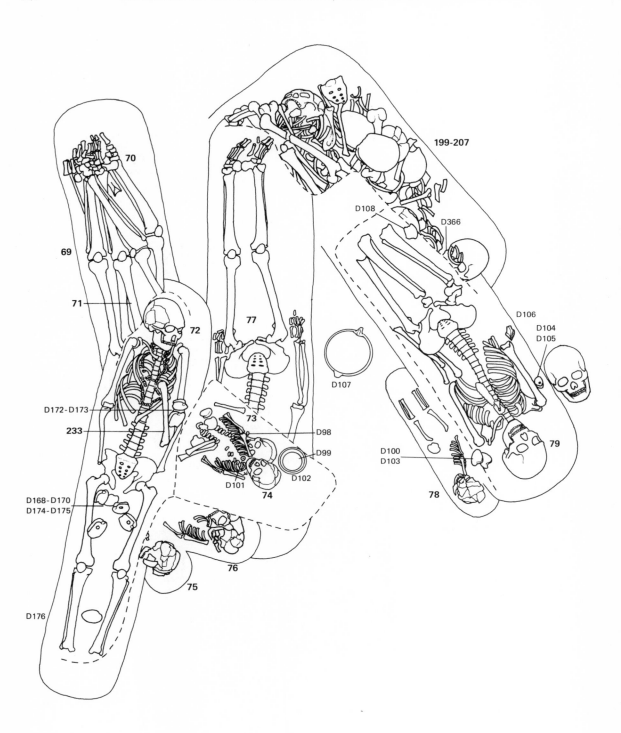

Figure 41.

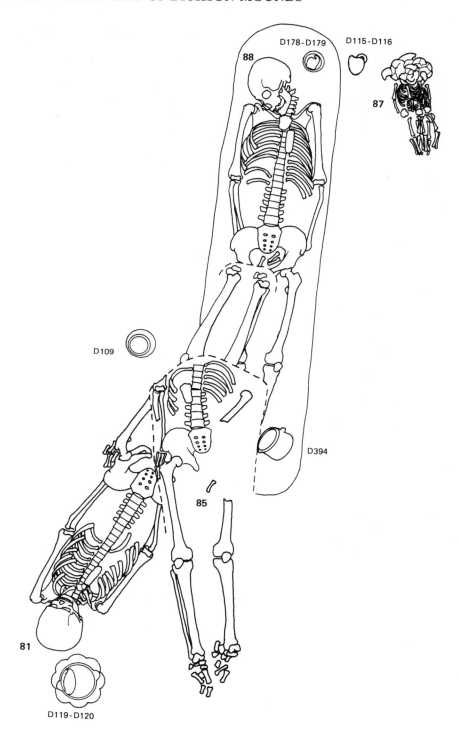

Figure 42.

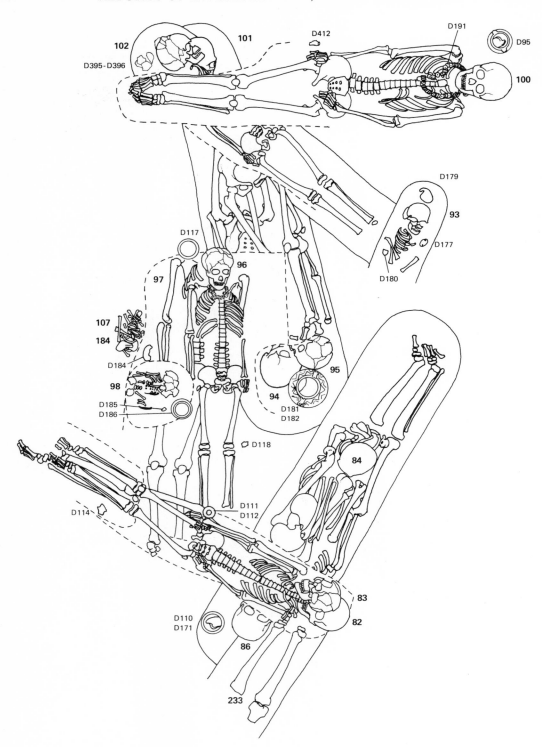

Figure 43.

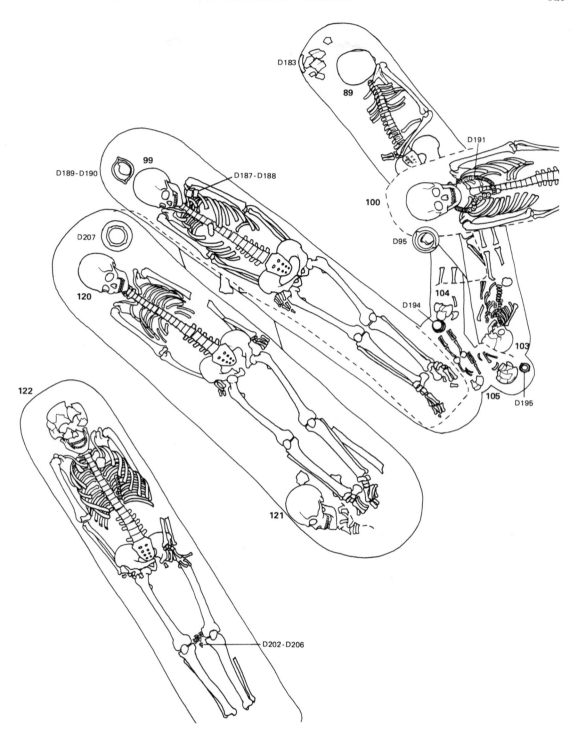

Figure 44.

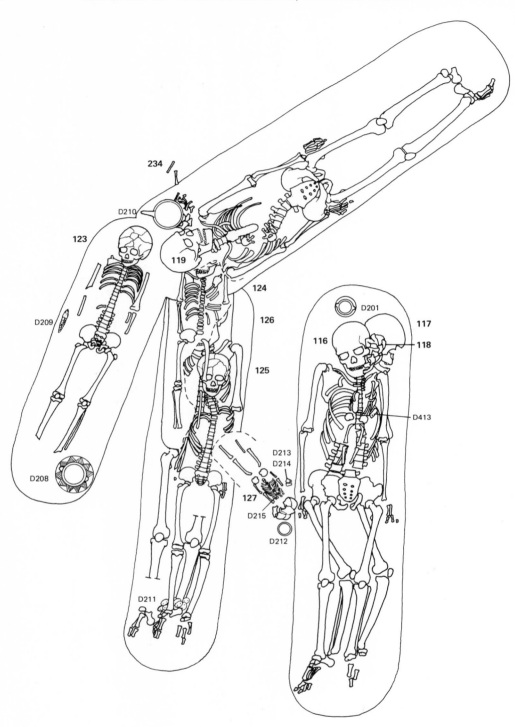

Figure 45.

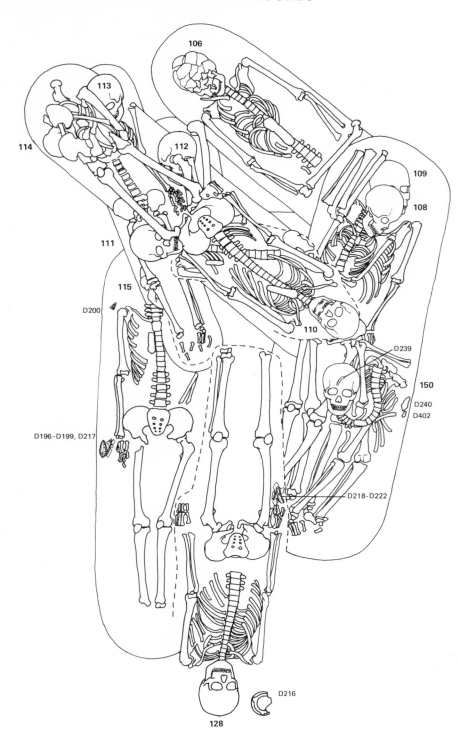

Figure 46.

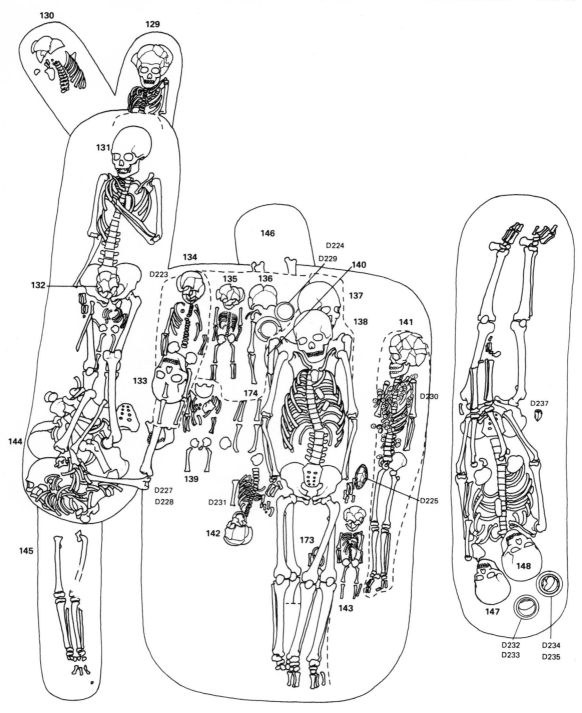

Figure 47.

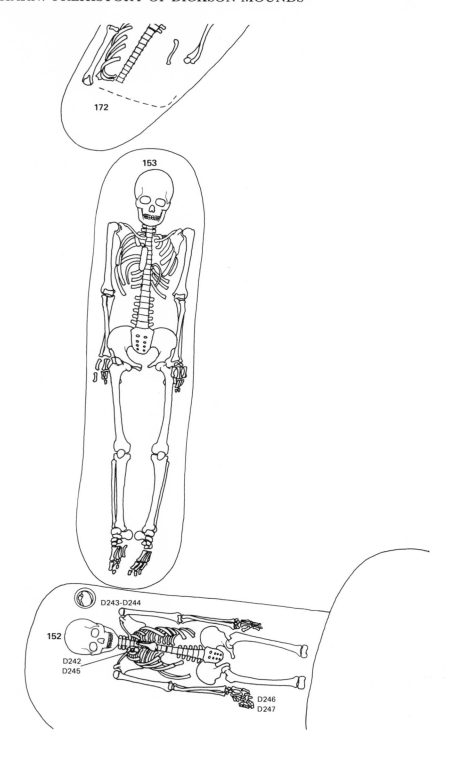

Figure 48.

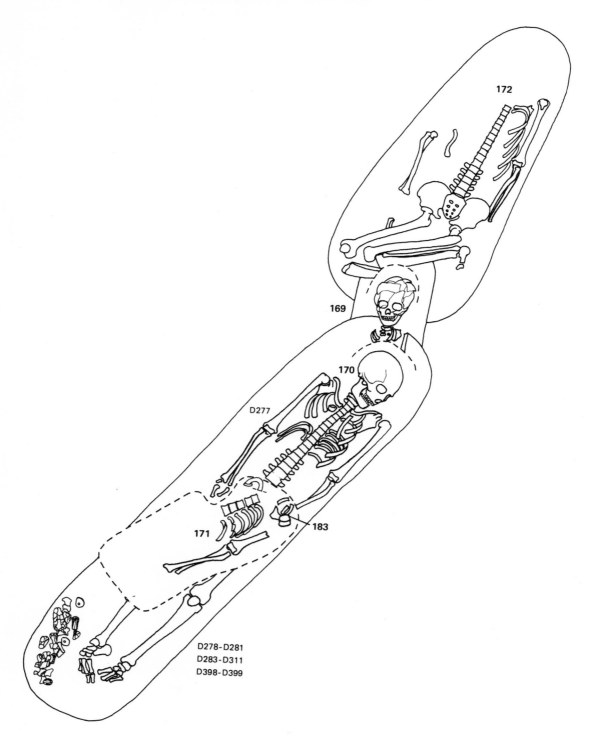

Figure 49.

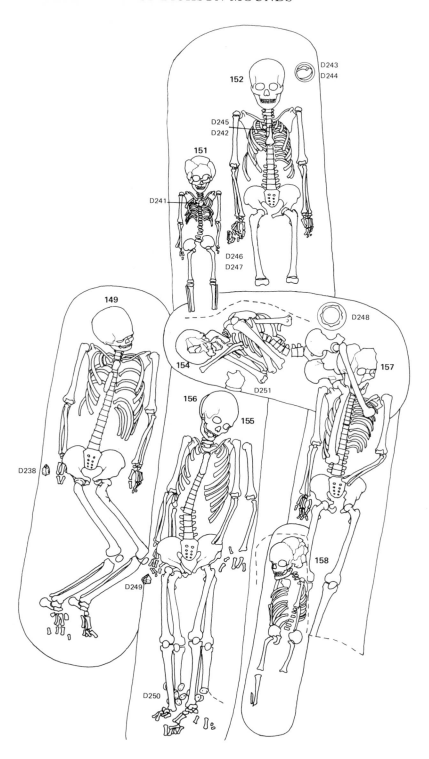

Figure 50.

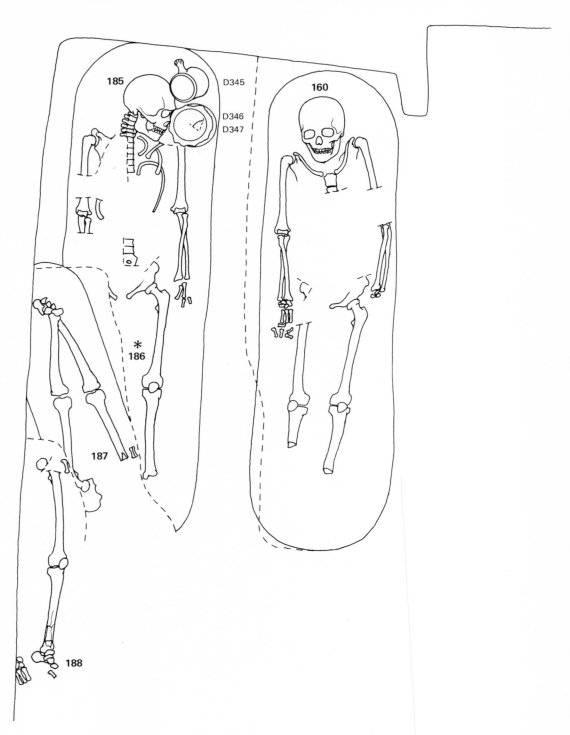

Figure 51.

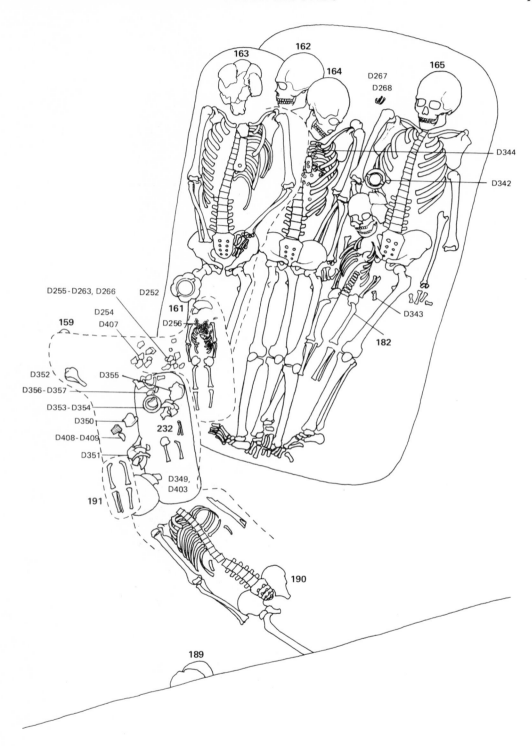

Figure 52.

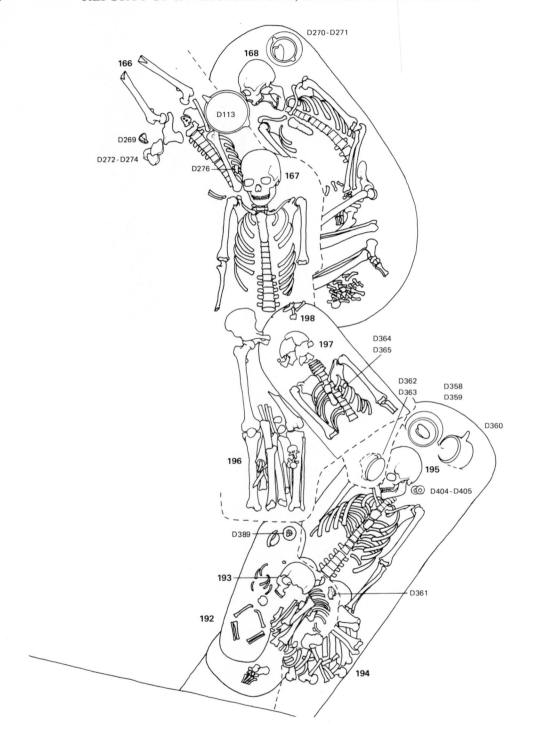

Figure 53.

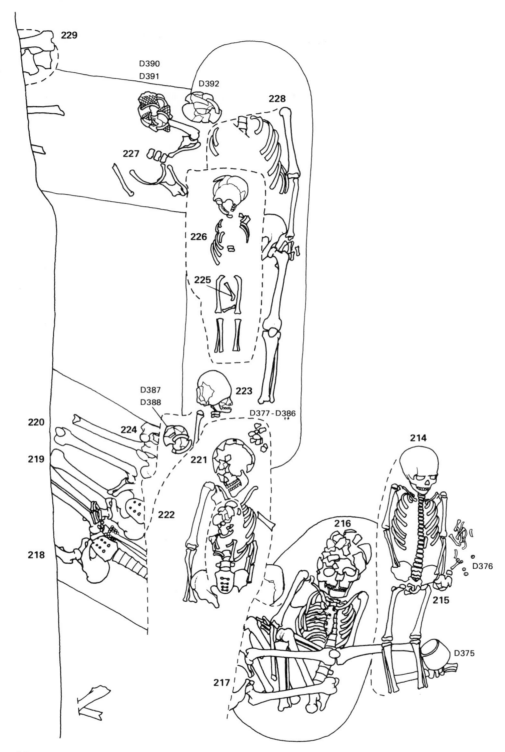

Figure 54.

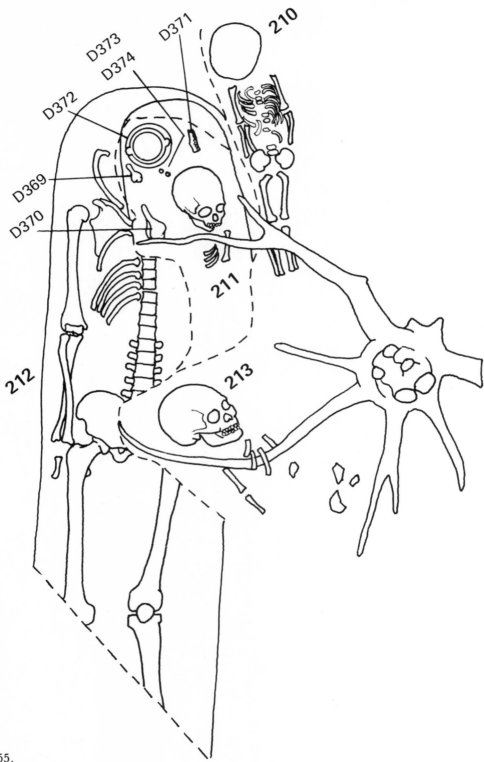

Figure 55.

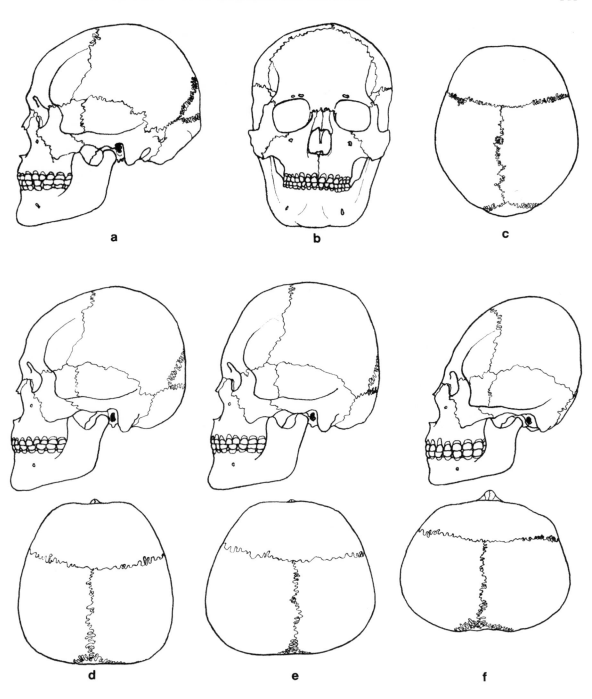

Figure 56. Typical skulls of the Dickson Mounds Cemetery: A-C, views of the skull of Burial 109, the adult male most nearly approaching the mean for Spoon River variant people; D-F, three degrees of artificial deformation of the crania.

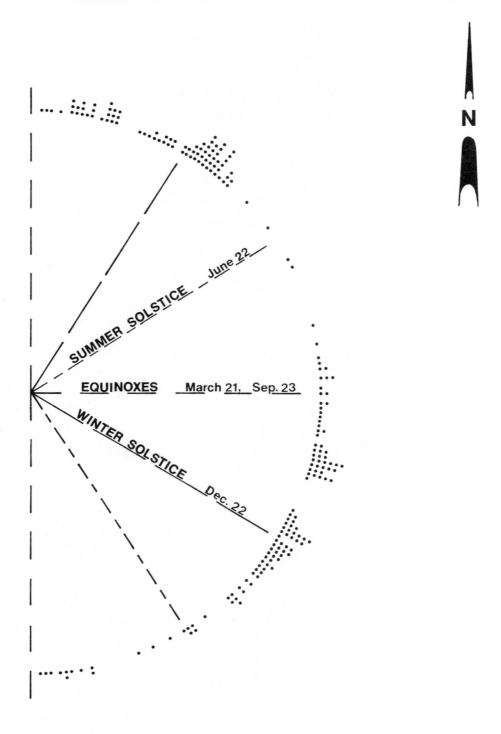

Figure 57. Sunrise angles and burial orientation.

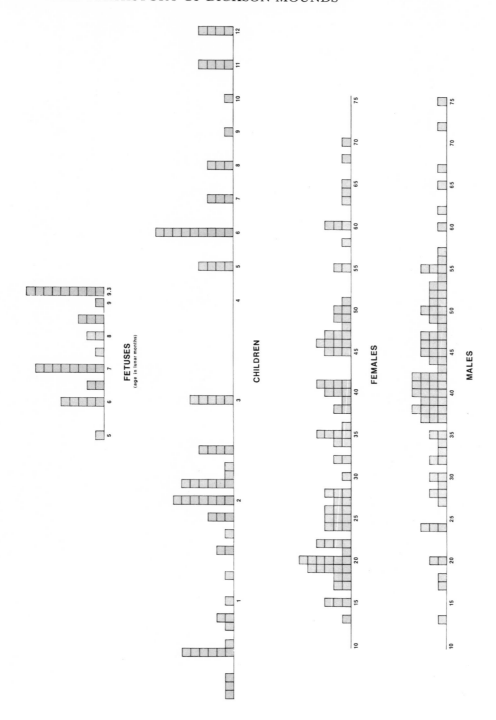

Figure 58. Mortality profile of fetuses, children, and adults in the Dickson-Mounds Cemetery. (Based on determinations made by Georg K. Neumann.)

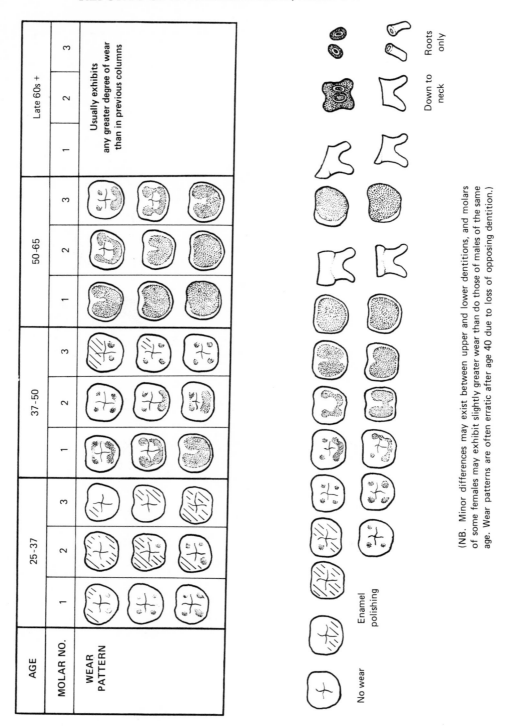

Figure 59. A tentative classification of age in Middle Mississippian skulls of the Central Illinois River Valley based on molar wear. (Model for diagram modified from Brothwell 1963.)

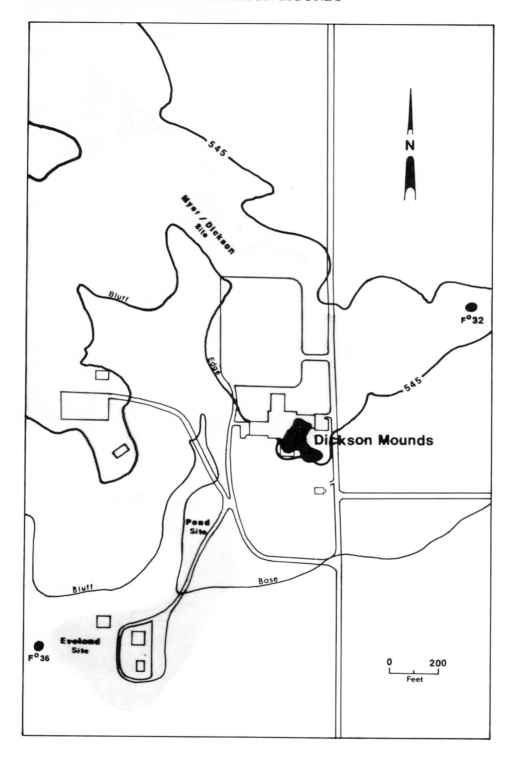

Figure 60. Map showing Dickson and adjacent sites. Shaded areas represent extent of village sites; blackened areas are mounds.

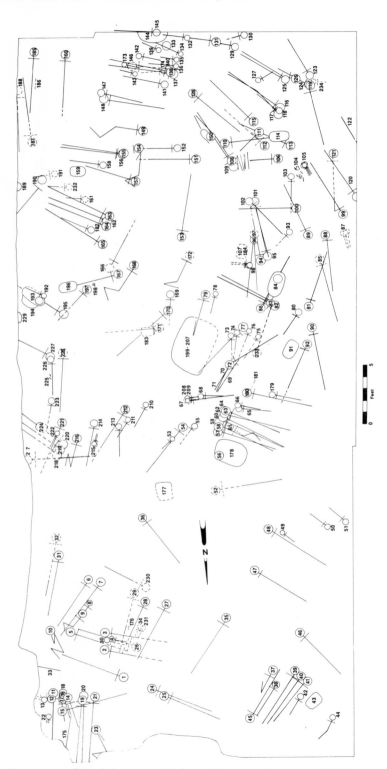

Figure 61. Map of locations of burials in the Dickson Mounds Cemetery F°34.

a. Don F. Dickson near tent covering original excavation, early April 1927. View to southeast.

b. Don F. Dickson and first temporary frame building over original excavation, ca. May 1, 1927. View to northeast.

PLATE 1

a. View of first temporary frame building from roof of second temporary frame building housing the expanded Dickson excavations. Tile block wall of permanent building under construction in background, December 1927.

b. First permanent building over the Dickson excavation, 1928-1968.

PLATE 2

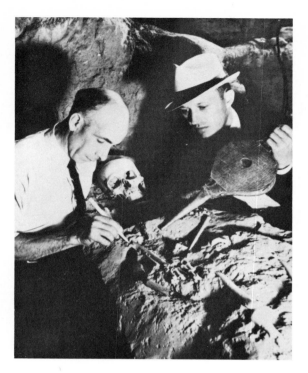

a. Marion H. Dickson (left) and Don F. Dickson in the Dickson excavation.

b. Thomas Dickson examining dog burial at University of Chicago excavations at Dickson Camp (F^{V}35) in 1932.

PLATE 3

a. Don F. Dickson and probably Raymond Dickson (right) in the original excavation, ca. 1931.

b. Don F. Dickson and T. W. Routson (right)
in the second excavation, April 1927. A
small A-frame hog shed protected this excavation for the short time that it was
exhibited.

PLATE 4

a. Beginning of excavation inside second temporary frame building, probably summer 1927. Artifacts were collected from nearby burials for photograph.

b. View of excavation from northwest, 1928. Note suspended catwalk in upper left corner.

PLATE 5

a. Don F. Dickson lecturing in the excavation, probably about 1930.

b. View of excavation from southwest, 1928. Note that excavation had yet to be expanded completely eastward.

PLATE 6

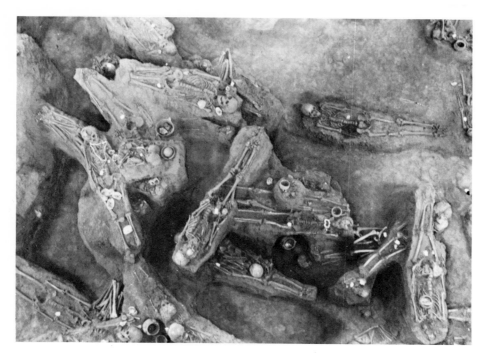

a. General view of burials, west-central area ca. 1930.

b. The Dickson excavation as it appears today.

PLATE 7